Scars and Time

Not everything heals
Marks of the past left on the skin and the mind
The clocks tick, time passes
Life fades life
Love dilutes the pain of damage inflicted in the dark
When light comes in so can lightness
Strength and power are enabled to grow
Not healed but lived with
In spite of, because of, for them, for me
I survived.

Lucy Baldwin

ISBN 978-1-914603-42-6 (Paperback)
ISBN 978-1-914603-43-3 (EPUB ebook)
ISBN 978-1-914603-44-0 (PDF ebook)

Published 2023 by Waterside Press Ltd
www.WatersidePress.co.uk

A catalogue record for this book can be obtained from the British Library.

Ebook *Gendered Justice* is available as an ebook including through library models.

Printed and bound by Severn, Gloucester, UK.

Gendered Justice

Women, Trauma and Crime

Lucy Baldwin

Foreword Professor Lorraine Gelsthorpe

❧ WATERSIDE PRESS

Contents

About the Authors

Dr Lucy Baldwin has more than 35 years' experience in social and criminal justice and is currently a Research Fellow and an Associate Professor at Durham University. She is also a qualified social worker and probation officer and has worked in a number of community-based and custodial settings. Her research and publications focus predominantly on criminalised women and mothers affected by imprisonment. Lucy is a survivor and victim of traumatic experiences and is passionate about facilitating women's voices in research, research ethics and trauma-informed ethical care in research. She is an ardent feminist and activist, and her work has contributed to policy and practice change in the CJS in England and Wales. She co-convened the international research network Women, Family, Crime and Justice (WFCJ). Lucy Baldwin is the editor of *Mothering Justice* (Baldwin, 2015) and author of *Motherhood In and After Prison* (Baldwin, 2022a).

Dr Charlotte Barlow is a Reader in Criminal Justice and Policing at the University of Central Lancashire. Over the past decade, she has worked on and led various externally funded research projects exploring issues such as police responses to coercive control, victim-survivor experiences of Clare's Law/Domestic Violence Disclosure Schemes, and agency responses to domestic abuse in rural communities. She is the author of *Coercive Control* with Professor Sandra Walklate (Barlow and Walklate, 2022) and *Coercion and Women Co-offenders: A Gendered Pathway into Crime* (Barlow, 2016). Charlotte's work on domestic abuse has featured in numerous journals, including the *British Journal of Criminology*, *Journal of Gender-Based Violence*, *Policing and Feminist Legal Studies*.

Dr Úna Barr is a Lecturer in Criminology at Liverpool John Moores University. Originally from Derry, she completed her PhD in 2017 at the University of Central Lancashire. Prior to this, she attended the University of Manchester and Queens University, Belfast for her MRes and LLB respectively. She is interested in feminist and abolitionist approaches to social justice. Úna's book,

Desisting Sisters: Gender, Power and Desistance in the Criminal (In)Justice System (Barr, 2019) is based on her PhD research. Alongside Kym Atkinson, Helen Monk and Katie Tucker, she is co-editor of *Feminist Responses to Injustices of the State and Its Institutions: Politics, Intervention, Resistance* (Atkinson et al, 2022).

Dr Natalie Booth is a Senior Lecturer at Bath Spa University. Her research seeks to understand how prison is experienced by family and friends of people incarcerated in England and Wales. She is the author of *Maternal Imprisonment and Family Life: From the Caregiver's Perspective* (Booth, 2020a) revealing the previously untold experiences of those charged with responsibility for looking after children of female prisoners. She also researches and writes about the maintenance of relationships and family contact during imprisonment, remand and pre-trial detention, mothers and women in prison, and developments in penal policy relating to women and families. She is co-convenor of the international research network Women, Family, Crime and Justice (WFCJ) and her research findings have informed policy developments in England and Wales.

Dr Sinem Bozkurt is a Lecturer in Criminology at the University of Westminster and is currently conducting research into the prison and post release experiences of racially minoritised mothers. In addition to her academic research, she has lived experience of prison which informs her practice. She also has several years' experience as a criminal justice practitioner.

Melanie Brown[1] is the mother of one daughter. She has lived experience of the CJS, and is passionate about advocating for and supporting penal reform. Melanie currently volunteers with women affected by the CJS and at her local food bank. She hopes to own her own cake making business in the future.

Abigay Green[2] is a mother of four children and grandmother of two. She has lived experience of the CJS and feels 'proud to have survived it'. Abigay now supports women in the CJS and feels she is able to use her negative experiences 'for good'. She loves to paint and writes poetry.

---

1. A pseudonym: see further *Chapter 10*.
2. Also a pseudonym: see *Chapter 10*.

Dr Nicola Harding is a Lecturer in Criminology at Lancaster University. Her research interests lie in feminist methodology and ethics, feminist criminology, fraud and financial crime and creative participatory methods of research. Nicola has lived experience of the CJS, and this informs all aspects of her research practice. She is passionate about facilitating voice and choice in research and is currently involved in a largescale research project related to gambling.

Dr Kelly Henderson has over 25 years' experience in the housing field. She is the Founder and Managing Director of Addressing Domestic Abuse (ADA). Kelly was the Domestic Abuse and Violent Crime lead for a local authority, coordinating the area's Multi-agency Domestic Abuse Partnership and Violent Crime Reduction Partnership. She was named 24 Housing's 'Housing Professional of the Year 2018' for her work and research on housing and domestic abuse and was named in the Top 20 Women in Housing: Leaders 2020. She co-authored *Housing and Domestic Abuse: Policy into Practice* (Irving-Clarke and Henderson, 2022). Kelly is a non-executive Director of Believe Housing, a trustee of the Alice Ruggles Trust, a founding board member of Women in Social Housing (Northeast) and an Honorary Research Fellow at Durham University.

Dr Yoric Irving-Clarke is the co-author of *Housing and Domestic Abuse: Policy into Practice* alongside Dr Kelly Henderson (above). His background lies in working as a practitioner in homelessness and supported housing services, including for women and children escaping abuse. His doctoral research explored the implementation of the Supporting People programme in England, and he maintains research and writing interests in policy formulation and implementation, and the philosophy of 'home' and housing generally. Yoric is the author of *Supported Housing: Past, Present, and Future* (Irving-Clarke, 2019). He worked at the Chartered Institute of Housing (CIH), leading on Homelessness and Domestic Abuse, also providing internal research expertise. He also represented the CIH on the National Domestic Abuse Policy and Practice Group. He is currently Policy Manager for a large housing association based in the West Midlands.

Dr Isla Masson is a Criminologist and Researcher at the Open University. Her research interests include women in the CJS, motherhood, incarceration, remand, care leavers and restorative justice. Her book *Incarcerating Mother-hood* (Masson, 2019) explores the longevity of short terms of incarceration on mothers. She is a trustee at the Boaz Project, a therapeutic work environment for adults with learning disabilities, and previously volunteered with the Independent Monitoring Board. She co-convenes the WFCJ research network.

Claire Morley has worked in the CJS for 17 years, and despite holding varying roles in prisons and probation at different grades, the commonality has always been her pursuit of practice which is gender specific, and trauma-informed. Most recently this has led to her leading three counties of the East Midlands towards the development of blueprints for Whole System Approaches which are supported by clear governance structures with lines of accountability. Internally within HM Prisons and Probation Service (HMPPS), Claire has led on the re-modelling of the gender specific resettlement model. This model has gained national approval and women's prisons and probation regions around the country are now working towards its implementation. The gendered practice model which is described in *Chapter 2* is one which is now adopted around regions and noted by the HMPPS central women's team.

Anna Motz is a Consultant Clinical and Forensic Psychologist and Psychoanalytic Psychotherapist who has worked in forensic settings for the NHS for 30 years, specialising in evaluation and psychotherapeutic work with criminalised women. She is a member of the Advisory Board for Female Offenders, under the Ministry of Justice. Anna was formerly the President of the International Association for Forensic Psychotherapy. She lectures internationally and works as an expert witness for the National Crime Agency. She has published widely in the field, including as co-author of *Invisible Trauma: Women, Difference and the Criminal Justice System* (Motz et al, 2020), exploring unconscious bias in the treatment of female offenders, particularly those from ethnic minority backgrounds. Anna is the author of *If Love Could Kill: The Myths and Truths of Female Violence* (Motz, forthcoming 2024).

Dr Kate Paradine has 25 years' experience of campaigning, strategy, policy and research in the charity, academic and public sectors. Most recently she was Chief Executive of Women in Prison (a national service providing and campaigning charity) and a co-founder of the National Women's Justice Coalition. She has led staff teams, boards of trustees and partnerships through periods of intense organizational and political change. She has a strong record of powerful advocacy for people whose voices are rarely heard and evidence-based lobbying for systems change. Kate, who is a Visiting Adjunct Fellow at the Stefan Cross Centre for Women, Equality and Law, University of Southampton, believes that the combined principles of feminism, abolition and anti-oppression hold the answers to building a new system of social justice for all.

Dr Christy Pitfield is Principal Clinical Psychologist and Clinical Lead for the Perinatal Mental Health, Health and Justice Directorate, Central and North West London NHS Foundation Trust. She has extensive experience of providing specialist consultation, assessment and treatment for women with histories of childhood trauma and working with complex systems to support clinical and non-clinical staff to work in a trauma-informed way. Christy has a special interest in working with women who present with mental health difficulties in the perinatal period, including those who self-harm and who are separated at birth.

Claire Rushton works as the Regional Strategic Women's Lead for West Midlands Probation Service. She has previously worked as a Probation Officer and an Interventions Manager at the Divisional Sexual Offending Unit where she specialised in working with women who have sexual convictions, before moving on to manage the UK's largest women's Psychologically Informed Planned Environment Approved Premises. Claire has volunteering experience as a counsellor at the Rape Crisis Centre, and has developed an interest in working with experiences of trauma and the links between criminal and social justice. She gained her Master's Degree in Applied Criminology, Penology and Management at the University of Cambridge. Her research informs a collaboration which set up a lived experience experts panel, a multi-agency delivery group for women and girls in the CJS and a healthcare project focused on improving health outcomes for marginalised women. She is undertaking research via the Griffins Fellowship Programme (with Claire Morley).

Dr Natalie Rutter is a Lecturer in Criminology and Policing at Leeds Trinity University. Her research interests focus on desistance, gender and probation delivery. She is passionate about challenging the stigma which surrounds those involved in the CJS, especially given the continually increasing use of social media and online technologies. In addition, Natalie strives to provide people with a voice within research through narrative, co-productive and visual methodologies.

Dr Monica Thomas is an Economic and Social Research Council funded PhD researcher at Cardiff University. Her PhD focused on the experiences of black mothers during and after imprisonment, using narrative black feminist methods. In 2017, she gained a Master of Science Degree in Social Science Research Methods (Criminology) at Cardiff University and is currently a Teaching Fellow within the Criminology Department at Bath Spa University. Monica has been involved in the co-development of several student-led projects, webinars and conferences relating to racialised and gendered experiences in Britain. She also has experience working with, and advocating for, imprisoned people and their families within charity and governmental organizations and is dedicated to challenging racial and social injustices within the CJS and wider society.

Acronyms and Abbreviations

ABFO	Advisory Board on Female Offenders
ACE	Adverse Childhood Experience
ADHD	Attention Deficit Hyperactivity Disorder
BAME	Black, Asian and Minority Ethnic[3]
BWS	Battered Woman Syndrome
CBT	Cognitive Behavioural Therapy
CJS	Criminal Justice System
CRC/S	Community Rehabilitation Company/Service
CWJ	Centre for Women's Justice
EPIC	Empowering People Inspiring Change
FOR	Families on Remand
HMIP	Her/His Majesty's Inspectorate of Prisons
HMP	Her/His Majesty's Prison
HMPPS	Her/His Majesty's Prisons and Probation Service
IPA	Interpretative Phenomenological Analysis
MDT	Multi-disciplinary Team
MOJ	Ministry of Justice
NPS	National Probation Service
PACT	Prison Advice and Care Trust
POWER	Positive Outcomes for Women: Empowerment and Rehabilitation
PRT	Prison Reform Trust
PSR	Pre-sentence Report
PTE	Potentially Traumatic Event(s)
SAMHSA	Substance Abuse and Mental Health Services Administration
TICP	Trauma-informed Care and Practice
TR	Transforming Rehabilitation
WFCJ	(Network for) Women, Family, Crime and Justice
WIP	Women in Prison

---

3. Please see: Adebisi, F (2019) and Aspinall, P (2021) in the *References and Bibliography* at the end of this work. Also discussion of the term BAME in *Chapter 5*.

Publisher's Note

The views and opinions in this book are those of the authors and not necessarily shared by the publisher. Readers should draw their own conclusions concerning the possibility of any competing accounts or explanations.

Acknowledgements

We, the collective authors would like to dedicate this book to the many women we have worked and/or researched with over our collective years, thank you. We hope this book will contribute to the longstanding fight for trauma-informed and gendered justice. We hear you.

Thank you to Professor Lorraine Gelsthorpe for agreeing to write our Foreword. We were honoured and delighted to be able to include the words of someone all of us hold in very high esteem, who has done, and continues to do so much to advance the cause of positive change in the CJS and beyond.

Special thanks to Abigay and Melanie for being willing to not only share their story but for contributing to the book. Thanks also to Dr Susie Atherton for her never-ending support, keen eye for detail and general willingness to be roped in! Similarly thank you also to Bryan Gibson at Waterside Press for his patience and support and his uniqueness and unfailing ability to surprise.

This book is dedicated to all those who have experienced trauma, and all those working with them, with the hope of making the world a better place for all.

Foreword

The concept of 'gender-responsive justice' has oft been described as a step-change in thinking about women in conflict with the law and what might be appropriate response. At the same time there have been endless debates about the relative merits of gender-responsive, gender-informed and gender-specific interventions and programmes. This edited collection of cutting-edge contributions reflects some of these debates, but more importantly teases out what gender-responsive, gender-informed and gender-specific interventions might look like in practice.

The key themes of the book revolve around the increasing criminalisation of women's lives, exposing the need to acknowledge a blurring of boundaries between 'offender' and 'victim' in the context of domestic violence and abuse, for instance, where women may have offended because of fear and control.

Criminalisation also generates stigma from which it is hard to escape. Drawing on the lived experience of some women, the authors collectively explore the ways in which 'criminalisation' processes penetrate women's lives in a myriad of ways, often making despair and depression inescapable. We also learn about the impact of trauma amongst racially minoritised groups of women, where every day 'micro-stressors' and vicarious experiences of racism because of broad social and structural racism compound the deleterious effects of criminalisation.

It is clear also that the processes of criminalisation through police arrest, police detention, court processing and punishment are agonising, whether this be the shock of imprisonment, concerns about care of children, or the exposing nature of unpaid work and media interest in cases. There is no escape from negative judgment.

The authors in this book, including women with lived experience and practitioners as well as academics, offer vivid and compelling accounts of women's experiences of criminalisation. The Government's Female Offender Strategy 2018[4] offered a template for policy development. Flawed as it was (with lit-

---

4. Ministry of Justice, Female Offender Strategy 2018: https://www.gov.uk/government/publications/female-offender-strategy

tle attention to young women, racially minoritised women, older women, intersectionality, and funding for example), and with damning assessment of progress from the National Audit Office early in 2022,[5] it was aspirational.

This edited collection is also aspirational with the bonus of learning from women who have experienced criminal justice directly, from practitioners who face everyday challenges of trying to ensure both protection of and support for the women with whom they work, or for whom they develop and guide policy.

The contributors recognise that interest and concerns about the plight of women in the Criminal Justice System are not new, but the book brings fresh impetus to change the system. They encourage implementation of a holistic approach, and suggest ways of ensuring 'justice' rather than injustice. As it is put by one of the authors, what is needed is an 'ethics of empathy' and compassion, in order to ensure that criminal justice is linked to social justice for women.

This is an important and inspirational book which should be compulsory reading for policy-makers and sentencers.

The Author of the Foreword

Loraine Gelsthorpe is Director and Professor of Criminology and Criminal Justice at the Institute of Criminology, University of Cambridge. She has wide interests in the links between criminal justice and social justice, looking at race, gender and social exclusion, women and sentencing, and women, crime and criminal justice more generally. Her research includes a focus on the effectiveness of youth and community penalties and on pre-sentence reports. She also has a strong interest in research methodologies and research ethics, human trafficking and the criminalisation of migrants.

---

5.   National Audit Office (2022), *Improving Outcomes for Women in the Criminal Justice System*: https://www.nao.org.uk/reports/improving-outcomes-for-women-in-the-criminal-justice-system

'If there is any institution where the need for insights and instincts of compassion appears to be self-evident, yet where it's appropriate role is fraught with uncertainty and unease, it is the CJS.'

Christopher D Marshall[1]

1. See Marshall, C D (2012: 283).

CHAPTER 1

Introduction

Lucy Baldwin

The need for compassion in the Criminal Justice System (CJS) seems at face value obvious (Marshall, 2012). Many of the crimes that come before the courts involve the injury, trauma, and suffering of victims or perpetrators — or perhaps, most often, both. The pursuit of 'justice' in courts often entails the exploration and understanding of the human experiences that provided the context for the 'offending'. Yet, often in the CJS we see compassion and sympathy reserved exclusively for 'victims' (Canton and Dominey, 2020).

Compassion can be defined as 'the experience of emotional pain and moral concern occasioned by the awareness of and the identification with other persons' suffering or unhappiness' (Marshall, 2012: 283). In the pursuit of objective, untrammelled justice, police and courts are duty bound to follow rules and procedures without being bound by emotional influences. Legal reasoning in the courtroom often seeks to focus on the rules of law, applied dispassionately and in a manner untouched by emotive and subjective considerations of cause.

However, we know that women who come into contact with the CJS, i.e. who become criminalised and labelled as 'offenders', have rarely escaped traumatic experiences in their lives. The lines between 'victim' and 'perpetrator' are often blurred, especially concerning women, yet compassion and recognition of the relevance of trauma in the 'offending' is often deemed to be more clear-cut. Many if not most women who coming into contact with the CJS, have experienced trauma as an adult, as a child or often both (Carlen and Worrall, 2004).

Many women enter prison with good reason not to trust, bearing the scars of a very much less than perfect life (Baldwin, 2022a). Thus, when working with women in the CJS, it would surely be neglectful to not acknowledge those experiences, to understand them and to explore how such experiences interact and intersect with women's 'offending behaviour', or an often more accurate description, their criminalisation, and indeed their desistance. Nonetheless, only relatively recently has the CJS begun to task itself to become 'trauma-informed', and specifically to become trauma-informed in a gendered manner.

Gelsthorpe and Canton (2020), in recognising the trauma histories of women in the CJS, ask important questions about how the CJS responds to criminalised women. Women who are most often victims as well as perpetrators of crime. They suggest (ibid) that often there is merely only a 'shadow' of care for criminalised women in the CJS, arguing further that 'there are differences between the rhetoric and reality of care, differences between policy and practice, and lived realities which expose the "dark side" of care' (ibid).

The chapters in this collection examine the paradox of compassion and care in the CJS, specifically through a gendered lens. Trauma, unsurprisingly, is a connecting theme through all of these chapters. Historically, women who fall foul of the law have been viewed as 'deviant', sometimes doubly and triply deviant if we add layers of culture, motherhood, and age. Feinman (1994: 7) suggests that there exists a universal fear of the 'non-conforming woman', arguing that a criminal woman is the epitome of this. Prison is a gendered experience (Liebling, 2009; Carlen, 1994; and see also Sim, 2009; Moore and Scraton, 2014). Carlen (1994: 136) argues that acknowledging and recognising prison as a 'State mechanism for legitimated pain delivery' per se is important, but in relation to how prison is experienced she argues that the impact is very different across genders. Moreover, that simply 'adding in' an exploration of variables such as race, class, or gender, is inadequate. Walker and Worrall (2000: 28) concluded that female prisoners suffer in distinct and 'special ways', specifically related to loss of fertility, loss of opportunities to be a mother and loss of children or relationships with children.

Women's experiences of the CJS and indeed prison are often compounded and complicated by their role as mothers, whether they have their children in their care or not (Baldwin, 2022a). Hairston (1991) and Enos (2001) argued that imprisoned mothers experienced profound suffering concerning the loss of their children, their mother status and role. Baldwin (2022a), Booth (2018) and Masson (2019) all discovered that imprisoned mother's found the 'stripping of the mother role' 'traumatic', 'traumatising', and with long lasting effects.

Confirming the gendered experience, women are more likely than men to be sent to custody for short periods (Baldwin and Epstein, 2017; Minson, 2019[2]). As such they are often unable to access any of the therapeutic or rehabilitative interventions offered to those on longer sentences. As Corston described, the short sentences may not be long, but they are long enough to cause women significant harm—long enough for women to lose homes, children and jobs, often compounding their already challenging circumstances (Corston, 2007).

As the world becomes more 'trauma-informed' it is important to consider what this means (or should mean) for women in contact with the CJS. Individual trauma 'results from an event, series of events, or set of circumstances that is experienced by an individual as physically or emotionally harmful or life threatening and that has lasting adverse effects on the individual's functioning and mental, physical, social, emotional, or spiritual wellbeing' (Substance Abuse and Mental Health Services Administration (SAMHSA), 2014: 7).

It is widely accepted that there are five Guiding Principles which are *safety, choice, collaboration, trustworthiness* and *empowerment.* Ensuring that the physical and emotional safety of an individual is addressed is the first important step to providing trauma-informed care. Trauma-informed practice can be an individual practitioner response, but it is also important that practitioners operate in a trauma-informed context and from within a trauma-informed organization. SAMHSA suggest that a trauma-informed organization *realises* the widespread impact of trauma and understands potential paths for recovery; *recognises* the signs and symptoms of trauma in clients, families, staff, and others involved with the system; and *responds* by fully integrating knowledge about trauma into policies, procedures, and practices, and seeks to actively *resist re-traumatisation* (SAMHSA, 2014: 9). The CJS and its partners must all be trauma-informed.

Covington (2007: 1) argues that 'Some of the most neglected, misunderstood, and unseen individuals in our society are the more than one million women in our jails, prisons, and community correctional facilities.' There is a growing knowledge base surrounding the importance and significance of a trauma-informed CJS. Trauma affects people from all socioeconomic backgrounds, class, culture, levels of educational attainment, location, ages, and racial or ethnic affiliation. Research suggests, however, that the more marginalised and

---

2.　See also https://shonaminson.com/2019/09/08/report-of-the-joint-committee-on-human-rights/

most vulnerable members of society are at greater risk of experiencing trauma. Women are also more likely to experience higher rates of multiple traumatic experiences, indicating that a gendered lens is important and relevant in understanding trauma, its causes, and its effects (Kubiak et al, 2017).

It is a tragedy, and a sad indictment and reflection of society, that some women, particularly women living with, or escaping traumatic experiences, have describe prison as 'the safest place I've ever been' (Bradley and Davino, 2002: 354). Bradley and Davino's research echoed previous research (see also Covington, 1998; Henriques and Jones-Brown, 2000). Bradley and Davino found that 'prison may at times provide a relatively safe environment for incarcerated women' (ibid: 356). This, they found was particularly true of women who had experienced multiple traumatic life events and/or who were escaping domestic abuse. This lived experience of criminalised women, and their feelings of safety in a space of punishment, adds to the significance and responsibility of prisons to be genuinely trauma-informed. However, it is also important to note that if society, services and particularly courts were more trauma-informed, then many imprisoned women would not 'end up' in prison in the first instance (Baldwin, 2015).

The impact, consequences and alterations in abuse survivors' thoughts, feelings and emotional regulation are often complicated and varied. When not seen through a trauma and gendered lens, these alterations or changes are often inappropriately and incorrectly labelled as pathological. This can have a distinct and specific impact on the perceptions of others leading to missteps in terms of interactions with others, including those in authority. As stated earlier, in the CJS all too often the trauma of the 'perpetrator' has often been ignored when it comes to understanding and working with people in contact with or in conflict with the law. Becoming trauma-informed in criminal justice entails becoming more astutely aware of the ways in which people who are traumatised have their life trajectories shaped by traumatic experiences, which for many criminalised women are often multiple and dating back to childhood and continuing into adulthood (Bradley, 2021). However, becoming trauma-informed is not just about *understanding* the impact of trauma, it requires deep consideration and considered action concerning the development of informed policies and practices which reflect this understanding.

Baldwin (2022a) and Bradley (2021) have highlighted that prison and the CJS per se can be the 'traumatiser', adding an additional layer of trauma to pre-existing trauma, although surprisingly this remains an under-researched area. A relatively newly emerging area of research is the trauma people with lived experience of prison are left with, specifically triggered by or originating from the prison experience (Piper and Berle, 2019).

Research investigating the relationship between trauma and the prison experience tends to focus on potentially traumatic events (PTEs) that might occur in prison such as prison rape, witnessing violence or witnessing suicide rather than the trauma of separation from children, the trauma of being in contact with the CJS, or from the prison experience itself. Piper and Berle (ibid) undertook a systematic review exploring the relationship between prison experienced trauma, PTEs and post-traumatic stress disorder (PTSD) outcomes, finding that experiencing prison can lead directly to PTSD. Similarly, Moore and Scraton (2014) explicitly argue that incarceration is a traumatising experience for women, one that is often experienced as 'destructive and debilitating', however how that translates post-release is not explicitly examined. Baldwin (2022a) found in her research with post-released mothers that traumatic effects (and in some cases diagnosed PTSD), were evident in mothers who had been involved in the CJS and ultimately prison, sometimes many decades after release.

Committing to a trauma-informed CJS is vital if we are to deliver more fair, intelligent, compassionate and importantly effective criminal justice. Furthermore, as well as adopting a trauma-informed approach to working positively with women in the CJS, the CJS must also recognise that effective interventions with criminalised women requires both the avoidance of re-traumatisation and the presence of respectful and supportive interventions to enable and facilitate women to repair and rebuild their lives. Bradley (2021: 255) calls for the 'Working with Trauma Quality Mark' to be introduced into Her Majesty's Prisons and Probation Service (HMPPS), as a 'quality assurance model in order to develop trauma practice, whilst providing a mechanism to demonstrate and celebrate aspects of good practice across HMPPS'.

Women are criminalised for living in and experiencing poverty and trauma every day in the United Kingdom. They make up five percent of the overall prison population in England and Wales. The total number of women in prison is most often between 3,200–3,800 but has risen exponentially over the last ten years.

Seventeen thousand children are affected annually by maternal imprisonment (Prison Reform Trust, 2019). Many women remanded to prison do not go on to receive a custodial sentence, in 2019 two thirds of women remanded (66%) did not do so — begging the question why they were remanded in custody in the first instance. Most women are imprisoned for a non-violent offence (77%). Reflecting the low risk of harm of most female criminality, most women will serve short or very short sentences. In 2019 62 per cent of women in prison were serving sentences of six months or less. It is in this context that the authors of this collection describe their research, practice and experiences of working with women in the CJS. The remaining chapters in this feminist collection explore the experiences of women before, during and after prison. All incorporate trauma into their discussions.

Chapter 2 'Adopting a Whole-Systems Approach and Why a Women's Specialist Team Model Makes Sense' by Claire Morley and Claire Rushton, two senior managers in the National Probation Service, opens the collection by presenting a robust argument why a gendered specialist whole system model for working with women is important. It examines the political, economic and educational legacy which provided the backdrop for the development of probation services for women. Using reflections from their own practice and long experience with women, the authors highlight the need for a trauma-informed, tailored Probation Service for women, one that accounts for and accommodates women's needs and individual identities — including their maternal and cultural identities. The chapter reiterates the importance of a women centred approach in a women centred environment and where relationships and consistency are recognised as important and valued. It concludes with the firm argument that in order to shift practice towards a gender specific and trauma-informed way of working, the trauma-informed core values must be taken on and supported as a priority. As already indicated these are *safety, trustworthiness, choice, collaboration* and *empowerment.*

In **Chapter 3** 'Desistance and the Stigma Machine: Being a "Good Woman"' Úna Barr and Natalie Rutter explore the desistance journey of criminalised women drawing on the concepts of 'stigma' and the pursuit of a 'good woman' identity. The chapter highlights how women in conflict with the law are made wholly responsible for their criminalisation. Further highlighting how 'policy and practice is neglectful of the often-overlapping structural conditions that surround both women's criminalisation and victimisation', the chapter goes on to argue that women, and especially mothers, feel the shame and stigma of their 'failure', despite the failures of society to support them in their desistance or to fully meet their needs. The chapter concludes with a stark reminder that the CJS is not a place to go for 'help', and that for the CJS to be fairer to women, then strides must be taken to address all that is lacking in social justice and that services for women must be gendered and trauma-informed.

Chapter 4 '"They Just Didn't Want to Help Me": The Criminalisation of Coerced Women Co-offenders' by Charlotte Barlow considers 'the influence of violence, coercion and love within intimate relationships on women's offending behaviour, particularly co-offending'. The chapter highlights how high levels of violence against women influences their pathways into crime and continued reasons for offending, arguing that women's actions are often influenced by fear. The chapter demands consideration of the victim/offender dichotomy concerning women who are labelled co-offenders but are in violent, controlling and coercive relationships, moreover highlighting the current failure of the CJS to respond adequately to women in such situations. The chapter reinforces the need to move away from criminalisation wherever possible and to reflect on how being more trauma-informed can better support women, divert them from a CJS response to trauma and facilitate more positive outcomes. The author argues this requires a holistic, gendered approach to justice and one where trauma-informed practice is situated in and addresses the broader societal harms and failures that currently, often unnecessarily, contribute to the criminalisation of abused women.

Chapter 5 '"Racism is Very Much There": Validating Racial Trauma in the Context of Criminal Justice' by Monica Thomas and Sinem Bozkurt examines how the CJS often fails to recognise or give weight to racism, and other racialised harms, as forms of abuse which the authors argue can lead to trauma and racialised harms. The authors argue that without validating the pain caused by racism, trauma-informed approaches and other strategies for support will continue to centre white women's experiences whilst further marginalising women positioned as racially *other*. The authors reiterate the importance of language and description and highlight why the use of the catch-all term 'BAME' can be problematic, advocating for the term 'racially minoritised' to be used instead. The chapter concludes with a call for an acknowledgement that 'racism is very much there'. The authors state that without this, being truly trauma-informed in the CJS, justice will not occur for racially minoritised women.

Chapter 6 'A Mother's Work is Never Done: Mother's Affected by Remand' by Isla Masson and Natalie Booth draws on their research project which explored the experiences of those with a loved one on remand. The chapter highlights the multi-layered emotions mothers, grandmothers and mother figures feel when supporting loved ones on remand to prison and who are simply 'left behind' to cope. The chapter reveals the shock, pain and ongoing trauma felt by these maternal figures, highlighting how little support or recognition there is for this invisible population who are also traumatised by contact with the CJS. The chapter calls for the impact on the wider family to be considered in the original sentencing, questioning the proportionality and justice of imprisonment for minor offences. It concludes with calls for additional research to explore the long-term impact of imprisonment, and particularly custodial remand periods (that may not have ended in a custodial sentence) on maternal figures and the wider family.

Chapter 7 '"And Still I Rise": Hope, Trauma and Imprisoned Women' by Christy Pitfield and Anna Motz describes the therapeutic work of the authors with women in prison. The chapter explores the traumatic trajectories of women entering prison, whilst also paying attention to the traumatising impact of imprisonment itself. Using case studies, the authors describe the impact of trauma-informed work in and on the system within which the women, and importantly therapists, are located. The authors argue trauma-informed practice means seeing the ways that incarceration re-creates trauma and finding alternative ways of managing women's pathways. It also reiterates the importance of being trauma-informed at every stage of a woman's criminal justice journey. Through Maja's case history, the authors illustrate how therapeutic responses to women in prison can offer both women and clinicians to help women break out of destructive cycles, borne of traumatic experiences. They argue that 'to do this requires care, sensitivity and willingness to bear the weight of past trauma, for the imprisoned women and the workers themselves', highlighting the importance of hope in the 'recovery' of women.

Chapter 8 'Women's Experiences of Presenting as Homeless Post Domestic Abuse: Homelessness Policy and Domestic Abuse — The Changing Legislative Context' by Kelly Henderson and Yoric Irving-Clarke examines homelessness policy in the United Kingdom, with reference to efforts to address domestic abuse. Drawing from the authors' research and case studies the chapter details women's experiences of homelessness and the homelessness 'system'. The chapter 'highlights how the failures and lack of understanding and responsiveness in the system, particularly for women escaping domestic abuse, contributes to women's trauma, often re-traumatising women during the system processes and assessments'. It calls for positive policy and practice change and reiterates the importance of housing staff receiving trauma-informed training and awareness, which the authors stress must 'happen alongside a determination to avoid the re-traumatising of domestic abuse victims/survivors in their attempts to access support and accommodation'.

Chapter 9 '"There's Nothing left, Nothing Left of You": Criminalised Women and Trauma', by Nicola Harding 'considers the social manifestation of trauma within a study co-produced with criminalised women as they navigate community punishment'. The author describes how she worked *with* women to tell *their* story. The chapter examines the presence of trauma within the individual and collective narratives offered by the women both before, during, and beyond criminalisation. It further examines how social responses to trauma were enacted by the women within the research space itself, and as they bore witness to each other's trauma narratives. The chapter highlights how criminalised women manage their trauma through the use of humour and telling their narratives through hope and imagination. The author argues these mechanisms for managing trauma are often misunderstood by criminal justice and calls for those who work with women in criminal justice to 'understand a little more, enabling the creation of trauma-informed spaces that condemn a little less'. The chapter argues that during the process of punishment and supervision within the community, women are expected to visibly manage their trauma, but the chapter reiterates how women manage that trauma is a personal choice and should not be solely dictated by the CJS processes of risk management. The author calls for creativity, flexibility and acceptance in community supervision processes and practice.

Chapter 10 'It's Not a Joke, It's My Life' by Lucy Baldwin, Abigay Green and Melanie Brown highlights the direct relationship between trauma and criminalisation. It combine an academic context and discussion with the lived experience narratives of Abigay and Melanie, written in their own words. The chapter seeks to redress the balance, if only in a slight way, in terms of facilitating criminalised women to have their own voice in traditionally academic spaces where they are normally written *about* (as opposed to *with*). Through Abigay's and Melanie's narratives the chapter illustrates the impact of trauma and how it intertwined with their criminalisation, their experiences in the CJS and ultimately their long-term outcomes and aspirations. The chapter reveals the 'missed and lost' opportunities to respond to trauma, dating back to childhood and which, if they had been acted on at that time, may well have meant very different outcomes for Abigay and Melanie. The chapter reiterates the importance of recognising and responding to maternal trauma and ongoing trauma triggered and compounded by the CJS. It echoes the need for trauma-informed practice at all stages of the CJS, and for maternal trauma to be included in that awareness and practice change.

Chapter 11 '"We Are the Ones": Joining Forces and Creating New Tools for Change: Challenges for Academia, Charities and Practitioners' by Kate Paradine calls for a sea change in the way academics, practitioners, charities and policy-makers work together to effect change. The chapter asks critical questions about why there has been so little progress concerning women's imprisonment, despite there being widespread agreement about what changes need to occur. It shames and critiques the never-ending patriarchy, bureaucracy and politics that gets in the way of working with criminalised women. Women who the author states are painted *only* as vulnerable and complex, *as opposed to* resilient and strong. The author asks why, 'for all the talk of "learning lessons" and reflective practice, remarkably little time is spent on questions like "Where are we going wrong?" and "What have we learned from failure?"' She further argues that 'we' need to focus on three areas for collective change; 'strengthening the case for prison abolition', simultaneously 'focusing on the long game of the "small victories" along the way', and 'speaking out for change together to amplify our collective voices and sharing power to create new tools for change'. Kate powerfully concludes, 'We can change things, but the real lasting systems change will only happen if *we* change. In the words of June Jordan, "We are the ones we have been waiting for. It all starts with us".[1]

In **Chapter 12** The collection concludes with final reflections on the whole of the contents of this book by the editor and encourages feminist action and activism. This, the 'Gendered Justice' collection, is aimed at practitioners as well as academics and it is hoped that it will go some way towards improving knowledge and assisting practice, especially in the area of trauma-informed practice. How 'we' in the system engage with women who come into contact with the CJS and related agencies can have a profound and significant impact on women's lives, and we must do all that we can to ensure that the impact is an informed and positive one.

Each of the chapters, as in *Mothering Justice* and *Motherhood In and After Prison*[3] before it, is interspersed with 'Pauses for Thought'. These ask readers to think wider than the text itself, but also encourage thought and prompt discussion (educators can use the pauses as the basis of a seminar). We, the writing team involved in this collection understand that positive change requires a united voice, a united passion and that is what we brought to this collection in the hope it will inspire others to join us and continue to pursue change. In the words of Ruth Bader-Ginsberg: 'Fight for the things you care about, but do it in a way that will lead others to join you'.[4]

---

3. Baldwin, L. (2015), *Mothering Justice: Working with Mothers in Criminal and Social Justice Settings*; and (2022a), *Motherhood In and After Prison* (both Waterside Press).
4. The late USA Supreme Court Justice during a question and answer session following an address to the Harvard Radcliffe Institute, 29 May 2015.

CHAPTER 2

Adopting a Whole-Systems Approach
Why a Women's Specialist Team Model Makes Sense

Claire Morley and Claire Rushton

Women's criminalisation is best understood in the context of traumatic histories involving abuse, neglect, substance misuse and marginalisation (Carlen and Worrall, 2004). The social complexities and discrimination underpinning women's pathways into crime are fairly well understood and discussed in detail elsewhere (Bloom et al, 2004; Morash, 2010; Malloch and McIvor, 2013; Moore et al, 2018). However until the 1970s women took only marginal space within Criminology (Newburn, 2007). It is accepted that women make up a small percentage of the offending population (5%). Yet, the impact of intergenerational crime along with other social costs related to the disproportionate numbers of women going to prison on short sentences means that the need to respond better to women is not only moral but also economic (Baldwin and Epstein 2017; Farmer 2019; Crest 2021). These sentiments inspired a wave of feminist researchers and, more recently, mainstream academics and frontline practitioners to highlight and challenge the differing outcomes for women in criminal justice settings. There is a collective call for change to a system that is designed by, and for, men. This disparity and the evident need to work in quite different ways for women has now been recognised and convincingly articulated by Baroness Corston in her 'Corston Report' (2007). Yet despite broad acceptance of the findings and recommendations of that report — 15 years later most of her recommendations remain unimplemented.

From the viewpoint of two of probation's regional women's leads, this chapter considers the organizational changes against a backdrop of a changing political scene in the context of working with women. It then looks at some of the ways we have operationalised our work with women across the United Kingdom, whilst considering the advantages and disadvantages of each model (including our own reflections of the impact of these). We argue that a whole-systems approach as advocated by Baroness Corston would be best supported through a specialist women's team model within the unified Probation Service. The proposed model outlined demonstrates the need for gender specific assessments and performance indicators so that practitioners can be supported in delivering truly trauma-informed, gender specific services.

Historical Context and Legacy

Although only making up a minority of probation's overall caseload (HM Government, 2022a), working with women can be a complex, tiring and difficult task. However, we argue that any 'difficulties' are compounded by structural issues rather than any uniquely gendered challenges, i.e. the women are not 'the problem' the structures and lack of resources are. For some officers, a preference for working with men was due to the belief that women were 'hard work and manipulative' (Morash, 2010). However, practitioner frustration is most often borne out of a limited support structure, incompatible assessment tools and incomplete training (Devitt, 2020). For many practitioners, there is a genuine desire to work well with women and to address the specific and gendered adversities women face; born from an understanding that criminalised women's 'chaotic lifestyles' are often a product of a background of trauma, vulnerability and poor emotional wellbeing. This frustration is worsened by organizational pressures to focus on outcomes, value for money (economic efficacy) and a preoccupation with a 'New Penology' and risk management (Worrall and Gelsthorpe, 2009; Annison, Brayford and Deering, 2015). Inadequate resourcing in times of austerity and the frequent programme of change further breaks down gender responsive progress (Goldhill, 2019).

This, however, has not always been the case. Throughout the 1970s and 1980s, staff were encouraged to offer creative support systems using relationships with local voluntary organizations (Worthington, 2014). Despite the increasing focus on economic principles, notably translated in the 'Statement of National Objectives' (Home Office, 1984), staff were still able to balance outcomes with the traditional notions of 'advise, assist and befriend' (Harris, 1992); and the inspirational work of feminist criminologists like Carol Smart and Pat Carlen continued to influence practitioners. During this time, probation's workforce was predominantly male. Female officers became 'specialist women's practitioners' by default[5] who would design and implement local, holistic strategies for working with women. In her reflections, Jill Annison (2016) summarised that these practices continued until the rise of new managerialism and 'What Works'[6] movements which was defined by a changing political scene during the 1990s.

In their Introduction to the *Handbook of Probation*, Lorraine Gelsthorpe and Rod Morgan (2007) go on to define the changes to the Probation Service throughout this period as 'seismic' (p. 1). Throughout the text, they discuss the 'culture of control' and the rise of the 'risky society' as defined by David Garland (2001); the reconstruction of public services and birth of 'managerialism' as articulated in 'Modernising Government' (Cabinet Office, 1999); and the politicising of crime through campaigns of 'law and order', most notably referenced in Tony Blair's New Labour speech where he declared that we should be 'tough on crime' (New Statesman, 1993). Gelsthorpe and Morgan (2007) argue that these social and political waves influenced a changing discourse from being an 'alternative to custody' to 'punishment in the community'. Although seemingly only a slight change of language, this shift signifies the attempts of the Probation Service to maintain a reputable organizational identity and role, against the changing political agenda and its desire for a more punitive response to criminality. With this, increased central governance, tightening of National Standards and public scrutiny of casework through 'high profile' enquiry reports, the Probation Service became a scapegoat for what had become an over-burdened and under-resourced penal system. Such moves led to penal populism (Bottoms, 1995; Raynor and Vanstone, 2016; Canton and Dominey, 2017) and a rising prison population.

Within the same timeframe, the Probation Service changed its training structure from a social work led qualification to the Diploma in Community and Criminal Justice, a probation specific programme rebranding officers as

---

5. In 1922 the 'Report of the Departmental Committee on the Training, Appointment and Payment of Probation Officers' (Cmd 1601) proposed that women should only be supervised by female officers (Annison, 2007).

6. 'What Works', also known as 'evidence-based practice' refers to a body of research interested in the effectiveness of interventions on rehabilitation. When referred to, consideration is often given to the Risk-Needs-Responsivity model outlined by Andrews and Bonta (1990) which sets out guiding principles for practitioners based on a person's risk levels, assessed offence-related or *criminogenic needs* and learning styles.

'offender managers' and bringing an emphasis on court order enforcement (Jordan, 2013). Finally, the 'What Works' agenda sought to guide the assessment and treatment of offenders and promised to reduce recidivism through reliable predictive risk assessments and effective cognitive behaviour therapy (CBT) group programmes (Bonta and Andrews, 2010). For women, this had disastrous effects. There was an assumption that generic risk assessments would be reliable for women even though they were based on data for men, and they focused heavily on pathological causes of crime rather than considering the socio-economic circumstances of women's behaviour or women's distinct and specific pathways into (and ergo out of) crime. Further, there was no room for a trauma-informed lens (Covington, 2007), at best little consideration of women's needs (Barry and McIvor, 2010) and, at worst, a translation of terms where needs were wrongly associated with risks, leading to an upscaling of treatment targets (Hannah-Moffat, 2005). This was evidenced via the reports and publications at the time such as HM Prison Inspectorate's Thematic Review into conditions of all women in prisons in England and Wales (1997) following a damming inspection of Holloway Prison. The Prison Reform Trust considered and reported on the social costs of women's imprisonment (2000) and the Fawcett Society asked for treatment of women throughout the CJS (2004). All these reports resulted in calls to the Government for changes in approaches to working with women.

Transitional Period

By 2007, the staff ratio had u-turned and around 70% of the probation workforce were female (Ministry of Justice (MOJ), 2007). Whilst in some areas women were consumed within generic, mixed caseloads, in others specialist caseworkers continued to hold 'women only' caseloads, known as the 'concentrator model'.[7] This did little to reverse the effects on women, and whilst many practitioners and academics alike called for radical change on the back of damning inspectorate reports and serious case reviews (PRT, 2000; Fawcett Society, 2004) it wasn't until Baroness Corston was asked to formally review

---

7. The allocation of women to practitioners who take on a specialist role as a specific point of contact for women amidst holding a generic caseload made of men and women.

the case for women that systematic discrimination of women throughout the CJS was formally brought to light. In her report, Corston argued that women's needs were being ignored and she stressed that treating them equally to men equated to 'unfair' treatment due to the disparity in offending needs and sentencing consequences (Corston, 2007). Of her 43 recommendations to the Government, many were finally picked up within the MOJ's commitment to women in their Female Offender Strategy, over ten years later (MOJ, 2018).

As part of this strategy, statutory and partnership organizations are obliged to work together in creating a 'whole-systems approach' to tackling the distinct needs of women through a National Concordat (MOJ, 2020). Despite these ambitions however, many of the recommendations are still outstanding (Booth et al, 2018), and there is significant progress to be made in certain areas such as accommodation and effective wrap-around services (Dominey and Gelsthorpe, 2020). Although the Transforming Rehabilitation (TR) agenda promised to better deliver services through direct commissioning to community organizations, underpinned by the Offender Rehabilitation Act 2014, low numbers, high costs and the fragmentation of service delivery prevented full scale take-up and produced disappointing results. It is not surprising therefore that compliance rates for women began to decline and the rate at which they were sent to prison on short-custodial sentences increased (Gelsthorpe, 2013; Stalans, 2015).

In her research 'Missing Voices: Why Women Engage With or Withdraw from Community Sentences', Sue Jordan looked at 'compliance thieves' and the extent to which probation contributed to women's disengagement with its sentences (2013). She found that women were at a heightened risk of breach for many reasons such as discrimination (Chigwada-Bailey, 2003), 'double deviance' (Carlen, 1988) and 'net widening' (Hedderman, 2012). In her recommendations, Sue Jordan asked for: gender specific training for staff; trauma-informed services via women's centres; and contextual court reports written by a known keyworker (Jordan, 2013). In summary, these recommendations point to the need for professionals to be confident in dealing with women, knowledgeable about the social circumstances of the woman and situated in a therapeutic allegiance, one which prioritises wellbeing over outcomes, meaningful compliance over enforcement.

Personal Practice Reflections

Our current professional roles are as Women's Lead, East Midlands (CM), and Women's Lead, West Midlands (CR). We have extensive experience of working with women both in a case working capacity as practitioners in the Probation Service and within management experience in Offender Management Units and a women's Approved Premises. This experience, between us, spans across counties from the North of England to and including Greater and Central London. Whilst this has provided first-hand experience of the challenges of gender responsivity in the Probation Service, we feel it is important to note the often-overlooked rewards and high levels of job satisfaction that practitioners can experience from engaging in a consistent, trauma-informed manner with women. The strength and resilience that women on probation demonstrate in the face of social injustice and life's adversities is something which is difficult not to be impacted by. It is simply inspiring and feeds our passion and drive for change.

Experiences of supervising women's specialist probation workers have allowed us to observe how this can also be the driver to specialist practitioners continuing their efforts to go 'above and beyond' to offer a service which *is* suitable for woman on probation. We can offer a personal perspective on the outlined probation history and largescale changes. We have observed women's programmes and models of practice developed in the Probation Trust times, dissolve at the point of TR. The feedback from women on these groups was unsurprising. Women benefitted from the flexibility of the programme and the mutual, peer support that groupwork provided, favouring this over individual supervision sessions where unequal power dynamics prevailed. Following TR and as the National Probation Service (NPS) and Community Rehabilitation Companies (CRCs) then formed, NPS were left working with between 3–4% of their entire caseload population being women. In real terms, when women were distributed across whole Offender Management Unit's probation teams, this would mean that a specialist women's probation practitioner in the NPS would only hold a maximum of four to five women on their caseload. The low numbers meant that despite repeated efforts to incorporate CRC women's services into NPS work, limitations on resource and the viability of this with such low numbers resulted in continuous failures to integrate gender specific services into NPS practice at a local or organizational level. Consequently, specialist women's workers tend to go 'above and beyond' in order to meet the gender specific needs of the women on their caseloads. We have met numerous women's practitioners who are simply inspirational in their commitment to deliver appropriate women's work in the face of an organization in which gender informed practice has not been a priority. This has been due to the impact of economies of scale coupled with women generally lacking the high-risk status which has traditionally attracted resource. Nevertheless, amidst high workloads and a target driven culture, this 'above and beyond' approach attracts increasing levels of emotional fatigue, vicarious trauma and longer working hours (Lee, 2017). In short, this is an unsustainable and inconsistent approach.

Whilst in isolation the approach can undoubtedly have significant impact, sadly despite the well-intentioned efforts of these committed practitioners women on probation have explained that the lack of structure and consistency between practitioners lends itself to: distrust in the service being exacerbated; attachment and rejection difficulties being triggered; and a distinct lack of clarity in 'what probation does'.

We have noted that sadly, within the various offices and regions, the lack of support for working appropriately with women has manifested itself into an aversion from staff to having women on their caseloads. Comments such as, 'Give me ten men over one woman' and 'women are so chaotic' are commonplace in probation offices and these have an impact on the way other members of staff and trainee probation practitioners view working with women. This is inadvertently leading to, what could feasibly be described as, a culture of the dislike of working with women. What is of concern is the impact that this culture then has on the practice of staff—particularly those who are very clear that they do not enjoy this work. Whilst double deviance is a term most commonly associated with court settings to described the harsher forms of punishment that women receive as a result of both their offence and the behaviour deviating from the social expectations that dictate how a woman should behave, Goldhill (2019) argues that double deviance can be seen in other professional settings as well. The described probation culture is an example of how this could develop. As stated earlier, we believe that much of the negativity surrounding probation work with women stems from under resourcing and underfunding—which means probation staff often simply do not have time to respond appropriately or fully to women's needs—which are often distinctly different to men's.

The investment by probation in the regional women's lead roles that we both now hold is testament to the desire and commitment by the service to tackle these issues face on. We would both describe our regional roles as a privilege to hold and strongly agree on the absolute importance of our work being a catalyst for change within the service. This includes not just the Probation Service's gender specific response, but also the necessity of a joined-up approach with other organizations to support staff to work more effectively with women, and ultimately achieving better outcomes for women and their families. A further contributory factor towards a more gender responsive service is the formation of a central HMPPS women's team which is playing a pivotal part in ensuring gender is something which is no longer de-prioritised due to the impact of economies of scale but recognised as a key aspect in achieving sustained desistance and reducing reoffending.

Sue Jordan was not the first to suggest that a whole-systems, holistic approach is key when working with women. In fact, much of the evidence, research and literature around women in the CJS concludes that, for efforts to be effective, a woman must be treated with a warm, genuine interest in her wellbeing and a desire to improve her social circumstances—as much as (if not more than) a need to address her 'criminogenic needs' (Annison et al, 2015; Sheehan et al, 2011; Jordan, 2013; Dominey and Gelsthorpe, 2020). Furthermore, it is more recently argued that it is important that a women's maternal circumstances and emotions are an important part of supervision and must also be accounted for (Baldwin, 2022a; Rutter and Barr, 2021; Pitman and Hull, 2021). Eaton (1993) referred to the need for a woman to 'believe that change can happen' before embarking on building motivation to change. To do this, a reciprocal relationship was needed that challenged the 'exploitative' relationships criminalised women are likely to have experienced beforehand. The role of trust and a therapeutic relationship between practitioner and service user is arguably important for everyone but seems to be essential if we hope for a woman to engage in a journey of desistance. In her research with criminalised mothers, Baldwin found that mothers under supervision felt 'monitored' rather than supported, and that the lack of trust in them as mothers made it challenging for them to trust in their supervisor's willingness/ability to support them. Baldwin (2015) talks about the importance of creating a space of 'emotional safety' in engagement specifically with mothers under supervision, but this concept translates to women more generally too. Trust in the working and therapeutic relations of criminalised (and often traumatised) women is an important part of creating and maintaining that safe space and facilitating positive engagement (Baldwin, 2022a).

Using the current language of a trauma-informed lens, we must ask 'What happened to you?' rather than 'What's wrong with you?' before we can hope to fully engage with the women that we work with or understand the reasons why they came to be before us (Petrillo, 2019). This is tricky given that at the very heart of a relationship between probation practitioner and service user is the role of monitoring and enforcement. A dilemma Worrall recognised well (1990). However, as 'trauma-informed practice' becomes more widely recognised it is seen as an increasingly legitimate way of engaging in our work. In a recent HM Inspectorate Academic Insights paper, McCartan stresses 'the earlier we introduce holistic, supportive, and appropriate social-emotional interventions, the greater likelihood of reducing the impact of adverse childhood experiences [ACEs] and trauma across the lifespan' (McCartan, 2020: 7).

In our role, we use of the powers of the concordat to mandate the need for each of these organizations to make 'thinking about women' a strategic priority. On the back of this, in most counties in the Midlands, there is now a multi-agency delivery group, sitting underneath each Local Criminal Justice Board (a regional multi-agency strategic group) where the key players, academics and often service users themselves, will work jointly to discuss trends and problems and figuring out appropriate solutions. Over recent months for example, we have spent time rolling out the new Community Rehabilitative Services (CRS) where third sector organizations take referrals to address social problems across seven pathways from Accommodation to Personal Wellbeing. For women, these organizations take a holistic approach in that the same provider can work to any of the pathways depending on the referral and the assessment outcomes. Whilst a whole chapter could be dedicated to a detailed explanation of this role and the CRS model, suffice it to say here that we continue to experience teething problems, not least owing to gaps in service provision (such as women on remand), quality (there continues to be a lack of appropriate accommodation for providers to refer into) and volume (after only six weeks of roll-out, a third of the annual capacity had already been used).

There is understandably then some reluctance for practitioners and scholars to get excited about these more recent efforts. Over the last few years, there has been an increased momentum to prioritise women and acknowledge the moral and economic principles upon which this work is necessary; notably through the creation of an HMPPS National Women's Team (made up of both prison and probation networks for the first time), and the creation of Regional Women's Strategic Lead Roles (our roles). More is still needed. For our efforts to be effective, we need a sustained commitment and investment in the systems that will back-up CRS. We need to acknowledge that whilst women continue to be transferred between several practitioners, whilst practitioners who often have no interest in working with women hold these cases, and whilst vicarious trauma and exhaustion of both practitioners and service users is not addressed, outcomes will continue to look bleak. Probation is engaging on a pre-sentence report (PSR) pilot in areas of the country to ensure that women receive such a report. There is the new publication of a 'women's toolkit', the first of its kind and which aids practitioners in working effectively with women in supervision. There is also a clear plan and ambition for regions to move towards adopting fully gender specific teams and the approval of a gender specific national reset-tlement model.

Re-thinking the operating models that support the supervision of women so that the necessary therapeutic allegiances can be fostered is imperative to this approach. Research (Jordan, 2013; Baldwin, 2022a) and our practice observations, have shown that woman would preferably experience one practitioner who, alongside partnership agencies, builds and works with a collaborative plan to improve the woman's social outcomes so that her desistance journey can be encouraged. The practitioners working with the woman must be trauma-informed, experienced, knowledgeable and passionate about their work and their relationships between practitioners and multi-agency partners. Only then will probation feel and look like a supportive and accountable network for the woman. Furthermore, as Corston and many others have advocated this trauma-informed[8] and gendered approach to women would ideally take place

---

8.   See this short educational resource about trauma-informed practice and trauma-informed organizations: https://vimeo.com/274703693

in women only spaces where multiple practitioners would work harmoniously to meet the needs of criminalised women (Corston, 2007; Baldwin, 2022a).

Towards a Trauma-informed and Gendered Service

There has always been a distinct lack of gender specific training for probation practitioners. A point noted by HM Inspectorate of Probation (2010) who recommended expedited training concerning working with women, with particular attention paid to developing professional judgement in relation to compliance and enforcement. There has been progress recently from the newly established HMPPS Women's Team, in the development of Positive Outcomes for Women: Empowerment and Rehabilitation (POWER). However the training is under review after it was rolled out following a delay in which the programme was de-prioritised as a result of the need to concentrate on staff training relating to the new, unified service. Understanding can be given to the need to focus on other areas of work given the huge organizational change that the service is, once again, experiencing. However, the de-prioritisation of women in the CJS in this circumstance seems again reflective of almost two decades of de-prioritising the evidence-base which supports a change in approach to the way we work with women in the CJS, which ultimately disadvantages women in contact with the CJS. Work is underway to develop a briefing and introduction to the POWER training which can be delivered to staff whilst we are awaiting the revision of the full training. This absence of practitioner and manager training in the understanding of factors specific to women in the CJS plays out in various ways for women at the receiving end of the service as well as for those who take on the women's lead role. In her research into the women's lead role, Dr Kerry Devitt (2020) identifies the practical challenges of the role in an organization in which rigid targets around enforcement are embedded. The practitioners in Devitt's research could clearly identify multiple difficulties in effectively carrying out the women's lead role, difficulties which were located in the lack of organizational support for such a role.

The structure of the aforementioned targets, alongside managers and staff who lack a gender specific knowledge base, lend to the high number of women who fail to engage with the Probation Service. Dominey and Gelsthorpe (2020: 405) identify that the support for women needs to be 'flexible, practical and pragmatic'. This approach is clearly at odds with the current measurables dictated by the service for the management of people on probation. The role of Women's Lead practitioner has no bearing upon these measurables and with no specific overview of what the role entails, practitioners are left trying to balance the incompatible paradigms of trauma-informed approaches and offender focused risk management work.

The recalls[9] for women in the Probation Service have significantly increased since the move to TR in 2015. The Prison Reform Trust (2018) states that the 'threat of being returned to prison for women serving sentences under twelve months is contributing towards the breakdown of trust between them and probation officer'. This view is echoed by an analysis of recalls of women in the Midlands National Probation Service during 2019–2020. The findings of this study demonstrated that women were recalled predominantly for lack of engagement and/or becoming estranged from their probation practitioner. The recalls were *not* as a result of risk escalation. Current probation practice does not adequately support the commonly accepted additional vicarious trauma and emotional fatigue of working with women.

▌▌ Pause for Thought

- Women's pathways into the CJS are often rooted in traumatic experiences in their past, societal inequalities and/or ongoing experience of being a victim. To what extent does a woman on probation have control over decisions that she has made in the past?
- How much control does she have over decisions that she is making currently — perhaps in the adherence to her licence conditions, or in the adherence to social care expectations of her mothering?
- Does a community disposal or licence account for the social injustices that she is likely to have experienced or does it focus on individual pathologies?

---

9. The recall to prison of someone who is on licence following early release or otherwise serving part of their sentence in the community: the decision to return them to custody for failure to adhere to conditions imposed on them during their time out of prison.

Devitt (2020) notes that longer term implications of Women's Leads frequently saw mental health implications for the staff in her study. The impact of this on the sustainability of a women's lead role is of concern. Furthermore, as this impact is commonly known to staff in the Probation Service, as noted within the practice reflections section, a culture of disliking working with women has become commonplace. Sadly, this has not been challenged and the rewards of working with women are infrequently celebrated. Therefore, the resulting lack of resilience in women's lead's roles, with low numbers of staff motivated to work with women, impacts on any level of consistent service delivery.

For the women experiencing this inconsistent model, they experience repeated transfer between practitioners, inconsistent practice between multiple probation staff and have discussed with us that they therefore lack confidence in the Probation Service. HMP Peterborough have established via their recall work, that women re-enter custody unaware of the reasons that they are there and unable to contact their officers in the community to discuss such issues. Thus, although well intentioned the concentrator model is exacerbating the distrust in statutory agencies, despite the complete passion and motivation of some of the Women's Leads to make a difference to women's lives. It is not difficult to reach a conclusion that a change in approach is paramount to achieving better outcomes for women. This chapter now moves on to discuss what an effective gender specific model of practice should look like for the Probation Service and to provide an evidence base as to how this will make a distinct difference to women in the CJS.

Movement towards a Women's Team model not only mitigates the risks described above, but additionally and crucially achieves better outcomes for women and their families and ergo society. Examples of whole system approaches which probation have ingratiated themselves within are strong evidence of this as demonstrated by the Greater Manchester Whole Systems Approach. Since their commencement in 2014, they have achieved reduced arrests for women by 45% and a 40% reduction in the number of adult women being sentenced to immediate custody across Manchester (MOJ, 2018). For the Probation Service specifically, a model of best practice will incorporate women practitioners holding wholly women's caseloads and gender specific and multi-disciplinary teams (MDTs) in women only environments (like women's centres). These teams would be supported by upskilled trauma-informed managers who are aware of the need to take a flexible approach when having enforcement discussions. Furthermore, principles and targets must be driven by objectives centred around the importance of gaining trust and engagement from women whom we should be expecting to distrust us. Seeing and working with the bigger picture of a woman's lifestyle, rather than just looking at factors linked to risk and reoffending is also crucial to its success.

Women's Specialist Teams

Given the acknowledged emotional fatigue, which is prevalent for practitioners working with women, a successful women's team in the Probation Service will provide a robust organizational response to support its staff with this aspect of the work (Lee, 2017). The trauma-informed approach which will underpin all work delivered to women on probation must be echoed in the management of the staff themselves, thus creating a culture of support and safe reflection. Supervision of staff working with women should have an equal focus on both the wellbeing of the member of staff and caseload management. Wellbeing considerations and support should go further than paying lip service to the needs of a practitioner and should be upheld in a trauma-informed organizational response (Lee, 2018). Devitt (2020) found examples of staff who were feeling the burden of women's work and also concerns regarding increasing staff sickness for practitioners when taking on this role. Simply talking about this with a line manager does not suffice to address the crux of the issue and changes in organizational priorities and measures to become gender specific, which are required so as to support staff taking on a women's lead role. This issue is also highlighted well through Knight's (2012) work which considers the extent of emotional literacy required for probation practitioners working with both men and women. In her thesis (ibid), Knight highlights the impact of emotional labour on staff when this is silenced or inadequately supported. Rather than just rely on supervision, seemingly provided to staff across areas in an inconsistent manner, she advocates for the joint approach of supporting staff by means such as debriefing, clinical supervision and reflective practice, and this needing to be prioritised equally alongside targets for practice.

Changes in how work is allocated to staff via the re-modelling of the workload management tool has allowed additional time to be allocated to staff according to the assessed complexity level of the individual. This was a welcome step forward in acknowledging that risk alone is not the only indicator of practitioner time and effort required. On its own however, this resource change is not enough to manage the impact that staff experience when working with women. The role of public protection, offender manager and the targets and measurables which these roles lend themselves to are at odds with the evidence base of what works with women. What works for women is evidenced as being the prioritisation of a strengths-based, relational approach in which practitioners deal with 'a woman as a woman first and an offender second' (HMIP, 2016). This approach is evidenced repeatedly in research and publications (Baldwin, 2022a; Dominey and Gelsthorpe, 2020; Jordan, 2013; Centre for Social Justice 2018; Goldhill, 2016; Rutter, 2021) and is one which requires a change in direction of the organizational priorities specifically when working with women. Asking staff to take on a gender specific, evidence-based approach within an organization focused on criminogenic needs and public protection is incompatible (Annison, 2013) and therefore cannot achieve the reduced reoffending rates of models such as the Greater Manchester Whole System Approach.

Lower caseload numbers, coupled with group reflective practice, clinical supervision and a planned working structure which prioritises reflective time for staff within their working week are measures conducive with establishing an effective and sustainable women's team model. Professional judgement is integral to effectively manage the diverse and dynamic needs of the women who we work with, and staff (and management) need to feel empowered and upskilled to exercise this.

For this response to have the desired impact, the character and interests of the probation practitioner is of equal importance. What we have seen in recent history is resentment towards the role when practitioners are pressured into a women's lead role in the absence of anyone else willing to take this work on, or purely in the pursuit of career development. Thoughtful recruitment into a women's team would include the considered response from the Probation Service as to where the practitioner's interests and strengths lie, how well developed their coping skills are, how well they work with other agencies and their understanding and commitment to a women's centred approach. The strength of a women's team, once established, will then lie in its staffing base. The staff and women on probation would then be included in the progression and evaluation of the team. Listening to their experiences of what is working well and what is not and incorporating their innovative ideas into the evolution of the team, both in the interests of the women on probation as well as the staff within the team.

As mentioned, POWER training for working with women in the Probation Service is being advocated by HMPPS women's team as a training programme of value and importance. Furthermore, now published is a toolkit for practitioners working with women. The toolkit is a result of a Women's Strategic Lead in the south-west region, who has collaborated with experts in the field to produce a package for staff to deliver to women they work with. The earlier identified lack of gender specific training has exacerbated poorer outcomes for women, and revolving door cases that have increased since the TR programme (Prison Reform Trust, 2018). The very notion of being in a Women's Team will support staff in developing a specific knowledge base and effective understanding of the appropriate, trauma-informed application of this knowledge via their day-to-day gender specific communication with other staff. Practitioners will additionally benefit from more specific training around key issues that women face such as the impact of motherhood, grandmotherhood and maternal trauma on their engagement with probation and their management of their sentence (Baldwin, 2022a). It is clear from Baldwin's work that the experience of prison on mothers is critical, yet an area which is discussed infrequently by staff working with mothers on probation. This as a result of the service's focus on criminogenic needs instead of the bigger picture and factors impacting on a woman's ability to engage. The gender specific Farmer Review (2019) further highlights the importance of strengthening familial ties for women and the significance that this plays in creating stability for a woman once released.

Operating Model

A women's centred approach is supported via a wealth of evidence. To translate what a 'woman centred approach' looks like for the Probation Service we can begin by understanding the need to shift practice to a hybrid and flexible model of offender management which acknowledges the 'bigger picture' of complexities that women can be facing.

Models which fail to consider the impact of outside influences on a woman's decisions and priorities are immediately setting themselves up to fail. Traditionally, the probation model has considered criminogenic needs, that is those factors directly linked to offending behaviour, as those which need addressing within the sentence plan. For women who are juggling the demands of multiple complexities within their lifestyles, failure to take these factors into consideration has a substantial impact upon the success of a woman's sentence. These complexities come in a range of guises, which must be considered whether linked to the woman's offence or not (e.g. substance misuse, relationships, mental health, chaotic lifestyle).

Baldwin's (2022a) research into maternal imprisonment and the post-release period reveals the impact of failing to acknowledge the maternal status and trauma of women who are sentenced to prison and who also engage with the Probation Service before during and after prison. She draws out how the impact of punishment is compounded by a woman's status as a mother as she is seen as even less deserving of care. This loss of care of women's children and grandchildren is so often the primary influencer to the women's behaviour and engagement and a source of great trauma. Having to engage in intervention work or sentence planning following an emotional call home to children is evidenced to leave women distracted and unable to engage in the process, yet with no acknowledgement from practitioners to their mothering. As Baldwin identifies, this can and does result in the mother actively disengaging from the processes of supervision or being emotionally unable to engage because of her maternal trauma and/or responsibilities. Yet this is rarely acknowledged — the woman is simply labelled 'disengaged'.

The effect of what is written down in our probation reports has a serious ripple effect for women who are also having to engage with social care to gain access to or care of their children. By taking a woman centred approach to probation practice and starting from a point of curiosity and a desire to learn what the woman defines as her main priorities and influences in her life, we can have positive interactions and acknowledge how parenting can impact upon engagement, instead setting up a plan of engagement which dovetails into the woman's lifestyle. This may include outreach work, home visits and phone calls, all of which, crucially fit in with the woman's lifestyle.

As noted above, Baldwin's (2022a) work is further echoed in the female specific Farmer Review (2019) in which relationships are discussed as a critical element in supporting and sustaining desistance from offending and stable lifestyles for women being released. This can be supported by the Probation Service creating measurables linked to objectives to develop positive relationships in all sentence plans for women.

Probation women's teams would be part of a larger MDT, which would allow for ease of information sharing and communication between professionals. Other organizations within this MDT will include social and welfare agencies which are crucial to effectively supporting a woman's stability in the community. A key aspect of this work would include the ability of Women's Lead practitioners in probation to delegate mandatory appointments to other agencies, empowering the woman on probation to have choice in who she wishes to work with, putting her choice at the heart of any response from agencies. Information sharing in this forum will increase the likelihood of practitioners being confident that where appropriate criminalised women are engaging with other services, or that there are more appropriate practitioners to gain the trust and compliance of the individual.

Recall to prison is extremely damaging to any attempts to rebuild lives in the community and the trust that a woman has in the Probation Service. Where a woman is steadily engaged with another service and there is no evidence of risk escalation, the probation practitioner can liaise with professionals as to the best way forward, rather than see the lack of engagement with the Probation Service as requiring enforcement discussions. Whilst this occurs on some levels currently in practice, the strengthening of ties to other organizations, particularly via a woman-centred, multi-disciplinary approach further increases the chances of working with a woman in the community and building the support network for her sustained stability.

Enforcement and Role Clarity

We have found that women with lived experience speak consistently of the difficulty they have placing trust in statutory organizations, and specifically probation practitioners. The impact of a recall decision should not be underestimated on women and their deteriorating trust in practitioners and the organization. We have found ourselves profoundly affected when a woman has told us of the injustices of 'the system' which are resulting in her frustration and feeling that she is being set up to fail. Women describe: the conflicting notion of enforced curfews which restrict access to suitable employment; the desire to gain accommodation to satisfy social care requirements, yet only being given access to a one bedroom property as she doesn't have full custody of her child (meaning in a one bedroomed space where she will not be eligible to have her children returned); the expectation that probation appointments will be a priority, when she is juggling the demands of parenting and an abusive partner. The mixed messages from probation exacerbate this situation and are borne from the dichotomy that is encompassed by the probation practitioner role—rehabilitation and enforcement, a dichotomy also felt, although arguably to a lesser extent, by the practitioner. Working in both a trauma-informed and enforcing role is challenging without further training and support for this. Greater clarity around the women's lead role within a women's team is therefore crucial to sustaining trust and engagement of the woman on probation.

In order to provide clarity to women and staff, the boundaries of a Women's Lead role must be clearly defined. Women's probation practitioners, as part of a multi-disciplinary response to women, can safely revert to the trauma-informed offender management, whilst relying on their colleagues within the MDT, who are better placed to work on more sensitive aspects of the woman's bigger picture. Gelsthorpe (2010) promotes the creative work with women's centres and partnerships between them and CJS agencies. Given the power of recall and enforcement held by the probation practitioner, which is acutely felt by women on probation, this clarity of role will benefit the working relationship and thus engagement of a woman on probation.

It is important to consider the recall and breach threshold through a gender specific lens, and role clarity is not the only response to rectify the issue of trust and engagement.

Hampshire's women's team explained that their recall rate for women on probation was extremely low. This was as a result of their understanding that women required a very flexible approach given the enormity and complexity of problems so often present in their lives (Gelsthorpe, 2009; Dominey and Gelsthorpe, 2020). They see that part of their role is outreach work and listening to other professionals involved to learn of women's engagement with other services. In cases where a woman has become estranged from the service, a gender specific, trauma-informed response would require the practitioner actively seeking contact with the woman, either directly or indirectly via other services. This approach acknowledges the social inequalities that women in the CJS so often find themselves victim to and moves away from viewing the estrangement as a result of individual pathology.

There is a benefit to an organizational acknowledgment of what is within and outside of the woman's control. This will go a long way to supporting the development of trust and engagement with a practitioner and the service. Therefore, recall and breach should be considered an absolute last resort and only in cases where there is clear evidence of risk escalation. This has been acknowledged by HMIP (2018) whereby they recognised that 'enforcement had the effect of compounding rather than lessening the sense of a revolving door between prison and the community'. In a similar vein, other authors support the assumption against the use of short sentences for women and recalls for women so often are for very short periods of time. The impact of a recall on a short-term basis, has the same detrimental impact on a woman and should be viewed comparably to the priority within in the Female Offender Strategy (2018) for the reduction in short-term sentences.

Principles of Practice

In order to shift practice towards a gender specific and trauma-informed way of working, the trauma-informed core values must be taken on and supported as a priority. These are *safety, trustworthiness, choice, collaboration* and *empowerment*. These are also the principles of feminist research. Repeatedly, practitioners have fed back in trauma-informed training that they wholeheartedly endorse the approach and are attuned to this style as it is akin to their motivational interviewing, pro-social modelling training and their understanding of the importance in developing professional working relationships. Yet they voice concern regarding effectively delivering on these principles as they can be over-shadowed by the abundance of desk-based tasks.

▌▌ Pause for Thought

- How can practitioners keep sight of the importance of a relational, trauma-informed way of working when they are tasked with conflicted and competing demands?
- How can practitioners tackle this on a long-term basis individually, within their team and challenge this within the wider organization?
- What is the impact on women specifically of failing to sustain trauma-informed and compassionate practice?

This pressure to have to 'do everything' (rehabilitate, assess, analyse, build rapport, enforce, complete intervention and so on) can be alleviated by co-working with partner agencies. Creating a working practice with women which has robust pathways between the Probation Service and other agencies working with the women supports role clarity, reduces duplication, shares workloads, and increases information sharing. Even in areas where a whole systems approach is not fully-established, strong partnership relationships can be created and supported by the organization at a governance level, thus creating a space to then supervise women in a consistent and trauma-informed manner as well as to ease pressure on themselves. This working style supports the core trauma-informed values by increasing choice and trustworthiness as the woman on probation does not have to re-tell her story repeatedly to different profession-als and is being giving consistent messages from multiple organizations. For probation practitioners specifically, who are not always best placed to support the woman through her rehabilitation whilst holding the powers of enforce-ment, this approach also enhances the safety that a woman is likely to feel in engaging with each agency.

Building trust with women on probation should be a key element in all trauma-informed work and given priority. For probation practitioners this can be achieved by changing the approach to understand that it is our responsibility to build that trust and create a plan of contact which fits into the woman's lifestyle. Resilience within the women's teams would also allow a consistent practitioner to be present for a woman to support the development of trust. On occasions in which a second practitioner is required to cover for sickness or annual leave, this should be a person known to the woman on probation. Pod working systems (a small team of around three staff members who consistently work with each other) support this consistent approach with officers working together to cover caseloads in the case of staff absence.

These principles should be supported by the structure of the working week reflecting a culture within the organization which upholds the essence of trauma-informed work. A working week which includes reflection time for staff and gender specific team discussions will promote best practice for women.

Conclusion

Permeating all levels of this model is the need to demonstrate to women in the CJS that the organization acknowledges the differences to which they are subject when faced with the prospect or reality of becoming involved in the CJS. This is done by changing the focus from individual pathology and addressing criminogenic needs, to one which acknowledges the aspects of a woman's journey which are in her control, and those which are not. This requires a response which is also brave enough to acknowledge Barlow's (2019) research into pathways into crime for victims of domestic abuse and the assumption of choice which statutory organizations adhere to when considering the decisions that the woman has made.

Conversely, taking a strength-based and gender specific approach which is rooted in trauma-informed responses from offender managers has the very real potential to make the substantial impact on women's lives. This is something which so many probation practitioners join the service with the intention and hope of achieving (Knight, 2012). Crucial to this model achieving sustainability, is that the trauma-informed response must be extended to practitioners themselves who are working with women in complex circumstances. What is simply inspirational is that women with lived experience and practitioners alike, despite the odds being against them, express so eloquently their passion, commitment and motivation to make a difference for themselves and other women in the CJS and their families. When this approach from women is supported by a gender specific and trauma-informed model, the capacity to achieve far-reaching outcomes becomes extraordinary.

CHAPTER 3

Desistance and the Stigma Machine
Being a 'Good Woman'

Úna Barr and Natalie Rutter

This chapter presents an insight into the qualitative desistance experiences of criminalised women. We are critical of the way criminalised women are 'responsibilised' to make changes in their own lives, shaped by the inequalities they experience under patriarchy and neoliberalism. The chapter particularly focuses on the concept of stigma, drawing upon the issues raised by Imogen Tyler (2020) in *Stigma: The Machinery of Inequality*. Tyler reconceptualises stigma as stigma-power (discussed below). We apply Tyler's theoretical understanding to two desistance narratives of women serving community sentences, Katie and Karen, who are representative of the women we met and interviewed during our respective PhD studies in the North of England. We note that the concept of the 'good woman' present in desistance research, policy and practice is neglectful of the often-overlapping structural conditions that surround both women's criminalisation and victimisation. We argue that criminalised women are stigmatised when they do not live up to the neoliberal and patriarchal expectations of what it is to be a 'good woman' which can affect their relationships and desistance from crime, as well as (and often more importantly) their experiences of harm. To finish the chapter, we consider how positive relationships and solidarity can inform anti-stigma struggles, to provide intersectional resistance to the 'stigma machine of inequality' (Tyler, ibid).

At the time of writing, the Conservative Government continues to move ahead with its plan to create 500 new prison places for women. This is despite the conclusions of excellent feminist work such as Baldwin's (2015) *Mothering Justice*, which focused on working with mothers in criminal and social justice settings. The concluding chapter included the proposal to 'reduce the number of women and mothers entering custody in the first instance, abolish short sentences and restrict remands in custody to only the most essential circumstances' (p. 278). Feminist organizations such as Women in Prison and Sisters Uncut have continued to argue how increasing prison places for women will shatter individual lives and destroy families and communities. Much of the desistance literature has been critical of the role prison plays in supporting criminalised individuals' desistance. As Barr and Hart (2022) argue, imprisonment is antithetical to desistance and entrenches harm. Further, the building of 500 new prison places also flies in the face of the Government's own Female Offender Strategy (2018) which referenced the harm imprisonment can cause to women's lives, families and communities.

As well as the expansion of the prison estate, we are witnessing the domination of neoliberal ideals of 'responsibilisation' and 'individualisation' within the Criminal Justice System (CJS). We saw this in the discourses of resilience that surrounded the Corston Report in 2007, and indeed these were cemented in the Female Offenders Strategy (above). Our combined research has highlighted the marginalisation and subjugation criminalised women face in every aspect of their lives. As is shown by other chapters of this book, women experience abuse, violence, trauma, poverty, shame and stigma before they are criminalised, within the CJS, and indeed following criminal justice contact. Stigma power is an essential component of the responsibilisation discourse and individualisation inherent in State policy around criminalised women. Whilst desistance literature has highlighted the importance of social bonds to friends, families and communities in shaping desistance from crime, these are often damaged by criminalisation alongside previous and current experiences of victimisation (Barr, 2019; Barr and Christian, 2019). However, there is room for hope, we argue, in relationships that challenge and contest this stigma.

Desistance and Stigma

The study of desistance from crime can no longer be said to be based only around the experiences of white heterosexual men. In particular there have been advances in the study of the gendered experience of desistance, largely from examination of women's perspectives (Rodermond et al, 2016; Hart, 2017; Österman, 2018, 2021; Barr, 2019; Barr and Christian, 2019; Gålnander, 2020;

Rutter and Barr, 2021). Critical examinations of the influence of power and social structures have tended to be confined to intersectional feminist explorations of desistance. As noted in Barr (2019), early theories around desistance tended to fall into three categories — maturational theories, social bonds theories or subjective theories emerging from the examination of narratives of criminalised people. Early narrative explanations located the experience of shame and stigma (LeBel et al, 2008). Braithwaite (1989) drew distinctions between re-integrative shame imposed by the CJS, where the internal self-worth of the individual was preserved and stigmatising shame, where both the (criminal) act and the actor were degraded. They noted (ibid) that experiences of stigmatising shame could lead to 'doomed to deviance' narratives (Maruna, 2001) which in turn meant it was particularly difficult for these individuals to desist.

Feminist theorists such as Probyn (2005) have argued that shame is gendered, particularly the case when women experience abuse, as so many within the CJS have, historically and contemporaneously. Probyn also argued that those who experience shame at a young age are likely to experience it in later life. Further, women are subject to being 'doubly demonised' when they are criminalised (Heidenshohn and Silvestri, 2012; Worrall, 1990; Leverentz, 2014) with Baldwin (2022a) arguing that, for mothers, the demonisation is threefold when they are shamed for breaking the social-, gender-, and mother-contract. Therefore, whilst desistance theorists (Maruna 2001; LeBel et al, 2008) propose that internalised stigma can be a barrier to living a crime-free life, feminist theorists add that this can be especially profound for criminalised women. Arguments highlighting that marginalising experience for women generally, and criminalised women (including mothers) particularly, adds to their experience of gendered harm.

Desistance and Relationships

Within early desistance studies, particularly those based on social-bonds theory, there was often reference to the 'good woman' (Laub and Sampson, 2001), usually a romantic partner or mother figure, who would influence men to 'go straight'. These supporting (literally as well as figuratively) characters were not examined in great detail in these initial desistance studies (Harding, 2017). This absence of investigation is particularly jarring when we consider that criminalised women's offending is often linked to the offending of a male partner and/or their histories of victimisation (Barr and Christian, 2019; Gålnander, 2020).

Alison Phipps speaks of the 'ideal neoliberal subject' as someone who faces adversity 'and makes the best of all situations' (2014: 34). The 'good woman' in early male-focused desistance analysis exemplifies this characterisation. As we will see in the narratives that follow from Katie and Karen, it is impossible to 'make the best of all situations' when women are facing intersecting inequalities relating to their experiences of criminalisation and victimisation and the related experience of stigma. The 'good woman' construction also affects their relationships.

Desistance research has evidenced and acknowledged how this journey must be understood within the context of relational networks (McNeill and Weaver, 2010; McNeill et al, 2012). However, research here has continued to focus on the male experience. Theoretically, relational desistance considers how change is seen by others (Nugent and Schinkel, 2016), while the argument around tertiary desistance highlights the importance of an individual's sense of belonging (McNeill, 2016). While this work enables recognition of wider structural forces that move beyond individualisation, it fails to distinguish the vulnerabilities and victimisation of criminalised women which are shaped by patriarchal structures, and how a sense of belonging can reaffirm what it means to be a 'good woman' within wider society. While women are more likely to emphasise the importance of relational desistance (McIvor et al, 2004) their experiences are largely formulated within relationships where they are the main carers of children. This reiterates their responsibility for family members, and the ideals of heteropatriarchy, with Booth et al (2018) raising the importance of considering the diverse forms of 'family' which surround the experiences of criminalised women's experiences. Baldwin (2022a) highlights how motherhood can intersect with desistance, being either a protective and motivating factor, or when children are removed to the care system, a risk factor.

In addition, research has noted that women can be coerced into criminal acts when involved in abusive relationships. Conversely, women can desist from crime entirely when they experience coercive control in abusive relationships (Barr and Christian, 2021). Research has shown the qualities of trust, being respected, not being judged, being understood and the importance of giving time, as fundamental in relationships that can be supportive of desistance (Rutter, 2019). Therefore, for criminalised women it is paramount to distinguish between relationships that can support desistance from crime and harm, and those that represent toxicity and a barrier to the process (Farmer, 2019).

Stigma: The Machinery of Inequality

Imogen Tyler argues that:

> '[S]tigma is designed, crafted and activated to govern populations on multiple scales and in diverse sites and … stigma production *from above* accelerates in periods of political and economic turmoil, often in response to particular demands of capital (and capitalists).' (2020: 269, emphasis in original)

Tyler describes stigma as 'a governmental technology of division and dehumanisation …' that corrodes 'compassion, crushing hope, weakening social solidarity' (ibid: 7). In examining stigma, Tyler refocuses the conversation on the production of stigma: 'where stigma comes from, how and by whom stigma is produced and for what purposes' (ibid: 8). This refocusing on the origins of stigma is important for critical criminology and desistance theorists in particular.

Tyler is critical of Ernest Goffman's much-cited work on stigma (1963/1990), noting that Goffman 'unplugs the concept of stigma from power: both the power-inflected micro-aggressions of the everyday social interactions he was ostensibly interested in, and the larger structural and structuring power relations which shape the societies in which we live' (2020: 22). By reclaiming the concept of stigma as a tool of power-relations, we can see beyond the interpersonal impacts of stigma and 'management' of spoiled identities, towards locating the production and weaponisation of stigma against socially undesirable groups of people (Ballantine, 2020).

Criminology and criminal justice in general, and desistance theory in particular, can learn from intersectional abolitionist feminism, which critiques, and aims to dismantle white supremacist capitalist heteropatriarchy (Hooks, 2009). As has been noted above, the 'difficulties' and 'vulnerabilities' faced by criminalised women have long been recognised by State research and analysis. Yet these reports are produced at times where women continue to be criminalised, while their services are cut at ever-increasing increments. It is within the State's interest to stigmatise criminalised women. For example, media crafting of welfare stigma is an essential mechanism of consent for austerity (Tyler, 2020) with neoliberal and heteropatriarchal constructions of 'the good woman' essential to the maintenance of stigma.

Yet, as Tyler persuasively argues, there is resistance to be found in stigmatisation. At the outset of *Stigma: The Machinery of Inequality*, Tyler uses a quote from a letter from Karl Marx to Arnold Ruge in 1843:

> 'Shame is already a revolution of a kind…Shame is a kind of anger which is turned inward. And if a whole nation really experienced a sense of shame, it would be like a lion, crouching ready to spring.' (Tyler, 2020: xiii)

By listening to criminalised women's narratives, we can locate the stigma-power of capitalist heteropatriarchy in their constructions of 'the good woman'. We can also locate the resistance against this stigmatisation and consider the collective effort required to challenge the stigma machine which creates inequality.

Background to Our Research

The research from which this chapter is based is discussed further in our *Probation Journal* article on 'Being a Good Woman' (Rutter and Barr, 2021). In brief, it is grounded in our respective PhD studies in the North of England, which both paid attention to the narrative experiences of criminalised individuals. Whilst NR's research employed a gender comparative sample to explore the role of whole relational networks in the processes of desistance, and particularly co-production (Rutter, 2019, 2020), ÚB's focused specifically on the desistance experiences of criminalised women (Barr, 2019). Both projects employed mixed methodological approaches with NB's focusing on conversational interviewing supported by visual and activity-based research and ÚB's employing ethnographic research at women's centres and semi-structured life-course interviews.

Research within Criminology, and in particular, desistance, has increasingly recognised the role and value of narratives, not only to understand experience and action but also the relationship to individual identity and the wider collectives to which individuals belong (Pemberton et al, 2019). Harding (2020a) raises the importance of recognising similarities and difference across an individuals' position within society, questioning how the knowledge privileged in criminal justice is often quantifiably deemed facts about criminalised individuals rather than the subjective experiences of criminalisation. It is therefore of fundamental importance that both researchers and practitioners listen. Also that they attend to the views of criminalised women (Burke et al, 2019) as narratives are central to our human experience, constantly changing and evolving over time (Presser and Sandberg, 2015).

Narrative analysis has been a key element of Feminist Criminology (Fleetwood, 2015; Maruna and Liem, 2020) sitting well within intersectional feminist approaches that draw attention to the patriarchal and neoliberal structures and discourse which provide the context to women's criminalisation, victimisation and desistance. Narrative Criminology has been particularly pivotal in explaining the onset and end of offending, with concentration on the relationship between structure and agency. By asking respondents to relate their life-stories, we can see the relationship between often-idealised pasts and imagined futures. We see the construction of the 'good woman' in descriptions of past selves, future selves and ideal others and we can note how these compare with women's understandings of their current identities.

Analysis of interviews with 29 criminalised women conducted between 2014 and 2019 form the basis of the arguments made in this chapter. In our *Probation Journal* article, we employed a thematic approach (Braun and Clarke, 2006) to analysis of our interview data, resulting in the emergence of four key themes within criminalised women's narratives in relation to stigma. These were: becoming a 'good woman'; shame, stigma and criminalisation; shame, stigma and victimisation; and relational networks. Conversely, in this chapter, we follow the feminist templates for narrative analysis set out by Carlen et al (1985) and more recently by Baldwin and her colleagues (2021c). We have chosen in this chapter to provide a case-study narrative approach to provide a greater insight into the experiences of Katie and Karen.[10] Whilst their stories are unique, sadly their experiences had much in common with many criminalised women we spoke to, particularly in terms of their experiences of stigma, criminalisation, victimisation, relationships and the role of stigma power in producing a particular construction of the 'good woman'.

Katie had no previous personal experience of criminalisation, but for Karen the experience was not new. Nonetheless, their convictions could be described as 'low level'. Both women were mothers, like most, but not all, of our interviewees, and their narratives were informed by what Baldwin refers to a Mothers Code of Conduct (2017: 30; 2022a), informing their perception of how they as women and mothers should, and importantly should not, behave. Their narratives present pockets of hope for the future through an examination of the small but significant ways the women have resisted stigma power.

Katie

I (ÚB) first met Katie[11] at her last group session at the women's centre. During both interviews, Katie was very emotional when talking about her offence and cried when relating her story in both interviews. In February 2013, following an arrest eleven months earlier, Katie pleaded guilty to a benefit fraud charge. It was her first and only experience of criminalisation. Since the arrest, Katie had attempted suicide on numerous occasions, her 37-year marriage had suffered, and she had been 'paranoid' and experienced panic attacks. At the first interview Katie said that most days she would not leave the house, although at our second meeting, a year into her 18-month supervision order, her mental health had improved somewhat. Katie clearly articulated her feelings of stigma from her experiences of criminalisation in our first interview:

'I feel like I've got "criminal" tattooed on my forehead. That's how I feel. And I mean I know it's not murder or anything, it's not child abuse or anything like, but it's still, I've still fraudulently claimed from the Government. And

---

10. Although Katie and Karen were both participants in ÚB's research, similar narratives were found throughout both our data.
11. Pseudonyms are given to the women and places named throughout our research.

that's…And people have said to me, "I can't understand it." And I've said, "Well if I'd had the courage to plead not guilty then this probably wouldn't have happened because I would have really fought…But now I'm struck with depression, anxiety…It's been horrendous, and I've no faith in the police now. Like I said, if somebody had have sent me a letter, I wouldn't have ignored it, I've never been like that. I've always been brought up to you know, know right from wrong. My father, he would never claim benefit or anything. My mother wouldn't, they didn't believe in it you know, so I weren't brought up that way. The only thing I'd ever claimed was maternity allowance, before the end of the nineties, when I went on disability allowance.'

At the time of interview, Katie was 60 years old and had lived in her hometown her entire life, other than a year spent in a nearby town in her teenage years when her father, a miner, had to move for work. Her mother was a weaver. Katie described her childhood as happy but strict, in that she was scared to do anything wrong. Returning after a year, Katie and her younger sister went to live with her grandmother whilst her parents ran a pub. Talking about her grandmother, Katie says; 'She was a big person in my life when I was younger… She was more like a mother really than my mother.' In later years, Katie found out that she had two uncles on her father's side who spent time in prison, but her father no longer spoke to them. Katie performed well in school but was forced by her mother to leave at age 15. She had wanted to go into nursing as a younger woman, but her mother would not allow it.

'She said, "If you live on campus, you'll end up being a prostitute because there's nobody there to tell you what to do and what not to do, so you'll just do what you want, because you're not very knowledgeable about boys." And that was her attitude. It was really difficult, really strict.'

Katie felt that her parents were stricter on her than her younger sister; her mother had explained that Katie had always been the favourite and that was the reason for the caution surrounding her behaviour. After getting married at the age of 22 to a former soldier and long-distance lorry driver, Katie followed the family tradition and became a licensee at a working men's club. She had three children, all girls. Katie and her husband also became foster parents once they moved back into her parents' large house. Following a hysterectomy, Katie put on a lot of weight. She became diabetic and needed a wheelchair to get about. As a result, Katie had to give up her job and started to claim disability living allowance. Her doctor prescribed a new drug, Byetta, which helped Katie control her diabetes and lose weight. As a result, in 2003/2004, Katie applied to go back to work; she went to college and began a catering course, with a key worker from the Job Centre assisting her. Following the course, Katie was offered a job supervising a cleaning team. Eventually, she started work at a local Michelin starred restaurant and hotel as a supervising housekeeper. Katie told me that, during the job interview, she had stated what she could and could not do and this was cleared with the Job Centre, who stated that she would be on disability allowance indefinitely unless there were any changes in her circumstances. Around this time, Katie began struggling in her work. She described it as arduous, despite being exempt from heavy lifting and buying equipment to help with the work. At home over Christmas, Katie had a fall and as a result started overdosing on prescription painkillers to help with the pain, and to help her do her job.

> 'I didn't want to let anybody down and I felt "Can I stop work? Can I go back to the way I were before, sitting in a chair and not being to get out?" And I thought, "No, no". So instead of taking six painkillers, I started taking between 12 and 16.'

She was not enjoying the work and felt that the other staff bullied her. Katie left work in March 2012. Two days later, she was arrested. During our first interview, Katie described in great detail the day of her arrest; the knock on the door at 6.30 am and her fear that her husband had been in an accident; her collapse in the police station; vomiting in her cell as she waited to be interviewed for six hours without food or water or access to her medication. During the interview process, she was shown police footage of herself out shopping, in college and taking her daughter to the hospital, walking without a walking stick in parts. She described being aggressively questioned about this for two hours, and eventually released on bail. In the three months following the arrest, Katie lost weight, and she began to get depressed, anxious and paranoid. In June 2012, she was told that either she would be charged in the next 12 months, or the case would be dropped. In the intervening period, Katie attempted suicide on numerous occasions. After Christmas, she received a letter informing her that she would be charged. Katie had seen a counsellor at this time who advised her that she was not mentally well enough to go through a court case. As a result of this advice, Katie pleaded guilty to the benefit fraud charge brought against her despite the wishes of her barrister. She received an 18-month supervision order, was ordered to pay £145 in charges and to pay back the £12,000 benefit, which she has been paying back at a rate of £5 per week at the time of interview.

After her arrest and charge, Katie was told she could apply for benefit again but was terrified of doing so due to fears of being re-criminalised. She had been constantly depressed and anxious, receiving a course of counselling at a local mental health unit. Katie and her husband were on an individual voluntary arrangement (IVA) to avoid bankruptcy, something which pre-dated the case. She described her financial situation as:

'knackered ... Well, we've just no money ... we're paying out £275 more than what we've got a month so we're really in dire straits.'

On the day that we had our first interview, Katie's youngest daughter was moving back into the home and Katie suspected it was to keep an eye on her, to make sure she did not do 'anything stupid'. Katie also lived with her grand-daughter and two grandsons; her husband came home on Saturday evening and left very early on Monday morning. When we met up for the second interview, her grandson's friend had also moved in with the family after being kicked out of his own home. At the second interview, Katie's 19-year-old granddaughter, Gemma, had been diagnosed with multiple sclerosis. Katie was extremely upset by this development. Katie felt her family relationships — particularly that with her husband — had broken down since her charge and arrest. In the second interview Katie described herself as 'friends' with her husband but stated that they were no longer in a relationship. Under the terms of the IVA debt solution, they had to live together. She also described a disconnect with her daughters as she felt they did not understand her depression. 'I said to my daughters; they're the same, you know, "I don't feel well"; "Oh get over it, stop being so stupid".'

Her relationship with her younger sister had also broken down. Her closest relationship was with a childhood friend, Rose.

'So we [Katie and Rose] went out for lunch and it was really nice. Yeah we caught up on things and we said we'd do it more often, go out once a month at least and so we can have a talk and she's really good, she's a really good friend and we've known each other since I was nine, so it's nice. She's there if I need her you know she's told me to ring her if I need her she'll come over. So that's nice to know that I've got somebody there besides the family that doesn't judge me. My family seem to judge me and "Oh pull out of it, stop being so daft" you know if I keep saying I feel really down today, "Oh don't be so silly." It's like they don't understand. So she's got lots of patience, Rose has, and it's nice.'

Katie was on a myriad of medication including antidepressants, diabetic medication and very strong painkillers. During our first interview, she described not getting out of bed all day most days but, by the second interview, had taken on a part time volunteering role at a local charity shop one day a week, as encouraged by her counsellor. She enjoyed being in the shop, where she managed the till and chatted to the regular customers. During the first interview, Katie stated that above all she wanted to leave England and ideally move to Spain. She had lost all faith in the police and CJS. This desire remained during our second interview but had been complicated by her granddaughter's illness.

'I do not want to stay in this country a minute longer than I have to do to be perfectly honest…I've never voted because there's nobody who I would have wanted to vote for. And after this experience, as soon as I can, live in another country than England…And I'd rather be Spanish or something than English. I just think it's not a just [country]…[begins to cry].'

Karen

Karen was 36 when we (ÚB) met for our interview in the Housing for Ex-Offenders Unit where she was living after meeting the previous week in the local women's centre where she talked openly about a previous violent relationship within a group session. During interview, Karen discussed her most recent offence, which was a joint enterprise offence for burglary. She had been staying at a friend's house when he woke her in the middle of the night to ask for help moving stolen goods into his flat. Karen had been in trouble with the police throughout her life, from a young age and ever since beginning her heroin addiction. However, this was her first burglary offence, her previous offences were 'just for being petty, just for stupid things … joy riding in cars, looking up to older lads … the wildness started really before I got into the drugs'. Notoriety within the CJS had ironically been a protective factor in the sentencing of the most recent offence. Her friend had been trying to suggest that she had been violent and threatening; 'but luckily the police have known me for years and they said, "look you know Karen's not like that". So, they didn't believe it because they know I'm not like that.' Karen received a six months' prison sentence followed by a six months' community licence which included working with probation, the women's centre and a Christian voluntary service once a week (which works to address 'personal, relational or sexual issues'). Karen noted that she had to move from her community where she knew everyone as heroin was an unacceptable drug: 'It's a no no on our estate, like a dirty drug sort of thing.'

Karen's family—her parents and her younger sister—had moved from Scotland when she was 'six or seven'. Karen's mother had given her father an ultimatum to leave his friends, Karen described the friends as 'gang-related'. They went to live with Karen's grandmother who was working in the local hospital at the time. She describes her family as a 'good Catholic family.' She did not speak to her sister and described their relationship as 'like chalk and cheese'.

> 'She's got everything that I wanted. At 36 I feel like I'm not going to get it now. My kids … I feel like I've lost them through the domestic violence. I wasn't strong enough to make a choice you know. They put me in refuges, in Bridgetown and things that. But I just blocked it out. I just got involved with bad things I felt like to punish myself, I felt I deserved it. I felt like I let my kids down. You know the choice I made to let my kids go to my mum's, I made that choice because it was best for them. If I had have dragged them from house to house … Paul [Karen's ex partner] was smashing houses up.

The kids were very close together, two of them are the same age now, they're both seven but they're not twins. So … age three and under you know it was hard work and then with him on top. So, for years, you know, I was, you know, family orientated and then when it all crumbled, I just went back to what I was like.'

Her relationship with her mother had been rocky and at the time of meeting Karen her mother had custody of the younger three of her four children. Karen described herself as being a 'boisterous tom boy' as a child and 'hard work.' She was excluded from high school at an early age and was out of education for a year before the education department forced her mother to send her on a residential course or else risk a fine. Karen ran away to London and lived in a property, which was attacked by 'yardies', it turned violent, and Karen ended up in custody. She stated that she was lucky to get out of London alive.

Karen had her first son with her partner of five years, Tom, at age 18. During this time she 'never went out, I was quite family orientated.' With the breakup of this relationship, however, she restarted offending and 'basically re-living my youth'. Karen also began forced street prostitution for drug dealers. She then met Sean and had three further sons during their ten-year relationship. Again, she 'settled down' for a few years, but, over time, Sean began to abuse Karen physically, mentally and sexually. Although the police were informed, Karen did not press charges 'so it looked bad on me for the children.' She was in and out of refuges at this time. She later went to live with her mum and three youngest children whilst her oldest son went to live with Tom's parents. Karen's mother then kicked her out of the house because of her drinking. Her children often blame Karen's mother for kicking her out and this resulted in Karen being unable to see her children.

'I've not been seeing them now because my mum doesn't like me seeing them, they get upset, they don't want me to go, and then they just take it out on my mum. Because they remember me and my mum arguing because my mum doesn't like me drinking.'

Nonetheless, Karen felt that her mum had being doing 'an amazing job' at raising her children.

'I'd love to move out of here, start having the children at the weekends and as they're obviously getting older they'll be able to make a decision you know, if they want to stay with me. But my mum is very strict, my mum actually wants to see me get accommodation, live properly, go shopping, live a normal life, do things that normal women do. I don't seem to have that in me, I just feel, you know, incomplete.'

After recently splitting up from Sean, Karen was not interested in getting into a new romantic relationship, as she was scared of what he would do if she were with a new partner.

'I'm too scared about him kicking off anyway, it just wouldn't be worth the hassle. But no it's not something…the relationship I want is that relationship with my family and my kids, that's all I want back.'

Karen does not work due to her health; she has deep vein thrombosis and anxiety issues with panic attacks which she related to being raped and locked up for two weeks by Sean. Karen appeared to shoulder the blame for all her 'decisions', particularly not leaving Sean when he was violent.

'I choose my paths. You know, I went seeking this different life, you know. When I first split up from my eldest son's father I sort of like went off the rails then as well…I know the choices I've made have had a domino effect on me and everyone around me, my whole family and friends. And I realise that now but it's a bit too late, I can't take those memories back for the kids, you know I can't…I've not been seeing them now because my mum doesn't like me seeing them, they get upset, they don't want me to go, and then they just take it out on my mum. Because they remember me and my mum arguing because my mum doesn't like me drinking. I'm quite confrontational when I've had a drink. So my mum kicked me out basically. And my kids were aware of that, they were hearing things so they resented my mum for that. She's done so well. She's done an amazing job. The kids are great. My eldest son, he's at his dad's mum's, and he's spoilt rotten, the conservatory is his games room, he's got a big 50-inch TV, but he doesn't want that, he wants to be with his brothers, he wants the family, and I've took that away from them through stupid choices I've made.'

Karen had been living at the accommodation for ex-offenders in the four months since her release from prison but hoped to get permanent accommodation soon. However, she felt that there was a lack of support for her from the agency who she felt were not doing enough to help her by getting her on housing lists for social housing, 'I feel like I have to tell her [accommodation staff] what to do which is shit really'.

Whilst in prison during her most recent sentence, Karen met a woman, Louise who was critically ill with cancer. Louise moved to Karen's unit two weeks after she came to prison. Karen was not happy with the treatment Louise received in prison. Because of, as Karen felt it, prison staff shortages, Karen effectively became Louise's carer:

'And one of the governors took a liking to me and basically said he respected the fact that I was sticking up for Louise because she used to be a very feisty woman but she was unable to do it for herself at that time. So, her medication got put up and things like that, she was more comfortable and that. And it made me take a big, big look at my life. I watched her kids come to see her, and her 12-year-old daughter, her youngest, you know she had to tell her daughter on a prison visit, you know, "I'm dying". And you know, it was horrible.'

Karen cared for Louise in prison, washing her: '... and basically just getting her up and back, getting her in the chair and making her feel like one of the girls for as long as I could. I used to take her round, push her round the prison.' Karen described this experience as 'an eye-opener ... You know just seeing her losing her family you know, seeing that she didn't have a choice.' Karen noted that her probation officer was 'amazing, she's firm but she's fair, she gives me a good kick up the backside when I need it. But I still feel like I've failed and I can't take back that time.' At the end of the interview, she broke down crying saying:

'I just put a front on all the time, and it's hard work, it's horrible. Deep down I'm so soft … I've to keep this front on because of the lifestyle that I've lived and I'm tired of it now, I'm drained, I've had enough … I'm living day to day at the moment, I'm not even thinking about the future. You know I was thinking about this the other day, you know when I was younger and little girls used to say, "when I'm older and I get married and …" I never had that in my head, I never dreamed of getting married and things like that. And I just feel like, my path was set out at a young age, and I followed it, and here I am now, you know in a train wreck.'

Discussion and Concluding Thoughts

Katie and Karen had very different histories with the CJS. Whilst the benefit fraud charge was Katie's first offence, the CJS was omnipresent in Karen's life from young adulthood and intensified at various points in her life. They lived in different accommodation and had varying levels of support from family members. They had different relationships with friends. Karen experienced horrific domestic abuse. Katie had not. Whilst Katie experienced the CJS as an unjust system, beginning with her arrest, Karen had some positive experiences with the police, in prison, and with her probation officer. Nonetheless, both described unjust experiences with the criminal justice and social justice agencies with whom they were in contact. Both women were mothers, and both had other caring roles, Katie for her grandchildren and foster children, and Karen in prison for her friend. Both women experienced problems with addiction and poor mental health. The clearest connecting theme of their narratives however was their experiences of stigma. This stigma related not only to their criminalisation, but was also experienced in connection to claiming benefits, using drugs and present in their narrating of experiences of motherhood, victimisation, and poor mental health. In particular, stigma connected to the apparent inability of the women to live up to the 'good woman' ideal set by society, and which is also present in the desistance literature. Stigma left the women feeling hopeless. As the desistance literature argues, this could pave the way to the 'doomed to deviance' narratives presented by Maruna (2001). Yet more importantly for Katie and Karen, was desistance from harm, including the harms of the CJS and their previous victimisations. Talking particularly about her experiences of criminalisation and the injustice she felt at her arrest and sentencing, Katie said:

> 'I go to see my probation officer and she says, "Oh take deep breaths in the morning and don't think about it." But if you're taking deep breaths not to think about it, you're thinking about it. And it's there all the time, it's always at the back of my mind. It just won't go away (starts crying), I keep thinking, "How long is it going to be for me?" Because I keep thinking, "What could I have done differently that I hadn't already done?" But it is, it's weird really, it still feels like a dream, it still feels like I'm going to wake up and it's not happened.'

What is clear is that there was a lack of holistic structural support available to Katie to help her deal with the trauma and stigma of her experience within the CJS. This mirrored Karen's traumatic victimisation experiences. Her experiences of domestic violence and the stigma she carried as a result of not leaving her ex-partner (as if this was a simple 'choice') created a hopeless 'doomed to harm' script which had real implications. Karen's narrative is replete with references to her offending being a personal choice. Yet it is difficult to locate within this narrative of abuse, rape and alcohol and drug addiction any moments of clarity, which would have allowed a rational choice to occur. It often appears that Karen's narrative is shaped by the discourse of others. Certainly, within the women's centre group sessions, which were observed as part of our research, there was, at times, a presupposition that crime was a rational choice for the women involved. The 'responsibilisation' of women and the discourse of 'choice' were particularly clear in observations of the 'Thinking and Behaviour' session where offending linked to 'quick and seemingly easy decisions' to solve problems and emphasis was placed on problem solving. At times, this led to overestimation of the choices and agency that the women had by women centre staff (see also Clarke and Chadwick, 2018). Discourse exists, often from a neoliberal 'feminist' position, which encourages women to see themselves as 'survivors' rather than victims (Phipps, 2014). This 'good woman' trope sees victims of violence and abuse as resilient individuals who can overcome victimisation, and, implicitly, are failures when they lack resilience, often in the face of overwhelming structural barriers. This can also result in a denial of victimhood. We see this reflected in criminalised women's own narratives.

Katie and Karen's narratives are also shaped by patriarchal and neoliberal constructions of the 'good woman'. The ever-present 'good woman' in Katie and Karen's narrative was not a benefit claimant, a drug user, a victim of domestic violence nor a 'criminal'. As we have argued above and elsewhere (Rutter and Barr, 2021) the dichotomy of offender/'good woman' is rooted in stigma politics and the operation of stigma power is clear in criminalised women's narratives. Stigma is not created in a vacuum nor in isolated social spaces. Stigma emerges from, and is reproduced by, structures of power including, in this case, hetero-patriarchal capitalism (Tyler, 2020). For criminalised women, society, and the CJS measure desistance by conformity to traditional feminine roles (Parry, 2013). Desistance is often associated with becoming 'an agent of neoliberalism' (Sim, 2018; see also Cederstrom and Spicer, 2015). We see this in liberal feminist constructions of 'empowerment' within practice, which individualises change and responsibilises criminalised women (Elfleet, 2021). We also see it in the desistance literature with its focus on paid work, which does not challenge the unpaid work of carers and voluntary workers, nor offer solutions to those who cannot work or are not given the materials needed to be able to do so. Further, male-focused desistance literature often places the burden of male desistance on their female partners (Rutter and Barr, 2021; Barr and Hart, 2022). This is clearly grounded in hetero-patriarchal constructions of the role of women in romantic partnerships.

Faith (2011) considers the bonds women make with other prisoners as a form of resistance, resisting 'prisonisation' and maintaining dignity (see also Baldwin, 2022a). For Karen, caring for Louise and her feelings of hope from being able to help make Louise's life more comfortable had a significant effect on resistance. Not only did she experience her own agency, but she also describes a 'wake-up call' regarding her own offending and drug use. However, once outside of prison, Karen's continuous victimisation at the hands of the CJS, her former partner, her accommodation providers and lack of family support at times diminished all self-efficacy which emerged from this 'defining moment'. The breaking of the stigma machine (Tyler, 2020) which Karen was able to achieve whilst in prison became a temporary solution once in the community and faced with the realities of stigma power.

Nonetheless, there are pockets of hope and resistance to the stigma machine in both Katie's and Karen's narratives. These emerged in both cases from their friendships with other women, Karen with Louise, and Katie with her friend Rose. These small packets of hope in interpersonal relationships alone were not enough for the women to move into a life free from stigma, as indicated in the final quotes of their narratives. The lack of structural support for the women to resist the stigma machine was evident in both narratives. Although deemed essential to desistance from crime, criminalised women often experience a lack of strong, positive relational connections (Singh et al, 2019) providing the context and environment for abuse, victimisation (Barr and Christian, 2021) and dysfunctional relationships (Booth et al, 2018). McNeish and Scott (2014) highlight that women's experiences of violence and abuse are often perpetrated by family members. However, the response is often only addressed at an agentic level, with the structural forces of patriarchy neither considered nor discussed (Barr, 2018).

Missed and lost opportunities to support women mean that women are regularly criminalised for being in poverty or 'offending' in the context of trauma (Baldwin, 2022a). The CJS must not be a place where women can go to receive help. It is a dangerous, violent system that lessens chances of receiving employment and family support, even where women are given community sentences. This is particularly true for women, and mothers, whose experiences of stigma are affected by gender dynamics. When women do receive community sentences, the focus must be on providing structural support to resist the stigma machine, challenging stigmatising understandings of the 'good woman' emerging from heteropatriarchal capitalism, encouraging friendship, love and support as well as the practical matters of housing, employment and trauma-focused support for victimisation. Desistance from harm is a collective struggle in breaking the stigma machine. Individualised responsibilisation, grounded in patriarchal and neoliberal arguments, must be resisted at all costs. We call, more widely for a 'reparative justice that supports the building of solidarity movements [in which we] ... rise in rage together against the stigma machines' (Tyler, 2020: 271).

CHAPTER 4

'They Just Didn't Want to Help Me'
The Criminalisation of Coerced Women Co-offenders

Charlotte Barlow

This chapter considers the influence of violence, coercion and love within intimate relationships on women's offending behaviour, particularly co-offending. Criminalised women more broadly are typically viewed to be wholly independent, rational agents or as lacking control in relation to their offending behaviour and thus having their agency completely denied. However, this dichotomy is problematic, as it fails to consider how violent, coercive and controlling dimensions of co-offending relationships may influence offending behaviour and experiences of agency. The importance of acknowledging such experiences in social context when attempting to understand such women's offending 'choices', and the current failings to do so in criminal justice responses, is explored. Furthermore, the chapter emphasises the need to move away from criminalisation in response to such women, offering a critique of both the victim/offender dichotomy that plagues the Criminal Justice System (CJS) and the limits of the law in providing adequate defences for women co-offenders who have experienced coercion, violence and abuse. It will also reflect on the challenges and opportunities of trauma-informed approaches in providing appropriate support for such women, particularly when these approaches occur in a criminal justice context.

Introduction

Feminist pathways research has identified that women's lawbreaking is characterised by structural, institutional and familial injustices and disadvantages, the most clearly gendered of these being their frequent experience of violence and sexual victimisation (Belknap and Holsinger, 2006; Batchelor, 2005). Coercion within intimate relationships has also increasingly been acknowledged as a potential motivating factor for female offending behaviour (Barlow, 2016; Jones, 2008; Ritchie, 1996). However, such experiences of coercion, violence and abuse are rarely understood by criminal justice professionals as a potential influencing factor on women's offending. As proposed by Sharpe (2016), it is not the intention of this chapter to identify such issues as a potential 'risk factor' for offending, as this essentialises and de-contextualises criminalised women's experiences from institutional injustices. Rather this chapter aims to highlight the significance of coercion and abuse for female co-offenders, particularly when they are in an intimate and abusive relationship with their partner/co-offender, and situate their experiences within the context of the social and structural conditions and constraints which shape women's lives. In doing so, the first section of the chapter discusses the ways in which rationality dominates legal explanations for offending. The second section explores the ways in which violence and coercion influences co-offending women's offending motivations. The third explores the ways in which the CJS and the law fail to recognise such experiences, leading to the increased criminalisation of women. Finally, the chapter critically examines the issues surrounding the focus on women's 'choices' within the context of such offending and considers alternative approaches to gendered justice.

'Malestream' Criminology and Rationality

What has been termed 'malestream' Criminology emphasises the male-dominated nature of traditional criminological perspectives and Criminology as a discipline. As highlighted by Walklate (2004: 24), early nineteenth century academics, such as Cesare Lombroso and Guglielmo Ferrero (1895), have 'framed the way in which thinking about males and females and masculinity and femininity has been constructed'. The deterministic and androcentric writings of such early criminological thinkers have had continued significance on criminological thought in more recent years. Gender is a key determinant of likely involvement in offending behaviour, yet the importance of gender has not always been reflected in the development of criminological thought, as such knowledge has historically assumed that crime is men's work and not women's (Walklate, 2001). The minimisation of women's motivations for offending and how this differs to that of men has led to an emphasis on rationality and rational choice pervading criminological thought and criminal justice practice. This reinforces rationality and agency being readily ascribed to men's motivations for offending, whereas women are either associated with being emotional, and therefore weak-minded, or are over-endowed with agency and rendered remorseless (Sydie, 1987). Criminalised women are often characterised as 'mad' in legal and media discourse, suggesting that offending influences are implicitly linked to irrationality, hysteria or mental health issues (Ballinger, 2000; Barlow, 2016). Such discourse represents any offending influences as non-agentic, and consequently represents women offenders as child-like or malicious when compared to male counterparts.

There is currently minimal scope for considering nuanced understandings of the ways in which intimate relationships, violence and abuse influence women's offending in legal and criminal justice practice. This is due to male-defined epistemology pervading legal thought, therefore legal terminology by its nature, such as 'rational man of the law', privileges the position and perspective of men (Yeo, 1993; Ballinger, 2021). However, as highlighted by Ballinger (2012: 452) 'to make assumptions about the population as a whole based on such constructions is to privilege the understanding of the world of the group which has dominated legal and public life: white, middle-class, heterosexual men'. This legal and public domination of the male perspective has led to all experiences and behaviour which fall outside these parameters to being 'othered' and consequently silenced (Barlow, 2016; Carline, 2005). Ballinger (2012: 452) argues that such principles lead to a double exclusion of the female experience, due to both the gendered nature of the law and men's experiences being viewed to be hierarchically more valuable. Consequently, women's experiences are 'othered' in criminological and legal thought due to both their sex and the gendered emphasis on rationality or choice being the principal motivation for offending.

However, such male-defined explanations for offending do not reflect the experiences of many criminalised women, particularly those who co-offend with a male partner. The relatively small body of research exploring women's co-offending has suggested that women often engage in more serious offending with a male partner than when they do so alone (Mullins and Wright,

2003; Koons-Witt and Scharm, 2003) and that they are more likely to engage in gender atypical offences when they co-offend with a man, such as robbery and murder (Becker and McCorkel, 2011). Scholars have also focused specifically on the experiences of women who are in an *intimate* relationship with their male co-offender. For example, Welle and Falkin (2000) have suggested that these women often experience 'relationship policing', which involves many aspects of their relationship and life, including participation in criminal activity, being controlled by their romantic co-offender. The intersecting inequalities of race and gender have also been considered in relation to co-offending women's experiences. Richie (1996: 133) has argued that an intersection of gender and racial inequality can lead women to be 'compelled' into a variety of criminal and deviant behaviours, with the notion of 'gender entrapment' helping 'to show how some women are forced or coerced into crime by their culturally expected gender roles, the violence in their intimate relationships and their social position in the broader society'. Moreover, Jones (2008) suggests that women who co-offend with intimate male partners are categorised in terms of their involvement in three key ways: acting as a result of coercion, offending 'out of love', and/or adopting an 'equal' role in the offending. I have also explored elsewhere the notion of a 'continuum of coercion' to explain how abusive, controlling and violent relationships with male, intimate partners/co-offenders may influence women's pathways into crime and offending decision-making (Barlow, 2016). This body of work collectively emphasises the significance of relationships on offending behaviour for women in particular.

Domestic abuse is increasingly acknowledged as a pathway into crime and continued motivation to offend for some women (Schaffner, 2007; Belknap and Holsinger, 2006; Barlow, 2016). For example, The Duluth Power and Control Wheel, designed as part of Domestic Abuse Prevention Programmes in the United States, acknowledges coercion into crime as a potential method of domestic abuse. Furthermore, the Corston Report (2007), which evaluated women's experiences of the CJS in the United Kingdom, also emphasises the importance of understanding the ways in which women's experiences of victimisation and domestic abuse influence their offending behaviour and criminalisation. However, an unintended consequence of such work and policy is that victimisation is increasingly viewed as a criminogenic 'risk factor' for women in the CJS (and actually the social justice system too), which consequently essentialises and pathologises women. This chapter aims to extend these arguments by considering the links between coercion, intimate relationships and offending for women co-offenders, whilst situating these discussions within the broader process of criminalisation and structural and social inequalities that such women experience.

Aspects of the analysis presented in this chapter are based on an empirical study conducted with Dr Siobhan Weare. We conducted semi-structured interviews with eight women who co-offended with a male intimate partner. The women were accessing a women's advice and support centre in the north-west of the United Kingdom at the time of interview. Semi-structured, in-depth interviews were chosen as the method of data collection as they allowed for women's narratives and subjective lived experiences to be most clearly communicated. This approach also reflected the feminist methodological and epistemological approach underpinning the project; and recognising the experiences of women from their own point of view (Harding, 1981).

The women had engaged in a range of relatively 'low level' offences, including theft, buying and selling drugs, drug use, and benefit fraud. The interviews were analysed using Interpretative Phenomenological Analysis (IPA). This method of analysis ensured that the women's lived experiences, and how they made sense of them (Smith, 2004) were centralised throughout the project. All of the women have been provided with pseudonyms. Rather than this chapter exploring the study in significant depth, as this has been done elsewhere (Barlow and Weare, 2018), key findings are used to develop conceptual ideas.

Co-offending Women's Pathways into Crime and Continued Influences on Offending

It is recognised that many women co-offenders may not be in an abusive relationship with their male partner/co-offender, and therefore may offend with greater levels of agency and adopt a more equal role in the co-offending behaviour. However, abuse, violence and control within a co-offending relationship were influencing factors for all the women's offending behaviour in the current study when in a romantic relationship with their male co-offender, despite such experiences not being part of the selection criteria to be part of the study. With this in mind, although various factors could influence women co-offenders offending, fear and love will be considered at length here.

As a result of patriarchy and high levels of violence against women in society more broadly, pathways into crime and continued reasons for offending for women are often influenced by fear. This is particularly the case if women co-offenders are in an abusive, violent relationship with their male co-offender/ intimate partner. Such abuse can be physical, psychological, emotional and controlling in nature (Barlow, 2016; Richie, 1996). All the women in our study experienced violence and abuse in their relationship with their male co-offender/ intimate partner. All the women also identified this abuse as an influencing factor on their offending behaviour. For example, Danielle stated that 'I just did whatever he told me to do. I was scared of him'. She referenced this in relation to her ex-partner pressuring her to smuggle drugs into prison whilst he was serving a prison sentence. Sarah echoed similar sentiments when discussing the reasons why she began and continued to co-offend with her intimate partner:

'He knocked the life out of me. I didn't know who I was. I was just this little coward girl who did as he asked.'

Three of the women also suggested that their partners were 'controlling' and 'manipulative' throughout their relationship. They suggested that this control often limited their 'offending choices', as their male co-offender exerted control over most if not all aspects of their lives.

For six women, their intimate, abusive relationships were clearly a catalyst for their offending. For example, both Rachel and Laura stated that they 'hadn't offended before' they met their romantic co-offender. Danielle also referenced that she 'wouldn't have offended if she hadn't have met him [her ex-partner]'. For these women, the relationships with their male co-offenders seemed to form the basis for their pathways into crime. It is important to acknowledge the potential coercive context of such women's offending. Welle and Falkin (2000) argue that women co-offenders may become involved in crime due to their fear of disappointing, angering, or disobeying their partner, highlighting the influence of fear on such women's offending 'choices'. The sustained and insidious nature of such coercive and abusive relationships mean that control can be exerted with or without the presence of the perpetrator, controlling such women's space for action (Kelly, 2003; Stark, 2007).

Jones (2011) also notes that male co-offenders often pressure women to take the blame for offences committed on their behalf. This was particularly relevant to Rachel's circumstances in our study. Rachel explained how her ex-partner 'threatened suicide' every time she tried to leave the relationship, evidencing his control and manipulation. She also discussed how he pressured her to commit benefit fraud, as they were struggling financially, mostly due to his gambling addiction. She suggested that even though he was the 'mastermind' behind the plan, he 'pressured' her to adopt the active role in the offending. Rachel said that 'he convinced me it was because he loved me' and it was 'always just pressure, pressure, pressure to do it'.

In such coercive circumstances, male co-offenders may also additionally exploit the social circumstances of women, particularly if they are addicted to drugs (Fleetwood, 2013) or living in poverty (Carlen, 1988). Three of the women in our study were addicted to drugs and highlighted a clear link between their drug-taking and relationships with their co-offenders. The specifics of the link varied for each of the women. The most extreme example was provided by Vicky who had never taken drugs before her romantic co-offender pressured her into doing so:

'At first I used to say that I didn't want to do it. He offered it me all the time, used to call me a pussy for not wanting any and eventually, I just couldn't be arsed with him being on my case all the time so I did it.'

Her ex-boyfriend became her drug dealer and then tricked her into taking heroin, intensifying her addiction:

'It started off with just weed and stuff like that and by the end he got me into heroin and all sorts. I remember one time he told me he had given me a bag of brown [weed] and I took it as normal, he started laughing and said it was fucking heroin. Fucking heroin. That was the first time I took it and it went from there really.'

This example highlights the importance of considering the broader context of such relationships when attempting to understand women co-offenders' behaviour and decision-making, rather than focusing exclusively on the offending act itself. Understanding the ways in which co-offending women's abusive and exploitative relationship with their partner and, in Vicky's case, addiction to drugs (or other influencing factors) may intersect to produce multiple, overlapping offending influences leads to a more nuanced understanding of women's lived experiences. Furthermore, recognising the context and influence of abusive relationships highlights their influence on such women's participation in offending. For example, after Vicky became addicted to heroin, she became dependent on her male co-offender to supply her with drugs. Consequently, he occasionally put pressure on her to take the blame for their or his offending when caught by the police in exchange for drugs, or she felt obliged to do this out of loyalty (as both her romantic partner and drug dealer). This highlights the added power dynamic and layered abuse in Vicky's relationship, due to her male co-offender being both her drug dealer and intimate partner.

As well as fear influencing women co-offenders' reasons for offending, emotions such as love may also impact decision-making. In our study, for Vicky there was a clear overlap between fear of her partner (discussed above) and the love she felt for him. She explained how she 'would have done anything for him' but also that she believed he 'took the piss out of how much I loved him'. She referenced this in relation to an occasion when she took the blame on his behalf after being arrested for theft and shoplifting they engaged in together. Love is particularly significant to consider in contexts when women take the blame or plead guilty to a crime they have not committed in order to protect the guilt of a male partner/co-offender. Research suggests that women are more likely to confess to crimes that they have not committed out of love or loyalty for male partners/family members (Klaver, Lee and Rose, 2008). This may explain how and why some women choose to protect their loved one by taking blame themselves (Jones, 2011). However, rather than separating love and fear as motivating factors for women co-offenders, they should be viewed as part of the same continuum (Barlow, 2016). Perhaps especially so in the case of women who have a history of abusive relationships or who have experienced historic abuse (which is the case for most criminalised and/or imprisoned women). In existing research as well as the women's experiences cited here, women co-offenders often report engaging in offending to avoid disappointing or angering their partner and/or due to loyalty and love. With this in mind, irrespective of whether the women committed a crime out of fear or love, the overlapping nature of such influences and influences should be considered.

Such influential factors also need to be located in the structural context of such women's lives. To varying degrees, the women in our study were economically disadvantaged, experienced mental health issues, had experienced childhood victimisation and abuse and engaged in substance misuse at some point in their lives. Such experiences of marginalisation need to be located within the broader context of gender inequality, adding further complex dynamics to the structural constraints the women experienced. It is within this context that the women's experiences of violence and abuse within their intimate relationship, and the subsequent influence this had on their co-offending, needs to be considered. Of particular significance are State, criminal justice and other agency responses (or lack of) to the women's experiences of victimisation (Baldwin, 2022a).

Criminalisation and Punitive State Responses

As previously discussed, all the women experienced extensive victimisation throughout their lives, yet none of them received effective (if any) criminal justice support for this. The women we interviewed reflected on being much more likely to be criminalised by criminal justice professionals for their involvement in offending, rather than supported for their extensive experiences of victimisation. For example, the women in our study suggested they felt that there was no point in contacting the police about the abuse they had experienced within the context of their intimate relationship as they felt that they would not be believed. Both Sarah and Laura described their 'hatred' for the police, due to previous negative and in their view harmful interactions with them. Vicky also stated that the police 'didn't want to help me' when she tried to report her experiences of victimisation, which led to a continued lack of trust in the police and broader CJS. Most of the women in our study were readily criminalised by criminal justice professionals, but their experiences of victimisation were minimised or not fully investigated. This is captured by Denise:

'It's like they see everything we have been through as an excuse, and we don't see it that way. I don't want their sympathy. I just wanted them to listen.'

Policing and criminal justice practices involve judgements about riskiness and perceived identities of 'victimhood', which are crosscut by intersecting inequalities such as race and class, ultimately leading to marginalised women more readily coming into contact with the CJS as offenders, rather than victims, irrespective of experiences of victimisation (Sharpe, 2016; Burman and Batchelor, 2009; Schaffner, 2007).

Furthermore, some of the fear experienced by the women was not only as a consequence of their abusive, intimate relationship, but also due to a lack of State support and fear of a punitive State response. For example, Denise reflected on her negative experience of prison, stating 'my hair went dead white. I was crying all the time, my blood pressure wouldn't go down'. She went onto say that the experience continues to affect her post-release, stating that 'if someone slams the door, I jump now. You know what I mean?' Prior to going to prison, Denise had mental health issues which she suggests were further exacerbated by the prison experience. Two of the women also reported being homeless after serving a short-term prison sentence for low level offences. One of the women appeared to be financially dependent on her male partner/co-offender and received minimal economic support from the State when released from prison. This meant that she had to make the 'choice' of returning to her abusive partner and likely continuing to engage in co-offending, or being homeless. Although returning to an abusive relationship may be perceived as an agentic choice, she made such choices within the context of broader structural constraints, such as economic marginalisation. This is arguably an example of a State-sanctioned negative consequence for such women, constraining their capacity for autonomy and independence and rendering them at greater risk of intimate partner violence (Sharpe, 2016). Additionally, as most of the women were known in some capacity to State authorities mostly due to their previous offending, some suggested, especially those who were mothers, that they were afraid to make social services or criminal justice practitioners aware of their experiences of victimisation, due to fear of their children being taken away from them or other negative repercussions (Baldwin 2015; 2022a). This therefore suggests that punitive responses and systematic failings by the State to recognise women co-offenders' experiences of victimisation added another layer of fear, which consequently influenced their offending motivations and criminalisation.

When considering the offending influences for the women in this study, previously discussed explanations of rationality are clearly not applicable, raising important questions about their perceived offending 'choices' (or lack of). Although some women recognised that they made a 'choice' to offend, others suggested they had 'no choice' (Danielle, Rachel, Laura) and all suggested that their choices were influenced by their abusive relationship with their intimate partner. This is exemplified by Vicky, stating, 'I felt like a prisoner in my relationship with him', which she believed consequently limited her perceived choices. The women's offending choices therefore need to be understood within the context of both their abusive relationships and their broader structural and social position in society. Rather than being a 'rational choice', the women arguably evaluated and drew upon the limited options available to them due to their social and structural positioning (Fleetwood, 2015).

The issues with translating such women's offending 'choices' into law are clearly evidenced by the lack of available defences that attempt to capture their experiences. There are three key defences in English Law that to differing extents have attempted to recognise the influence of coercion on women's offending. These are battered woman syndrome (BWS), marital coercion (abolished in 2014) and duress and all three would not capture the experiences of the women discussed here.

Duress is a defence which, if successful, results in acquittal for an individual compelled to commit an offence through fear of immediate serious physical violence from a duressor. However, despite this technically being a defence that can be used by women who suggest they have been coerced into crime, women are much less likely to use this defence in comparison to men. Abused women themselves often do not recognise the coercion and abuse they experience within their relationship, and often occupy a false world created by the perpetrator. Loveless (2010) also suggests that the defence is likely under-used by women who are coerced by an intimate partner because such abuse can easily be perceived as falling short of duress. For example, men may be more likely to experience coercion through a clearly identifiable threat of serious harm (i.e. a particular incident), rather than by sustained abuse or the 'incremental destruction of self-esteem characteristic of prologued domestic violence' (Loveless, 2010: 2).

Furthermore, even defences which directly attempt to include the experiences of women whose offending may have been influenced by a violent intimate relationship fall short. BWS is recognised by the World Health Organization as a sub-category of post-traumatic stress disorder (PTSD). It involves symptoms of depression resulting from persistent domestic abuse, resulting in extreme fear and co-dependency on the abuser.

BWS also faces many similar critiques to the defence of duress. Firstly, the inclusion of the term 'battered' by implication excludes women who experience non-physical coercion and control (Bettinson, 2019). Furthermore, although a gendered approach is important when attempting to understand experiences of coercion (Burman and Brooks-Hay, 2018), including only women's experiences in the defence of BWS means that male victims experiences or those relationships which fall outside of the heterosexual model (such as same-sex relationships) are excluded (Bettinson, 2019).

Finally, marital coercion (Section 47 of the Criminal Justice Act 1925) was a stand-alone defence before this was abolished in 2014. The defence stated:

> 'On a charge against a wife for any offence other than treason or murder it shall be a good defence to prove that the offence was committed in the presence of, and under the coercion of, the husband.'

There were various notable issues with this defence. Firstly, a woman had to be married to rely on it, the husband had to be present at the time of the offence, thus contradicting research which suggests that abuse and coercion can occur without the physical presence of the controller (Stark, 2007); and furthermore, that the defence denied women's capacity for agency. The defence was abolished in 2014 as it was suggested that this was no longer applicable or relevant in modern society due to significant advances in gender equality since the defence was created in 1925. However, not all women have experienced such equality. Indeed, there is a significant proportion of women who for social, religious and cultural reasons cannot effectively exercise their own free will and may feel that they have to obey their partners if coerced into criminal behaviour (Barlow, 2016). Furthermore, completely abolishing the defence of marital coercion means there is now no alternative comparable defence that coerced women can use. Such issues notwithstanding however, the defence itself was not fit for purpose to reflect the experiences of all women whose offending was influenced by their abusive intimate relationship. These issues collectively highlight that even in the unlikely event that a woman's experiences of victimisation and abuse are recognised within the context of their offending by criminal justice professionals, the probability of this being reflected in law is low.

Furthermore, even looking beyond specific defences, women's experiences of intimate partner abuse are rarely fully considered in mitigating circumstances.[12] For example, for the women discussed here, although intimate partner violence influenced their motivations to offend, they may not have been directly coerced into crime in a legal sense, therefore the defences of duress and BWS would not be applicable. The fact that at least 63% of women in prison have experienced domestic abuse (Prison Reform Trust, 2017), highlights the inherent issues with the law in reflecting such women's experiences. The Centre for Women's Justice (CWJ) suggests that although the introduction of the coercive control offence in England and Wales recognises the consequences of domestic abuse in intimate relationships, the criminal law still does not provide an adequate defence to those who commit offences as a result of abuse.

The role of the State, law and criminal justice organizations more broadly in exacerbating experiences of victimisation and adding to the harms such women experience is often ignored or minimised. It is argued here that the structural constraints many female co-offenders experience, combined with inadequate and harmful State and legal responses to their experiences of victimisation, increase their feelings of fear and desperation, rather than provide empowering support. When considering the offending influences of female co-offenders, the fear of their abusive partner/co-offender is therefore not separate or separable from their fear of punitive and harmful State responses and their broader social and structural position in society.

---

12. Mitigating circumstances presuppose that there has been a conviction, following which they may be put forward in an attempt to reduce sentence (of whatever kind).

The Preoccupation With 'Choice'

In legal and criminal justice policy and practice, there is an emphasis on rational choice as being the key motivating and influencing factor on decision-making processes. For the women interviewed in this study, their choices were not based on rationality, but rather were at least to some extent influenced by their relationship with their male co-offender, their broader structural and social positioning in society, as well as fear of negative, punitive State and legal responses (Clarke and Chadwick, 2018).

Failing to understand the ways in which the violence and abuse within their intimate relationship influences such women's offending behaviour has led to a preoccupation with 'choice' as a central component of theorising and understanding their experiences. This is also reflected in law, with BWS and duress focusing on capacity for rational choice. Such debates also extend to feminist theorising, with Maher (1997) suggesting that criminalised women are typically viewed to be either wholly in control of their offending behaviour or irrational and 'out of control' of their offending decision-making. However, this dichotomisation of choice is a reductionist approach, and does not apply to all criminalised women. The dichotomy of agency leads to over-simplistic and limited understandings of many women co-offenders' experiences. However, as argued by Mahok et al (2013: 3), dichotomising experiences of agency 'requires us to deny, or at least obscure, the extent to which social relations of inequality and domination continue to structure our lives'. This highlights the emphasis on individual, 'rational' choice and autonomy within existing understandings of agency and choice serving to minimise experiences of abuse and the ways in which deep-rooted, gender inequality and oppression impacts upon women's pathways into crime and continued influences on offending (Ballinger, 2000; Sharpe, 2016). Rather than focusing on simplistic binaries, such as 'agent' or 'victim', the complex ways in which experiences of choice and agency are entwined and intersected with race, culture and gender should be better understood.

It is not the intention of this chapter to suggest that influences deny the agency of women who offend, but rather to understand the ways in which coercion and intimate partner abuse impact upon offending motivations for women who co-offend with a male partner. The preoccupation with women's perceived 'choices' often leads to an avoidance of situating such choices in context (Clarke and Chadwick, 2018). This consequently encourages a lack of understanding of the factors which may influence offending decision-making at both a micro (i.e. abusive, intimate relationship with co-offender) and macro (violence of the State) level. Recognising that women may have agency (albeit to varying levels), whilst simultaneously understanding the ways in which coercion and abuse may influence offending choices, enables our understanding of co-offending to move beyond notions such as 'He made me do it' and rather allows an exploration of how structural, social and cultural context may impact such women's perceived offending 'choices' and behaviour. According to Madhok et al (2013: 157):

> '[W]hat matters most is not whether something is chosen, but what it is that is chosen and whether it is worthwhile and beneficial, or at least not detrimental, exploitative and destructive.'

For the women in this study, although they all made a 'choice' to offend, they each argued that their offending 'choices' were at least in part influenced by their relationship with their male co-offender/partner and their broader social and structural positioning. This collectively highlights that when attempting to understand women co-offenders' experiences, the 'preoccupation' with choice and rationality needs to be re-considered. Theorising and understanding should re-focus to consider the role of coercion and abuse, centralising this in social context and women's lived experiences.

Furthermore, when considering the extent of women co-offenders 'choices', the violence and injustices of the State and the ways in which these limit offending choices need to be better understood. As previously discussed, women's experiences of abuse within their relationships were often exacerbated by punitive State responses or lack of support and recognition for experiences of victimisation. The women co-offenders discussed here are not 'ideal victims' (Christie, 1986) due to their participation in offending activity. Rather than their offending 'choices' being understood within the context of their abusive relationships, they were criminalised by criminal justice professionals and other State authorities, which further increased the harms they experienced. However, it is argued here that reducing experiences of victimisation to a potential offending 'risk factor' for such women is problematic. Although trauma-informed, gender-responsive approaches to justice are increasingly acknowledging women's experiences of victimisation, they do so by targeting individual women's potential 'risk', rather than acknowledging issues with institutional practices (Sharpe, 2016). Such approaches focus on encouraging women to make better 'choices', which serves to 'responsibilise' such women for their experiences of victimisation and ignores the role of the State in maintaining or exacerbating the harm women experience (Clarke and Chadwick, 2018; Baldwin, 2022a). It is argued here that the influence of violence and coercion should be situated and understood within the context of punitive State practices, which criminalise marginalised women, minimise their experiences of victimisation and consequently fail to meet their needs.

Conclusion — Moving Forward

Co-offending with a male, intimate partner often influences women's offending behaviours (Becker and McCorkel, 2011) and potentially their pathways into crime (Barlow, 2016), particularly if this relationship is abusive and violent. This chapter has examined the influence of the coercion, abuse, love and fear within such relationships on women co-offenders' offending behaviour and continued influences on offending. In particular, the women in this study suggested that their abusive, toxic relationships with their male co-offender made them feel afraid to anger or disobey their partner, therefore limiting their perceived offending 'choices'.

Feminist pathways literature has made important contributions to knowledge in understanding the ways in which women's social circumstance and experiences of victimisation can influence their offending behaviour (Belknap and Holsinger, 2006; Daly, 1994). However, experiences of victimisation for women offenders are increasingly identified as a 'risk factor' for future or continued offending, rather than developing a nuanced understanding of the ways in which abuse influences such women's lives. There needs to be a greater understanding of the complex interplay between micro-level (i.e. experiences of victimisation and abusive relationships) and macro-level (i.e. State harm, structural and social positioning) influences and the ways in which these impact female co-offenders experiences and 'choices'.

One way of achieving this level of understanding is to develop a holistic, gendered approach to justice. Although a difficult task, this kind of radical approach is necessary to ensure that the overlap between victimisation and offending, and the harms of criminalisation, are more effectively understood (Carlen, 2008). These kinds of approaches need to go beyond simply 'adding women' into the existing system, and would require centring women's experiences of victimisation and additional structural constraints, such as race, disability, indigenous status and sexuality. This would involve moving away from a process of criminalisation, and considering what a truly trauma-informed, community-based approach would look like. Some existing trauma-informed practice focuses on individualising women's experiences, prioritising a 'risk factor' approach to dealing with women's victimisation, reinforcing broader preoccupations with risk which pervade the CJS (Carlen, ibid). However, women's experiences of trauma and victimisation need to be situated within the broader context of structural harm. Trauma-informed approaches should focus on empathy and tailoring support provision in a needs-led way, rather than centralising risk. This is particularly important for marginalised groups, such as migrant women, who face punitive responses within the context of current harmful and punitive immigration policies and laws in the UK (Canning, 2020). By situating trauma within the broader context of structural harm, a gendered approach to justice could be imagined. At a minimum, to achieve this approach, holistic, informed and tailored partnership working is required, centring the support of specialised services, such as the domestic abuse sector. In conclusion, gendered approaches to justice need to go beyond the individualised, 'risk'-focused approach currently dominating policy and practice and rather situate such women's choices within the context of broader State, institutional and structural harm, thereby ensuring gendered and needs-led support is available to women to prevent unnecessary criminalisation.

CHAPTER 5

'Racism is Very Much There'
Validating Racial Trauma in the Context of Criminal Justice

Monica Thomas and Sinem Bozkurt

Although racism and racial discrimination are experienced across multiple stages of the Criminal Justice System (CJS) (HM Inspectorate of Probation and EPIC, 2021; Lammy, 2019; Phillips, 2012) the trauma that may result from these specific experiences is rarely discussed and acknowledged. This is reflected in the development of 'trauma-informed' approaches for working with and supporting women involved in the CJS which often fail to recognise or give weight to racism, and other racialised harms, as forms of abuse which can lead to trauma. Without validating the pain caused by racism and racialised harms, 'trauma-informed' approaches and other strategies for support will continue to centre white women's experiences whilst further marginalising women positioned as racially *other*.

In this chapter, we start with the premise that racism 'is very much there' (Sadia, an Afghan and Pakistani mother). So, rather than having to prove its actuality—which we already know—we can start to explore its emotional and physical impacts. To do this, we draw upon the concept of racial trauma. Racial trauma refers to psychological, emotional, and physical harm caused by experiences or anticipated experiences of racial prejudice, marginalisation, and discrimination (Boachie, 2021; Carter, 2007; Comas-Diaz, 2019; Hardy, 2013; Harrell, 2000). However, racial trauma is not experienced in isolation. For women who are racially minoritised the intersection of both their gendered and racialised identities, as well as other possible marginalised identities, can result in multiple and unique forms of oppression within the CJS and wider society (Cardale et al, 2017; Chigwada-Bailey, 2003; Cox and Sacks-Jones, 2016; Corston, 2007; Farmer, 2019; Lammy, 2017; Thomas, 2021).

In her study of 'Black Women's Experiences in Employment', Crenshaw (1989) explains that a 'single-axis framework', marginalises black women in questions of race and sex because the experiences of otherwise privileged individuals are the only ones evaluated. For example, while a black man has the benefit of being a 'man', he must contend with the prejudice that comes with being black; on the other hand, white women, whilst also enjoying the privilege of being white, are nonetheless marginalised as women. However, the experiences of those who face both racism and sexism, those of being racially minoritised women, or black women, in Crenshaw's case, meet at the intersection. She states that this emphasis on the most privileged members of a group marginalises those who are burdened in multiple ways. Ultimately, Crenshaw claims that black women are most often invisible in both feminist theory and anti-racist policy debates, given that both are based on a limited set of experiences that do not always accurately reflect the intersection of race and gender.

Guided by Kinouani's (2021: 1) statement that 'racism causes harm. Harm to the body and harm to the mind', this chapter begins to reflect upon racially minoritised women's experiences of, and responses to, racialised and gendered harms during sentencing and imprisonment through the lens of racial trauma. These reflections will be informed by our ongoing PhD research relating to 'The Experiences of Black Mothers In and After Prison' (MT) and 'The Experiences of Racially Minoritised Mothers In and After Prison' (SB), my own personal lived experiences of sentencing and imprisonment (SB) as well as an exploration of existing research, reports, and inquests.

The chapter begins with a reflexive note on the importance of language when discussing, and understanding, the varied experiences of women who are racially minoritised. Following this, racial trauma is defined and then considered in relation to its emotional and physical impacts during sentencing and imprisonment. The chapter ends with a concluding argument advocating for an acknowledgment and informed understanding of racialisation and racism within trauma-informed practice. As with the other chapters in this collection, this one includes 'Pauses for Thought' which ask you, the reader, to further consider the arguments, points and information given.

The Importance of Language

Before looking more closely at racial trauma we feel it is important to express and justify our current position on language relating to identities that are racially minoritised. In this section we problematise the use of the term 'BAME' within the context of the CJS by outlining its negative consequences for research and practice.

Adebisi (2019) distinguishes between two separate issues relating to the current use of the term BAME, the first being misuse and the second inadequacy. The use of the term to describe an individual person is an example of misuse, as an umbrella term should not be drawn upon to describe a singular person (ibid). An individual cannot be BAME and to describe someone as such is to render their personal identity and particular lived experiences invisible (Aspinall, 2020). In relation to this particular critique, it is the wrongful application of the collective term BAME that is highlighted rather than an issue with the actual term itself (Adebisi, 2019).

However, BAME as an umbrella or collective term has also rightly faced criticism for its inadequacy (ibid). The term itself is inadequate as it condenses a wide range of differing racial, social, political, cultural, and historical identities into one 'tidy' homogenous acronym of lived experience (Thomas, 2021), whilst also presenting a false sense of harmony between all racialised groups which fall under the catch-all title. Selvarajah et al (2020: 2) emphasise the way in which this homogenisation is 'embodied in the pronunciation of "baym" which acts to "flatten important social and cultural differences between groups, while erasing the uneven power structures within which they are situated" through its simplistic and crude tone.' The way in which 'baym' so easily rolls off the tongue and can be used so quickly and without thought feeds into both its misuse and its inadequacy. The term provides comfort. It allows for the complexity and nuance of racialised identities and experiences to be glossed over or mentioned only in brief. As Adebisi (2019) states, 'It allows you *to check that one box and be done*' and it is this superficiality which can add to the trauma of invisibility.

Language is important as it both shapes and reflects the way in which we understand the social world (Wetherall et al, 2001). The normalisation of BAME in everyday talk within certain institutional and political settings has consequently impacted the way in which racialised identities are understood and conceptualised within them. The safety and comfort that the catch-all term seems to provide for people wanting to describe particular groups within society has come at the cost of rendering individual identities invisible and at worst invalid (Aspinall, 2020). I have felt this most during my current PhD research with black mothers who have experienced imprisonment in Britain (MT). I am constantly having to reiterate, reclarify and justify my specific focus on black mothers, with the assumption often being that I might actually, or *should* actually, mean 'BAME' mothers. As a black-mixed-race academic, the very fact that people can now hear the word 'black' and interpret this to mean 'BAME' is alarming. It is as though people have become so used to 'one BAME person [standing] for all BAME people' that anything which troubles this notion is seen as out of the ordinary (Adebisi, 2019).

Consequently, women who are racially minoritised often face a triple type of erasure within academic literature relating to the CJS. As women they are often overlooked or sidelined in research which largely exemplifies and prioritises the experiences of men. As women who are not white their racialised experiences are often lost or unexplored in women-centred research which attempts to be 'colour blind'; and as women viewed as BAME they are often misrepresented in research which seeks to depict a universal BAME experience. Going beyond these forms of erasure a further exclusion exists within women-centred criminological research in Britain, not least because women scholars who are racially minoritised are underrepresented in a field dominated by white authorship thus shaping the type of research that is produced and the conclusions that are made.

In relation to understanding the variation of women's lived experiences within the CJS, the homogenisation of all non-white racialised identities under the heading BAME is thankfully becoming increasingly problematised (HM Inspectorate of Prisons, 2020; Cardale et al, 2017; Farmer, 2019). There is an increasing acknowledgement that women from differing minoritised racialised backgrounds are likely to have distinct needs and experiences from one another (HM Inspectorate of Prisons, 2020; Cardale et al, 2017; Farmer, 2019; Thomas, 2021). For example, the types of prejudice and discrimination experienced by Roma women within the CJS are likely to differ from that of Chinese women; as reflected in the differing arrest rates, treatment, sentencing patterns, sentence lengths and experiences of imprisonment between differing racialised groups (Cardale et al, 2017; MOJ, 2020).

There will of course also be differences within these broader racialised categories, as women have multiple identities which intersect with one another shaping experience (Farmer, 2019; Baldwin, 2022a; Thomas, 2021). In my research despite all of the women identifying as black or black-mixed-race and there being some sense of an overarching collective experience, there have also been distinct experiences reflective of the differing cultural identities, ages, sexualities, complexions and immigration statuses of the women (MT). Consequently, our understandings of racialised harms and racial trauma within the CJS should not be one-dimensional but should be responsive to the complex, intersectional and diverse nature of identities and experiences.

After much discussion between us, we have decided to use the term 'racially minoritised' within this chapter as a broader reference to women whose racialised identities are often positioned as 'other' within the CJS and wider society. The expression 'racially' is used as despite certain groups being classified in terms of their perceived racial, cultural, geographical and/or religious origins or affiliations 'a racialised component exists in all these groups' perceived [inherent] differentiation to other racial groups' (Milner and Jumbe, 2020: e419). Racialisation thus refers to the process by which people are constructed as belonging to a particular group based on both 'physical and cultural traits' (Garner and Selod, 2015: 12; Meer and Modood, 2009; Miles, 1989). Gunaratnum (2003: 15) argues the term racially minoritised provides 'some sense of the active processes of racialisation that are at work in designating certain attributes of groups in particular contexts as being in a 'minority'. It constantly reminds us of the relationship between racialisation and power (Gunaratnum, 2003; Salvarajah, 2020; Milner and Jumbe, 2020), recognising we are not 'minorities' in any biological sense but rather we are minoritised through oppressive social constructions and processes surrounding race and identity. An important distinction.

Notably, therefore, the term describes a 'social process' rather than an identity, and people will experience this process differently depending on their individual identities (Milner and Jumbe, 2020: e419). We must, wherever possible, 'name and recognise' the actual identities people hold for themselves (Selvarajah et al, 2020: 3) to understand the particular contexts in which they must navigate their lives. Importance is thus given to validating self-identification[13] and individual experiences. It is advised that this individualised approach should also be extended to working with, or supporting, women within the CJS as when developing trauma-informed practice it is important to recognise, and be responsive to, the differing racial and cultural contexts in which trauma may be experienced, interpreted, and defined (Thomas, 2021).

❚❚ Pause for Thought

- In your use of language and of the term BAME have you/do you stop to consider the experiences of differing racialised groups?
- What do you think the challenges are for promoting understanding in the general public about what you have just read? — Will it change your own language?

Defining Racial Trauma

As highlighted in the introduction, racial trauma is understood as the embodied response to experiences, or anticipated experiences, of racism and racialised harms (Boachie, 2021; Carter, 2007; Comas-Diaz, 2019; Hardy, 2013; Harrell, 2000; Kinouani, 2021). These experiences can take place in many forms (Carter, 2007; Harrell, 2000), intersect with other life stresses (Harrell, 2000), span across the life course and be passed on through generations resulting in ongoing and reoccurring 'injuries' (Comas-Diaz, 2019: 1; Kinouani, 2021). Harrell (2000: 44) distinguishes between six differing types of racialised harms or as she defines them 'racism-related stress[es]', further reinforced by Kinouani (2021), which may result in subsequent trauma:

---

13. Self-identification provides an insight into the racialised identities people are willing to share with others (Campbell and Troyer, 2007). It is acknowledged that there are other forms of racialised identities such as 'observed' (what other people see/treat you as) and 'internal' (what you hold just for yourself) and these intersect with one another to shape our lived experiences (ibid; Pirtle and Brown, 2016). Whilst all these identities are necessary to consider, it is extremely important when working with women to take the time to know and understand how they personally self-identify as misclassification or misnaming can in itself be a form of racialised harm (ibid).

1. **Racism-related life events** — Individual incidents of racism which have a distinct beginning and end to the experience (e.g. a personal experience of police brutality or racial discrimination during sentencing).

2. **Vicarious racism experiences** — Witnessing or hearing about racism happening to family, friends, or strangers (e.g. seeing a friend be racially discriminated against whilst in custody or being exposed to incidents of injustice and violence via the media such as the publicised death of Sarah Reed whilst in prison custody).

3. **Daily racism microstressors** — Everyday and reoccurring aggressions which remind an individual of the negative stereotypes and assumptions surrounding their observed racialised identity (e.g. probation staff misinterpreting black women's mental health needs as anger management issues due to harmful stereotypes surrounding black femininity).

4. **Chronic-contextual stress** — Stress caused by having to 'adapt and cope' (Harrell 2000: 46) within a particular environment or context which is characterised by structural or institutional racism. This may be magnified within settings where there are very few people who share the same racialised background as oneself (e.g. being held in a prison environment that does not cater for, or understand, one's own cultural needs).

5. **Collective experiences** — Observing, *feeling* or being conscious of the cultural, social, and political impacts of racism on one's own racialised group(s) (e.g. being aware of discriminatory treatment by police and becoming hypervigilant, fearful or alert to the possibility it may happen to oneself or others).

6. **Transgenerational transmission of group trauma** — Historic trauma that is passed down generationally within families and communities. Differing racialised groups, communities and families will have distinct experiences shaped by their personal, historic and cultural contexts (e.g. the mass imprisonment of particular racialised groups).

Racism and racialised harms can be experienced at individual, institutional and/or systematic levels. When thinking about the impacts of these harms, it is argued that research often focuses on 'the social, economic, and political effects of racism' (Carter, 2007: 14) rather than the embodied physical, psychological, and emotional reactions people may have in response to these negative experiences (Carter, 2007; Harrell, 2000). Racial trauma can thus be understood as a 'hidden wound' that is rarely asked about, understood and validated (Hardy 2013: 25). Reactions to racial trauma can manifest in many forms. They can be physical such as headaches, bodily aches and pains, high blood pressure, and heart disease; psychological such as hypervigilance, depression, anxiety, psychosis, self-harm, intrusion, flashbacks, internalised devaluation, and silencing; or emotional such as anger, fear, distrust, rage, frustration, and distress (Carter, 2007; Carter and Pieterse, 2020; Hardy, 2013; Karslen et al, 2005; Kinouani, 2021).

Despite being based on men, Smith and Lee's (2019) research provides an initial framework for thinking about the relationship between power and racial trauma within the CJS. Smith and Lee (ibid) interviewed 40 young black men living in an economically marginalised neighbourhood in America and identified that the majority of these men had persistent feelings of frustration, anger, annoyance, fear, anxiety and hypervigilance due to continuous personal, and vicarious, experiences of disproportionate and violent policing (see also Aymer, 2016) as well as physical injuries from police brutality. It was found that the 'lack of control, defencelessness and helplessness resulting from the power' imbalance between the individual experiencing harm and the individual/institution perpetrating the violence intensified the trauma (ibid: 171). In contexts such as the prison, the unequal power dynamics between those imprisoned and the staff/institution, as well as the confined nature of the environment, have also been found to impact the way in which racism is experienced whilst also restricting the way in which it can be mitigated or responded to (see Wilson, 2003).

When considering women's racial trauma within the context of criminal justice it is important to recognise that experiences of marginalisation, prejudice, discrimination, and racism which occur within this system will not necessarily stand alone but often form part of an ongoing experience or re-experience of racism and disadvantage throughout the life course. Therefore, such experiences are likely to intersect or coincide with other forms of oppression, violence, and subsequent trauma. This is supported by HM Inspectorate of Probation and EPIC's (2021: 6) report focusing on racial equality within probation, which recognises that by the time people who are racially minoritised become subject to probation 'many have experienced financial disadvantage, early trauma, crime and violence in their communities, family and friends becoming caught up in the CJS and acts of racism'. Negative racialised experiences during sentencing, supervision and imprisonment may thus be shaped by previous, ongoing, or anticipated experiences of harm which will in turn influence the way in which racial trauma is felt, understood, and responded to.

Moreover, the report which consisted of 81 interviews with both men and women identified gendered differences in the way that race based stress may be experienced (HM Inspectorate of Probation and EPIC, 2021). It was found that as well as dealing with their own experiences of racism and disadvantage, the majority of the women interviewed also felt responsible for protecting others, particularly men and boys, from the potential risk of racism (ibid). Hypervigilance is a recognised response to racial trauma as there is a heightened sense of alert and anxiety in an attempt to guard oneself or others against perceived racialised threats (Boachie, 2021; Joe et al, 2019; Smith and Lee, 2019). For example, in an ethnography with black mothers in America who had formerly experienced imprisonment 'hypervigilant motherwork' was identified as a common mothering strategy used to protect children against disproportionate threats of violence and harm in their communities as well as State intervention (Gurusami, 2019). Developing an appropriate understanding of racial trauma in relation to women's sentencing and imprisonment must recognise the multiple ways in which stress and trauma may be experienced either personally, vicariously or collectively within and across these contexts.

▌▌ Pause for Thought

- Do you feel racism is widely acknowledged as a form of abuse?
- Have you ever received training relating to how to recognise and support someone who may be experiencing racial trauma?

Sentencing: Same Offence — Different Outcome? (SB)

'The most important decisions in the justice system are made in our courts. They are where life-changing judgements are made about innocence or guilt.' (Lammy, 2017: 31)

The justice system has been built on the basis that the law will be impartial and applied fairly to all. However, in practice, it has been well-documented that both gender (Gelsthorpe, 2007) and race (Uhrig, 2016) can have an impact on the sentence individuals receive. Whilst women are more likely than men to be remanded in custody and subsequently serve a custodial sentence, there are also racialised disparities in the types of sentences women receive.

According to Uhrig (ibid) black women presenting at Crown Court are 25 per cent more likely than white women to be sentenced to custody. Significantly, they concluded sentencing was proportionate for women belonging to other groups[14] that are minoritised. Black women were identified as being 2.3 times more likely to receive a custodial sentence for drug offences than white women. This is argued to be 'traced back to a combination of disproportionate arrest and disproportionate custodial sentencing' (ibid) and, ultimately, the 'double layer of discrimination' that black women face, which includes both sexism and racism (Crenshaw, 1989). However, statistical data depicting racialised sentencing outcomes does not capture the lived experiences of women who may face, or feel that they have faced, unfair and unjust treatment because of their observed racialised identities. Placing emphasis on hearing and validating personal lived experiences is vital for addressing the trauma that may stem from feelings of injustice. Acknowledgment is necessary.

In my personal experience (SB), I was facing judicial proceedings for breach of trust in my position as a prison officer, as articulated in Bozkurt and Aresti (2018). I was given a suspended sentence at first, but the case was taken to the Royal Courts of Justice after an appeal by a Member of Parliament, a *white, middle-class, male.* Importantly, a white female prison officer had gone through a

---

14. Please note, that the constructions of racialised categories used by the MOJ in this report are highly reductionist being: 'white', 'Asian', 'black', 'Chinese and other ethnic' and 'mixed'. These may not represent the identities people hold for themselves. Additionally, there is no recognition of gypsy, Roma and traveller identities, so sentencing outcomes for these groups remain invisible in this context.

similar ordeal a few months before me. Her suspended sentence was also upheld on appeal, and she was back in front of the Court of Appeal. The appeal judges in her case, however, concurred with the original sentencing judge and did not reverse the decision. Although the outcome of her sentence was explicitly stated during my appeal hearing, my sentencing judge's decision was overturned, and I was sentenced to two years and eight months in prison. Notably, I had entered guilty pleas to two counts of conveying unauthorised articles into a prison, whilst the other white female officer did so to two counts of misconduct in a public office, conveying prohibited articles into a prison and possession of cannabis. Therefore, despite pleading guilty to a higher number of charges the white female officer received a more lenient sentence. In addition to this, a black female prison officer was also convicted in that same year for one count of possession with intent to supply a class B drug (cannabis) and was given a three years and four months custodial sentence. A sentence longer than both the white female officer and I, despite the lesser charges. Overall, therefore three similar offences with three different outcomes occurred within the same year.

My argument was not, and never will be, that I did not deserve a punishment, I accepted guilt and cooperated throughout. However, it was the courts' inconsistencies and clear racial discrimination that infuriated me, adding to my trauma. I felt that, because I was Turkish, I did not receive the same leniency as the white female, but I also did not encounter as severe punishment as the black female. I was in the middle, almost as if there are *shades to sentencing*. There is a growing body of literature within America focusing upon the impacts of colourism within sentencing (see Squire and Newhouse, 2003; Pizzi et al, 2005). For example, in their research focused on black women during sentencing, Vigilone et al (2011) found that black women with lighter skin often received shorter custodial sentences than women with darker skin. Conversations surrounding racial injustice therefore must recognise how colourism may also shape experiences and treatment (Walker, 1983).

Concerns of racial bias impacting the court process were also evident in some of the women's accounts across both of our PhD findings. In my research, several of the women spoke about their experiences with racial discrimination (SB), but Dominique commented specifically about the contrasts in treatment she received at her court hearing:

'Erm, throughout prison you were definitely dealt with differently because of your colour. You were, you just weren't treated fairly. Erm, for example in my proceeds of crime case, there was 13 of us in the case and three of us were of ethnic origin. All the white people didn't get any extra time, but us ethnics, all got 15 months and a 30,000 pound bill. All exactly the same and none of the white people in the case got that. I mean that was the most extreme that I've seen that I was like there's just no other way or no other reason for this, it had to be our colour. The white people never got an extra day.'

Discrimination at sentencing is a 'racism-related life event' (Harrell, 2000) that has caused trauma and rage in my case. Hardy (2013) states that this is a deep emotional reaction to feelings of devaluation and degradation. It develops over time because of a build-up of suppressed emotions brought on by injustice and voicelessness. Furthermore, in her online blog, Katz (2020: para 1) defines 'injustice trauma' as 'a specific type of experience that occurs when other people make decisions and do actions that unfairly impact others'. She describes the feeling of this as being 'heavy, constricted like you want to break free and scream or cry. It sits on your chest and clenches your throat'. Arguably, this can be linked to the felt impacts of perceived racial discrimination at sentencing as it is a type of injustice that is rarely questioned or challenged, ultimately rendering the already disadvantaged, completely powerless.

Prisons as Sites of Racial Trauma

Using the lens of racial trauma, this section of this chapter re-examines two interview transcripts from conversations I had with Trish and Kayla (both black British mothers) to focus on some of the traumatic impacts of racialised marginalisation, prejudice, and discrimination for black women. It is necessary to highlight here that not all the black women I spoke with felt that prejudice or racism impacted, or played, a notably influential part in their experience of imprisonment. The next section looks closely at not only prisons as places of racial trauma but the experience of Annabella Landsberg, a black mother who died whilst in prison custody and emphasises how racialised violence within the prison system can have fatal consequences which are often not spoken about.

In relation to women's imprisonment, the prison estate has long been recognised as a repressive space which gives rise to new, and exacerbates existing, traumas. For women who are racially-minoritised, racial prejudice, discrimination and subsequent racial trauma can be understood as an additional burden which may influence and impact on their experiences of imprisonment. Our research (MT and SB) has identified several ways in which the prisons estate has failed to recognise and accommodate the culturally distinct needs of women. Women have also shared with us numerous instances where they have been marginalised and discriminated against due to adverse perceptions of their intersecting racialised, classed, religious and sexual identities held by prison staff or other women in prison. Therefore, through the lens of racial trauma, the prison becomes understood as a site of 'chronic contextual stress' (Harrell, 2000).

Chronic-contextual stress refers to trauma which is triggered by having to adjust and survive within in an environment in which racialised identity is known or felt to be marginalised and oppressed (Harrell, 2000). It is argued that these feelings are often exacerbated in environments where people are positioned as the racial minority (ibid). For Trish, the institutionally white nature of the prison environment led to constant racialised hypervigilance. During her imprisonment she was constantly aware of the fact she was navigating the system as a black woman and therefore may be particularly vulnerable to differential or harmful treatment, as reflected in her quote:

'Straight away I was aware that I was black, straight away and that was on my first night in prison.'

Trish's heightened consciousness of her racialised identity appeared to be influenced by several factors such as being in the racialised minority amongst the women in prison, a lack of black prison officers and staff, and a persistent sense that prison officers had misjudged her as a troublemaker solely based on harmful stereotypes surrounding the colour of her skin. Racialised hypervigilance was also present within the narratives of other black mothers who were alert to, and felt they had to continually mitigate against, marginalisation and or differential treatment during their time in prison.

Hypervigilance was not the only indication of racial trauma prevalent within the women's narratives. Kayla expressed feelings of hurt, sadness, and distress because of the unfair and discriminatory treatment she received whilst previously imprisoned. In one example, Kayla described prison officers unfairly labelling her as threatening, resulting in the disproportionate and unjust use of physical force against her, with such assumptions linking to stereotypical understandings of black femininity as something hostile, strong, and forceful (Chigwada-Bailey, 2003). Voicing her feelings towards the prison officers, Kayla expressed this as follows:

> 'I'm saying just because I'm black and I'm voicing my opinion it don't mean that I'm going to go 0 to 100 and start punching up people. That's where you people are going wrong. You don't need to lock me in. The same way you ain't locking in that likkle white girl down the bottom cuz she's shouting off her mouth. There's four of you and you are walking her to the room, but you wanna try and twiss me up and put me in my room?'

The way in which Kayla's voice was not heard, but instead was wrongly translated and responded to as aggressive and threatening has harmful ramifications for both her body and mind. Through physical restraint her body was hurt, regulated, and removed and through not being heard her voice was silenced and repressed causing emotional pain and embedded trauma. As she later reflected:

> 'You're just trying to express yourself [begins to cry] because you're so hurt and that. Like I've got tears in my eyes for fuck's sake how you going to tell me I'm being aggressive?'

It is also important to recognise that 'potential damage of racism lies not only in the specific incident, but also in the resistance of others to believing and validating the reality or significance of one's personal experience' (Harrell, 2000: 45). During our conversation, Trish highlighted feelings of frustration and anger at personal as well as vicarious incidents of racism not being taken seriously by staff. In one example, Trish had complained to an officer about a racist slur being used against her friend (a black mixed-race woman) by another woman on the wing. She recalls the incident being downplayed by the staff member and other women with remarks such as, 'I don't think she meant it in that way' and 'She didn't call you it'. Not being believed is yet another way in which black women's experiences are silenced and repressed within the prison environment resulting in emotional harm.

The consequences of mistreatment, discrimination, and subsequent trauma experienced prior to and during imprisonment can also be fatal.

Annabella Landsberg

Annabella Landsberg died in 2017 a death that was preventable. Attention is given here to the way in which a combination of particular racialised, gendered and health-based discriminations within the Prison Service, and other social agencies, led to a series of catastrophic failures in the duty of care towards her as well as acts of violence being committed against her. When reading this account please also be mindful of the vicarious trauma experienced by Annabella's family and friends; as well as others who have heard about or witnessed her treatment within prison.

Annabella Landsberg was a 45-year-old black mother to three children, who had moved to England from Zimbabwe after being the survivor of a gang rape. She was also living with HIV. In 2007, she suffered a brain injury due to tuberculosis, and her family noticed her behaviour became more 'childlike' and 'challenging' (INQUEST, 2019). Yet she did not receive adequate support from mental health or social services for the multiple traumas she had experienced and instead became subject to police intervention (Frazer-Carrol, 2019). In February 2016, Annabella was sentenced to four years and six months in prison and after spending time within two other women's prisons she was transferred to HMP Peterborough in May 2017. By this time, she had also been diagnosed as having type 2 diabetes However, medical staff at HMP Peterborough had failed to adequately conduct required medical checks and so were not aware of her diabetes diagnosis (INQUEST, 2018).

During her time in HMP Peterborough Annabella was seen as challenging and anti-social by staff and as a result was placed in segregation on two separate occasions. Consideration does not appear to have been given to her brain injury, mental health needs and previous traumas as potential causes of her behaviour; and her history of attempting to overdose was not raised when determining whether she was 'fit for segregation' (Prisons and Probation Ombudsman, 2018: 15). Whilst in segregation, on 2 September 2017, staff used physical restraint against Annabella who was then left on the floor of her cell for 21 hours and did not get up to eat or drink. The Prisons and Probation Ombudsman report (ibid: 12) found that staff did not adequately check on her, as they thought she was faking her illness and 'attention seeking'. On September 3, a nurse entered Annabella's cell whilst she was still on the floor and threw water over her, later stating to officers that she expected Annabella would get up now she had left the cell.

At 3.13 pm on September 3 an ambulance was called for Annabella after a senior nurse was informed that no-one had carried out the necessary clinical observations for her despite the use of restraint. The senior nurse reported that, when entering the segregation unit, the atmosphere was 'jokey' and officers had remarked that Annabella was 'playing around' (ibid: 13). At the hospital, Annabella was found to be suffering from multiple organ failure and severe dehydration and tragically, on 6 September 2017, she died from complications relating to diabetes. It has since been acknowledged that the 'delay in providing medical assistance inevitably impacted on her chances of survival, but that had signs of her having high levels of glucose been acted upon prior to midnight on September 2 she would have survived' (INQUEST, 2019: 10).

As a result of misogynoir,[15] Annabella was seen as someone dangerous in need of control, punishment and force rather than in need, or worthy, of care. This is reflected in the failure to provide her with appropriate and necessary support for both her mental and physical health prior to as well as during her imprisonment. But also, in the violent, forceful, and neglectful way staff treated her. Even whilst in intensive care, prison officers placed Annabella in chains for 90 minutes out of fear she may become *challenging* or *threatening*. Assumptions surrounding black femininity as something resilient, strong, and disruptive meant that Annabella was not perceived to be vulnerable by those responsible for looking after her; a societal view that exposes itself in the racist treatment of black women and girls across a number of institutional settings. Speaking on the death of Annabella, the Director of INQUEST (2019) stated:

'Annabella was a black woman with multiple vulnerabilities. That she came to die a preventable death in such appalling circumstances is shameful.

---

15. Misogynoir refers to prejudice aimed specifically towards black women as shaped by the intersection of anti-blackness and misogyny (Bailey and Trudy, 2018).

Distress of black women in prison is too often disbelieved and viewed as a discipline and control problem. Annabella needed care and therapeutic support but instead suffered dehumanising, ill treatment.'

It is important to acknowledge, that the circumstances of Annabella's death are very similar to a number of black[16] and black mixed-race women who have also died in prison custody signalling a systemic problem. However, one death is always one too many.

 Pause for Thought

- We would like you to take a moment to think about Annabella and her loved ones.

Conclusion

After much debate on whether we should propose suggestions for supporting healing, we decided that it is not appropriate for us to do so yet in the context of this chapter. Institutions cannot support healing without first acknowledging the existence of the trauma itself and, in some cases, their role in causing or perpetuating it. We therefore argue that the first step is for institutions and services to recognise that 'racism is very much there'. After all, if you do not accept that something exists how can you deal with it? As highlighted at the start of this chapter, trauma-informed practice is becoming increasingly drawn upon to support women involved in the CJS. Its goal is to recognise the impact of trauma on an individual and, as a result of that recognition, to provide appropriate support. Such practice shifts the focus from 'What's wrong with you?' to 'What happened to you?' (HMIP, 2020) and aims to recognise strengths and skills, build confidence, and re-educate. This also helps embed

---

16. We have referred specifically to black women here as the stereotypes, assumptions and violence which characterised Annabella's treatment were linked to harmful perceptions of black femininity. We advocate for further and more in-depth research to consider the way in which differing prejudices and racisms may have impacted upon the treatment of women from other minoritised backgrounds.

new coping skills to enable behaviour recognition and regulation rather than re-traumatising with blame and sanction (ibid).

I (SB) took part in a trauma-informed course whilst serving at HMP East Sutton Park. I found that the taught processes of both acknowledging trauma and finding coping strategies were based on universalised assumptions of what women would experience such as domestic abuse and sexual violence. Whilst these are common issues faced by women universally, it must be noted that racially-minoritised women may also endure racialised harms which may inter-sect with, or be separate from, other forms of trauma they have experienced. For example, in addition to other traumas, I also had the layer of what I had gone through at sentencing (see earlier in this chapter). However, this was not an area that I was able to bring up and address in the course, nor did I feel comfortable doing so. Additionally, in the experiences of Annabella Landsberg it can be seen that rather than providing trauma-informed support the Prison Service treated her with blame and sanction, causing us to ask, 'Whose trauma is being used to inform practice?' Annabella had complex needs relating to her health, history of abuse and the trauma of imprisonment and racism and yet there was no support or care to help her cope with any of these.

Ultimately, trauma-informed practices, along with the CJS overall, need to be both culturally and racially sensitive. After defining racial trauma and discussing its existence in both courts and prisons, we now propose that the 'hidden wound' (Hardy 2013: 25) must be understood and discussed before any healing can begin. There needs to be a greater understanding of the many cultures which racially-minoritised people belong to, as this has an impact on their experiences. It is apparent that colour blindness does not work. Instead, we need a system that is both racially and culturally sensitive.

CHAPTER 6

A Mother's Work is Never Done
Mothers Affected by Remand

Isla Masson and Natalie Booth

Based on interviews from a wider project exploring loved ones' experiences of supporting those on remand (Booth and Masson, 2021), this chapter explores the *negative* impact upon mothers, and grandmothers, who maintained contact with incarcerated adults who have experienced remand. It is suggested that despite their family members being over 18 years of age, these *maternal* women continue to provide support to their adult children, potentially to the detriment of themselves/their own health. The interviews with women, who self-identified as mothers, stepmothers, foster mothers and grandmothers, indicated a number of ways in which they themselves had been *traumatised* as a result of the emotional toll following their (grand)child's remand. This included shock relating to the offence/enforced separation and the emotional and practical impact of visitation. It is argued that the harm caused by the incarcerated has a ripple effect, and extends not only to the person in prison, but to loved ones not found guilty and not sentenced; we illuminate how and why, for mothers and grandmothers, this is particularly acute/traumatic.

Introduction

The proverb, 'A mother's work is never done', has been chosen to frame this chapter following the authors' reflections and analysis of data regarding the emotional burden, placed either by themselves or others, on many women attempting to support those in prison. Semi-structured interviews were carried out with 16 women, who self-identified as mothers, step or biological, foster and grandmothers.[17] We chose to explore the experiences and voices of both mothers and grandmothers as, for many, the love and roles adopted by these maternal figures is intergenerational (see Baldwin, 2015; 2021b for further discussion regarding the relationship between incarceration and grandmothers). The interviews explored a wide number of topics and issues relating to the support provided by these maternal figures to their adult (grand)children who were in prison with experience of remand. This group of mothers and grandmothers comes from a wider data set of 61 loved ones[18] (Masson and Booth, 2018) who support those who were, or had been, on remand in England and Wales (for more information regarding the Families on Remand (FOR) project please see Booth and Masson with Dakri, 2021: 412–422). Interestingly, most of those interviewed for the FOR project identified as female, demonstrating the gendered nature often relating to supporting those in prison (Booth and Masson with Dakri, ibid; Codd, 2008; Lanskey, C, Lösel, Markson and Souza, 2018: 181–195; Baldwin, 2022a). There were other relationships in this larger sample of women beyond mothers and grandmothers, for example partners, sisters and aunties. However, it is the unique aspect of mothering which is central for this chapter. As such, we focus on the often-negative experiences, the ongoing trauma experienced by maternal figures, who have chosen to remain in contact with and support their incarcerated adult (grand)children.[19] We suggest that even if they are supported by others to maintain this contact, and perhaps accompanied by others on prison visits, there is a significant mental load taken on by these women. The (grand)mothers[20] continued to worry about their children, which subsequently took a toll on them.

Women experience a variety of pressures to uphold society's expectations relating to motherhood (Oakley, 1976; Hays, 1996). Conversations on this matter focus on decisions (whether entirely agentic and/or shaped by other circumstances, such as fertility) around whether to have children and/or if they

---

17. Rosie, Connie, Sinead, Bindu, Zabina, Jackie, Camilla, Janet, Scarlett, Wynnie and Marina (all mums); Heather (a step-mum); Tracey (a foster-mum); and Muriel, Marie and Stella (all grandmothers).
18. The authors use the term 'loved ones' to include any/all significant others of those in prison beyond heteronormative and traditional definitions of the 'family' that might only include biological and legal kin.
19. Hereafter the term children is used in this chapter to denote both adult children and grandchildren of the mothers we interviewed.
20. Hereafter the term mothers is used in this chapter to denote both mothers and grandmothers we interviewed.

are in a position to have children. There are strong assumptions of what a 'good mother' does or does not do. When women are not deemed to have fulfilled an appropriate mothering role, as is often the case with imprisoned mothers (Baldwin, 2015), they experience more punitive sanctions by the State and society. When it comes to pregnancy and motherhood, women are often on the receiving end of unsolicited 'advice'. For example, when people find out they are pregnant they are told, amongst many other things, that they should rest now, or get as much sleep as possible as when the baby comes they will be up all night looking after their infant (BBC News, 2019). In reality, sleep or good mental health are not always achievable in pregnancy or for those wanting or trying to conceive. Motherhood and mothering attract significant and widespread societal judgement, for example regarding what pregnant women should or should not be eating or drinking, how babies should be fed, or immunised and whether women should or should not be working when they have young children (Masson, 2019; BBC News, 2018 (regarding discomfort of breastfeeding in public)). Baldwin (2020: 95) refers to this as a Mothers Code of Conduct. Motherhood and expectations of mothers have no end date, and, for many mothers, when their children grow up (in that they reach 18 years of age and legally become adults), they do not stop worrying about them or mothering them; there is no cut off point — *a mother's work is never done.*

Positionality of the Authors

Both the authors for this chapter have researched the impact on motherhood and mothering within criminal justice settings for their doctoral projects and subsequent research.[21] However, increasingly the topic of what is deemed to be a 'good mother' has become more personal. Whether this relates to our relationships with our own mothers or becoming mothers ourselves. Our relationships with our research have significantly changed; something that our friend, colleague, and editor of this book — Dr Lucy Baldwin — suggested might happen. Rather than standing at the periphery and applying the issues with an academic lens, we are now personally immersed within this mothering world, feeling

---

21. Please refer to the *References and Bibliography* regarding the authors' relevant publications.

ourselves the judgement from others with regards to whether we are doing or saying the 'right' things. Equally it has made us conduct our research from a different point of view; reflecting on the process and experiences of the mothers we interviewed by drawing on this new frame of reference. For instance, in the early stages of data collection for the Families on Remand (FOR) study we sat outside a prison visitor centre eating lunch and de-briefing from what were often difficult conversations with loved ones. Acknowledging the huge upheavals and pressure being described to us, we spoke about whether we thought we would be able to put our lives on hold, like many from the project appeared to have done, for our loved ones. An important follow-up question was would our responses have been different or more strongly felt if these loved ones were our children? It is with these reflections in mind that we explore in this chapter the under-discussed ongoing impact of mothers affected by remand, and focus on both the initial shock relating to remand as well as the harm related to visits.

▮▮ Pause for Thought

- How can we all, as members of the public, reduce societal pressures on women to conform to ideal standards of 'good' mothering?
- How and why is it important to consider and explain the positionality of the authors?
- How might the authors' own histories and/or assumptions shape their research endeavours?

Literature Review

One of the most prolific and well-cited concepts in Criminology relates to the argument first introduced by Sykes (1958) and subsequently applied to over 50 pieces of work (Haggerty and Bucerius, 2020) articulating how imprisonment is painful, often referred to as the 'pains of imprisonment' (Masson, 2019). Likewise, there has been increasing recognition that these pains do not stop at the prison gates but are experienced also by the loved ones of the incarcerated, sometimes considered as 'referred pains' (Lanskey et al, 2018), and furthermore that these pains extend beyond the reach of prison (for example, Condry, 2017; Booth, 2020a; Baldwin, 2022a). International research has unanimously reported how imprisonment can cause problems socially, financially, emotionally, psychologically and physically for loved ones (for reviews, see Weaver and Nolan, 2015; Booth and Masson with Dakri, 2022). While a considerable proportion of this research has explored the effects of imprisonment for children, partners and parents, this chapter seeks to contribute new insights into particular, maternal pains of imprisonment for mothers outside of prison, who are supporting their adult children during and after remand. This focus draws on findings from the FOR study which sought to address the gap in the knowledge base as, despite this growing interest in prisoners' families, familial experiences surrounding remand remain explored to a lesser degree.

Remand in custody is a different form of incarceration as the detained individual is either un-convicted and awaiting trial, or convicted and awaiting sentencing,[22] often due to the serious or violent nature of the offence charged (ibid). It is argued that the remand of a loved one may evoke different emotions for those left in the community, for example shock or trauma, due partly to the serious or violent nature of offences involved for many remanded. It is also suggested that the immediacy of separation that follows remand, as well as the uncertainty of the duration and outcome of the incarceration, can change and likely intensify the adverse experiences of loved ones. Taken together, we argue that this process can be a form of ongoing trauma for mothers, who due to societal, familial or personal pressure often assume and experience further stresses when their child is remanded.

The term 'trauma' has substantially developed and broadened in recent years (Haslam and McGrath, 2020), but for the purpose of this chapter we are using the definition by the charity Mind (n.d) as this acknowledges how trauma can be instigated by 'stressful, frightening or distressing events'. These events can directly affect the traumatised individual and/or be witnessed as happening to someone else, and can include feelings of powerlessness, fright and/or being unsupported. As will be demonstrated, the term 'trauma' can be applied to the experiences of mothers supporting their imprisoned adult children on and/or after remand. We already know that loved ones of prisoners report how the

---

22. For more information about remand, see https://www.gov.uk/charged-crime/remand

initial period of separation following incarceration can be an exceptionally painful, shocking and worrying time (Masson, 2019; 2021). When their adult child is remanded, mothers may be less aware that a loss is imminent, and therefore have less time to prepare mentally and practically for the abrupt separation that occurs. The remand also instigates a series of unknowns for women outside, especially when this is their first experience of familial imprisonment, as they attempt to gather information about the prison detaining their child (see also Loucks, 2005; Booth, 2020a). In the days and weeks following the separation, mothers outside are often focused on re-establishing contact with their child and, over time trying to navigate the penal systems and processes to maintain this contact, for instance through prison visits.

Prison visits can be a 'double-edged sword' insomuch as they provide rare opportunities to meet face-to-face and interact at a more personal and intimate level, whilst also having the potential to evoke emotional and practical stresses. International research on prison visitation has described, in considerable detail, both the more positive and negative aspects of visiting experiences for prisoners and their loved ones (e.g. see Comfort, 2008; Chui, 2010; Brunton-Smith and McCarthy, 2017). However, as the maternal experience of supporting their imprisoned adult children has received much less attention, not much is known about these particular pains. That said, the mother/child separation caused by a mother's incarceration has received considerable focus in recent years (Baldwin and Epstein, 2017; Masson, 2019; Booth, 2020b; Baldwin, 2022a). This growing body of evidence has reported how challenges with contact sometimes centre around the complete lack, or lower frequency, of face-to-face contact or because visiting has caused yet more disruption and upset, especially at the end of the visit and as the looming (re)separation occurs. It is not a great leap to suggest that mothers visiting their incarcerated adult children would not experience similar emotions. Regardless of the age of their child in prison, mothers will likely have adverse reactions and feelings owing to separation brought about by incarceration. As previously stated, this is because motherhood is a lifelong role and commitment that does not end when a child reaches 18 years of age.

The growing evidence analysing maternal imprisonment has highlighted how visiting can be an exceptionally painful experience for mothers separated from their children, and their families outside (Baldwin and Epstein, 2017; Masson, 2019; Booth 2020b; Baldwin 2022a). Negative experiences and emotions around visiting were often felt differently, but perhaps equally as painfully by those inside prison, but also, and as our research has shown, by the mothers outside too.

Mothers described how, being able to 'see' their child in person could also reveal truths about how they were coping, and vice-versa. One imprisoned mother discussed by Martin and Powell (2023) described how the visit had exposed how poorly her child was being looked after by her caregiver. Unsurprisingly, this revelation led to increased concern and worry about their health and wellbeing, and is a reaction that we might expect any mother to have if and when they believed their child—of any age—was not being well cared for. However, as the maternal experience of supporting their imprisoned adult children has received much less attention, not much is known about these particular pains. This again despite motherhood often being a lifelong role and commitment that does not end when a child reaches 18 years of age.

As such, it is important to consider how mothers on the outside who are separated from their adult children experience prison visiting. Given that the sample for our study was mostly recruited via prison visitor centres, all the mothers interviewed were visiting loved ones and can help shed light on this previously under-researched maternal experience. The following section is split into two distinct but interlinking themes:

- first the initial shock and subsequent impact on maternal mental health; and
- second the impact of visits and how many of these mothers prioritised the needs of their loved ones rather than their own.

Both of these themes will be supported with the voices of some of the mothers interviewed and will include 'Pause(s) for Thought'. It is hoped that these will provide an opportunity for the reader to reflect upon the findings and consider ways to improve their own or wider practice.

Findings From the Families on Remand Project

Initial shock and subsequent impact on maternal mental health

The vast majority of the maternal figures interviewed said there was a significant impact on their own mental health as a result of their loved one's initial arrest and subsequent period of remand. Several spoke of the initial 'shock' relating to this terse separation, often because they were unaware of the original alleged offence or were not expecting their loved ones to be detained in prison. For example,

> 'It was very, erm, surreal, no, disorientating really, very surreal, very unreal, everything about it, you know, you're just thrown into something like that it's hard to get your head around.' (Wynnie, mum)

Likewise,

> 'I wouldn't have thought it in a million years … it were all on the news and everything.' (Marie, grandmother)

For Janet, the incarceration of her son was particularly painful as it was her birthday, when they should have been celebrating, 'It was a horrible day to be sentenced'. In the future this annual reminder for Janet will be particularly acute.

Importantly, it is suggested that this initial shock might have been greater for those with this maternal role, compared to other women providing support in the larger FOR sample (for example, partners). This is because although several had close relationships with their children, these children were all adults now, and therefore they did not have the same insights into their day-to-day activities, which some partners/wives had. This was articulated by one partner from the wider research group, Ariel:

> 'It was a lot more shocking [for his mum and dad] than it was for me because obviously I kind of knew what he was getting up to, but his mum and dad didn't. So for them, it was just like a whole brand new thing.'

This sudden confrontation related to alleged criminal activities, and the consequences of this evoked a mixture of many intense emotions in a short period of time. Sometimes this had long-term implications as was the case for Sinead who explained how her son's remand was taking both a mental and physical toll:

'I'm surviving...I'm staying alive. That sounds really corny, but that's as far as I'm going, I'm staying alive. I don't look well, my hair's falling out, my weight is phenomenal, erm, I'm borderline depressed erm...I'm just a lost soul on autopilot, I mean you can hear my tummy rumbling! I'm literally starving because I've suffered with my eating.'

For some of the mothers interviewed, the shock relating to the alleged offence and subsequent incarceration meant they initially chose to distance themselves from their children. This was either because the trauma was too much as they struggled to accept their imprisonment and their new family circumstances, or because of other commitments, including other demanding responsibilities like caregiving or paid work. For example:

'When it happened I believed everything that I was told that had happened and I said "I'm sorry I can't deal with this" and I hadn't spoken to him for 12 months, I didn't want anything to do with him.' (Camilla, mum).

Walking away, even temporarily, was a means to re-insert some control into the mothers' lives and remove themselves from the hurt and disappointment they were experiencing. Maternal shame is commonplace for women in contact with the CJS (see Condry, 2007; Baldwin, 2015). Such shame may also be experienced as a result of society's views of their child's actions, with Sturges and Hanrahan (2011: 986) suggesting that 'mothers live under the glare of public judgement, and understandably, they may internalise society's verdict as their own'. Therefore, it may be that this distancing was a mechanism to reduce or remove feelings of internalised shame and blame, and/or to provide time to find a way to conceptualise what their child had been accused of. Understandably some mothers may struggle to process and accept the charges against their child, and may decide they are unable to provide support either in the short and/or long term. As Codd (2008) rightly argues, this is their decision and should be respected. However, for Camilla, time provided an opportunity to re-conceptualise her son's imprisonment and led her to realise the benefits of reconnecting with him:

'I sort of came around to the realisation that, you know, perhaps I should get in touch with him and you know, my friend said "Look, he's your son, what happens if something happens? You'd never forgive yourself" and I did, I think it was so much relief because I think he thought I'd finished with him.'

As will be demonstrated later, for several of the interviewed mothers, their need to perform their mothering role and the responsibility they felt to do this, meant they often suppressed their own emotions and needs. Bindu, stated there were:

'All sorts of different issues going on in our life and so I'm thinking, "I can't deal with this" so I thought I'm blocking myself off from my son for a while because I can't let this business fail now and because I'd invested money in it...I was torn whether to support my life and my business, or support him.'

Choosing to remain in contact was not always a simple decision for the maternal figures outside. It should be remembered that the overall duration of remand is unknown, creating uncertainty about the length of time that the women would need to balance prison contact with other aspects of their lives. Likewise, those on remand are entitled to more regular visits than those who have been sentenced,[23] which may add to the pressure experienced by mothers deciding whether to support those on remand. Scarlett spoke about how she had to juggle visits and supporting two sons with looking after her grandchildren and disabled husband.

'There's not much time for us, not much time for me and my husband, do you know what I mean? We just want it all to slow down so we can get a life'.

---

23. Please visit: https://www.gov.uk/staying-in-touch-with-someone-in-prison/visiting-someone-in-prison

Another mum, Connie, spoke about how she was being pulled in lots of different directions to support both her son who was awaiting sentencing, as well as her partner who was in hospital. Providing support to an unwell partner is exceptionally demanding under any circumstances but the added toll of her son being in prison, as Connie explained, resulted in her feeling as though: 'I'm not in the right frame of mind for doing any of it'. The combination of the initial shock and other life circumstances made it particularly difficult to put on a brave face. The change in family circumstances because of her son's imprisonment was immense on top of her partner's hospitalisation, her closest loved ones had both been institutionalised—she had 'lost' both men in her life with whom she had previously lived. However, in contrast to those interviewed who temporarily walked away, in order for Connie to take control over this unprecedented situation it was felt that remaining connected to both loved ones was essential. Despite this, Connie explained that she felt 'nervous' about her first visit and was quite conflicted at this early stage by both 'wanting to come and not wanting to come'. Ultimately, what spurred Connie into visiting was the overwhelming need to see her son and the concern—or possibly a form of 'mum guilt'—that he may think she had abandoned him during his time of need. 'I wanted to see him obviously and I didn't want him to think that we didn't want to see him.' In fact, linking back to concerns about those being in prison not making it, for Connie, her age added another layer to what she was experiencing:

> 'One of the major things that is worrying him and me as well is that, depending on the sentence, I mean, I'm 73 and he's frightened of me not being around [when he is released from prison].'

Others spoke about deep seated worries that they would not be alive when their children were released. Here the remand and potential extended period of time due to a lengthy prison sentence did not mean that mothers were just separated from their children, but that they might not have any further opportunities to be together in the community at all. The mothers' awareness that they might only ever have contact within the restraints of prison was an incredibly upsetting feeling that weighed heavily on them.

For many mothers in the study, there was an ongoing psychological impact of this trauma that was not contained to the initial shock of the incarceration but resulted in recurring nightmares and crying as well as depression and not being able to leave the house or see others.

'He phones me every day and erm, he always says "I love you loads mum and I'll speak to you tomorrow" and I just end up crying and then I can't stop crying, every day…it's horrible' (Janet, mum).

Echoing previous research (Chui, 2010; Turanovic et al, 2012) another mother, Jackie, felt the experience was: 'Like having a loss in the family, a death or something'. However, as argued previously by both Hames and Pedreira (2004) and Booth (2020a) there is less sympathy relating to this grief, compared to others like divorce or death. Sometimes the emotional turmoil the mothers on the outside felt impacted their ability to work and to financially support those in and outside of prison. For example, for Marina, the impact of her daughter's incarceration was that she no longer felt like 'herself'. Due to the stress Marina felt she was under, she had to take extended leave from work: 'There's no possibility to go to work because, well, for example, I'm no use today so well, I stopped work'. It took a long time for her to be able to return to part-time work and, as discussed later, Marina's daughter in prison, and son in the community took steps in order to protect her and not further damage her mental health.

Bindu's mental health had similarly deteriorated to such a degree that she felt unable to work following the remand of her two sons. Having previously been the director of her own business and medication-free, she explained about being nine months into the remand of her loved one:

'I'm on like ten different tablets morning, noon and night for pain for my knee, for my shoulder, for depression, I'm on Prozac, I'm on sleeping tablets, I'm on tramadol so, I'm just a mental wreck…I just stay in the house all day, I just don't do nothing, I just sit there and pray, I'm just praying, my Qur'an, I'm praying on the prayer mat, I just don't do anything.'

The trauma and impact of their children's imprisonment was experienced differently by the mothers and consequently produced different outcomes;

some mothers had become more guarded, while others became accustomed to the routine. For many mothers the impact and trauma were not constrained to the initial periods of remand and individuals, but also to their experience of the CJS more broadly (Masson, Booth and Baldwin, 2023: 132–136). Scarlett, who had been providing support to her sons for at least five years at the time of interview owing to their repeat offences and periods on remand, said:

'I think I've learned to have a hard, a tough skin now, at first when it first started happening it was like buckets and buckets full of tears and whatsit, it's draining, but then I think you just toughen up to it all, do you know what I mean? You just have to, you just have to or you'll just get sectioned won't you?'

These different experiences shared here show how the negative impact and level of trauma experienced was multifaceted, often having a ripple effect on the mothers own lives. This was not only during the initial arrest and remand period, but continued during the extended period of incarceration and, where applicable, after conviction/sentencing. As discussed below, this initial and ongoing trauma was also found in the mothers' narratives concerning prison visits.

❚❚ Pause for Thought

- To what extent do you think criminal justice practitioners and academics should view those in a maternal role, and attempting to support those on remand, as victims of trauma? Do you think they are?
- How much should the trauma of maternal figures be taken into consideration when choosing to remand individuals in custody or on bail?
- Think about the implications for mothers if they do not want to be the 'bail address'.
- What can be put in place to better support these loved ones' mental health?

The Impact of Visits

It was not uncommon for those with maternal roles in this study to describe aspects of the visiting experience in a negative way, especially when asked about their first prison visit and/or their first time visiting a new prison after a transfer (see Masson and Booth, 2022: 463–483, for the impact of systemic penal practices). Visitation evoked a wide range of emotions, however sometimes the visiting mothers had to try and quash their own emotions, and not visibly display any trauma in order to protect their children in prison. For them, the best thing they could do as a mother or grandmother given the circumstances was to continue to put the experiences of their loved one first. Yet, the language used to describe the initial visit clearly articulates the emotional toil these experiences brought, with chosen words including: 'traumatic' (Bindu, mother), 'intimidating' (Tracey, foster mother), 'stressful' (Zabina, mother), 'horrible' (Janet, mother), and 'surreal' (Wynnie, mother).

Those supporting their adult children towards the start of their time in prison, for instance on remand or shortly after conviction, were more likely to describe visiting as a more emotionally challenging experience. For Bindu this was because she was observing how prison was having an adverse impact on her son's emotional and physical state, commenting that: 'I was horrified because he'd gone dark, he's lost so much weight, he was smelling'. Bindu's husband discouraged her from visiting her sons because of how painful and distressing it was for her. He reported how it took several days for her to recover from each visiting experience which significantly contributed to her previously discussed depression. After several months of her sons being on remand, Bindu made the difficult decision to discontinue the visits as they remained too traumatic, and she felt unable to adapt or become accustomed to the visits.

Another mother, Jackie, continued to visit but was similarly concerned about the state in which her son would appear during visits when he was detained in a local, remand prison. The offence for which he was accused made him a vulnerable prisoner,[24] and he was often the target of verbal, physical, and sexual

---

24. A vulnerable prisoner (VP) is an individual who is deemed to be particularly at risk of bullying because of either the nature of their offence, known 'enemies' and threats within the prison or circumstances surrounding their offence.

abuse. As such, Jackie's experience of visiting at this time was tainted by an overwhelming concern for his safety:

'The visits were awful, every time we visited we didn't know what we were gonna get, how he was gonna be, whether he was gonna come out holding himself or limping or whether he was going to be able to come out at all.'

In instances when the prison environment was causing considerable suffering, several revealed techniques that their children had adopted to try to conceal or reduce their mothers' exposure to harm. It might be said that their adult children were trying to protect their mothers from the full reality of the prisoner experience which, as we know from previous research, is painful and characterised by several deprivations (Sykes, 1958). For instance, Jackie explained how her son 'tried to hide a lot of things' from her or, when this was not possible owing to physical injuries that would be seen during the visit, would ask her not to cry so as to not draw attention to his bullying out of fear of further sanctions.

Jackie: 'They don't want you to be upset, don't want to cry and make him look weak so I said "ok."'

Interviewer: 'Don't want you to cry?'

Jackie: 'Yeah because he says if we cry, you know, it makes it look like he's said something to us to make us cry, and if it's like that with us, it makes him look [pause], so you've got to be careful.'

Interviewer: 'Keeping up that pretence on his behalf?'

Jackie: 'Yeah, and the one day he phoned me up and he said to me "When you come in, I don't want you to get upset, I don't want you to cry so just pass it off for now, I'll talk to you and tell you what happened."'

Due to concerns regarding her display of emotions potentially putting her incarcerated son at risk, Jackie was forced to 'be careful' and keep her emotions in check, which was incredibly difficult and forced her to minimise her own maternal trauma. In a slightly different way, Sinead's son who suffered from severe mental health problems instructed her not to visit at all. Not only was this out of concern for her wellbeing as she made the long journey to/from the prison using public transport, but also to protect her from seeing the extent of his deterioration.

> 'He won't let me go because I've got to catch the train and then it's an after-noon visit and it'll be dark and I'll be on the train and it'll be cold and that was the initial excuse but now, he's deteriorated that much, he won't let me see him because he knows he's ill.'

This protective stance was also taken by Freddie and his imprisoned sister who, between them, carefully managed the flow of information to their mother, Marina, so as not to further upset her. 'When I knew something, I'd tell my mum a couple of days later because my sister would tell me not to tell her'. When he did give the information to his mother, he summarised it, to further protect her from the painful details. While not all mothers reported having distressing visiting experiences, and not every adult child was playing this protective role, many reported the emotional pressure that regular visitation inflicted. For grandmothers Marie and Stella, however, the impact that visiting brought to them was considered minimal in comparison to what their incarcerated grandson had to navigate on a daily basis.

> Marie: 'It's awful isn't it? These prisons are terrible aren't they? But we're just visiting aren't we?'

> Stella: 'Yeah, we just learned to take each month as it comes.'

Again, it seems as though the mothers felt their own pain and trauma was less than or trumped by their child's trauma. As such, to be 'good mothers', and in order to consciously or subconsciously conform to socially acceptable maternal ideals the mothers suppressed their own emotions, pain and trauma.

Linking to the previous argument that sometimes individuals became accustomed to the prison environment, for some, visiting seemed to become less acutely painful over time. For example, sometimes visiting experiences improved following prison transfers as was the case for Jackie when her son was moved away from the remand prison, and certainly as her familiarity with the prison processes and rules increased. Wynnie explained how she often told other parents new to visiting that, while the situation remains imperfect, the experience will improve to some degree:

> 'I've known mums, I've known dads who were looking at long sentences who've said "I don't know if I can do this" and I've said the only thing I can tell you is that it does get easier, and it does get easier, it's never ideal, it never will be [pause] but it does get easier, it never gets harder than the first time … it just becomes a part of your life.'

With her son being in prison for 12 years, three of which were on remand, Wynnie was in a good position to comment on the longer-term experience of visiting. She had been the only person to visit her son during this time and had travelled to many prisons to maintain this face-to-face contact. Likewise, many with this maternal role were the only, or main and most regular, visitor that their children had. This finding might be explained by the mothers' enduring commitment to their maternal role and the needs of the child to be prioritised over their own interests and the broadly held view that *a mother's work is never done*—however old your child is.

Despite the emotionality associated with contact and visiting for them personally, many of these maternal figures wanted to continue supporting their imprisoned child and viewed prison visits as an important way to achieve this. Even though their children may have been accused or convicted of criminal offences, and as mentioned previously sometimes quite serious offences, those interviewed considered their support essential to their child's health, wellbeing, recovery and/or future. We should remember that motherhood is a role, a commitment, a responsibility that many women assume not only during their children's formative years, but through adolescence and into adulthood, and for many carries through to their children's children (Baldwin, 2022a).

The face-to-face contact afforded by maternal visits was considered particularly vital for the delivery of this support in the initial period of separation following remand. Foster mother, Tracey, explained why a visit soon after her son's remand would have more effectively steadied the family at this time of confusion and change, and provided support to her son saying:

> 'It's immediate so it's like a rollercoaster, you're stood still and then you're off and there doesn't seem to [be] any sort of way to have any contact to find out what's going on until it's happened so that I think needs addressing'.

Muriel talked about the role that she felt she had during her grandson's imprisonment and the way she could continue mothering during this period. She considered how mothers, and other loved ones, had a responsibility to remain in contact as a means of not abandoning those in prison, and reiterated how this contributed positively to their incarcerated loved ones' mental health. As already stated, this is not necessarily a view shared by all, but the emphasis Muriel placed on what they are 'supposed' to do indicates a strong connection to gendered, social expectations of motherhood.

> 'They're getting bored with each other, they don't see nobody, and I know some of them have done wrong, but you're not supposed to push them to one side when they've done wrong, I don't believe in that. You can't push them aside. It's all said and done, it's happened and that's it, I mean there's good and bad in everybody, but the point is that they are not seeing their families or their friends like normal. We need to occupy their minds, they're locked up.'

It is important when considering the harms of incarceration, including remand, to consider how societal expectations and pressure to be a 'good mum' may negatively impact women outside, especially as our study revealed, they prioritise the experiences and needs of their children over their own physical and mental health.

▌▌ Pause for Thought

- To what extent do you think it could be traumatic for mothers and grandmothers to visit adult children in prison?
- How can those with maternal roles be better assisted to address their own emotional needs whilst they support those in prison?
- What can be done to further support those who have chosen to not maintain contact and not visit their children or grandchildren in prison?
- What do you think you might do in this situation?

Conclusion

As academics we sit in a privileged position to highlight the injustices in our CJS, and to champion change for those subjected to such a punitive administration. Through this chapter we have illuminated some of the ways in which mothers and grandmothers who remained in contact with loved ones in prison on remand, and after sentencing, experience trauma. Deciding whether to remain in contact with someone who has been accused of an offence, and sometimes quite a serious offence if a remand in custody is considered appropriate, is a very difficult position to be in. It is made particularly difficult for various reasons, including the vicarious trauma of witnessing the harm experienced by their child in prison, emotions potentially related to the trauma the child may have caused, and also their own trauma—which is felt directly through their own experiences as mothers and grandmothers supporting their loved one in prison.

The decision is made especially complex for maternal figures as there are additional societal pressures with which to conform. Whether external or internalised, these social pressures can result in substantial maternal harm. The mothers outside experienced deterioration in their mental health following the initial shock of their adult child's imprisonment, as well as ongoing struggles as they navigated the emotionality of prison visits and support. Although these maternal women do not represent all mothers or grandmothers who have experienced their loved ones' period of remand, we have seen how the enduring pain caused by these punitive sanctions can and should be characterised as a traumatic experience (Mind, n.d.). When considering prison as a form of contemporary punishment, it is important for everyone in society to reflect upon whether the ongoing trauma to so many people — often women — is proportionate. Indeed, repeat interviews might help to better identify and articulate the longevity of this harm, as the narratives and analysis presented in this chapter are drawn from aspects of the one-off interviews in the FOR study. While the findings do support the extant literature (Condry, 2007; Booth, 2020a; Baldwin, 2022a), it would be interesting to see whether the issues identified are just the tip of the iceberg. Likewise, for the purposes of this chapter we have focused on the initial shock relating to the offence/enforced separation and the emotional and practical impact of visitation, but data analysis signalled that the negative impact was attached to other aspects related to attempts to continue to provide support, and to continue to mother.

The longer-term implication of imprisonment is something that has been the focus of research exploring maternal imprisonment (Masson, 2019; Baldwin, 2022a; Baldwin and Mitchell, 2022), but it is argued here that this ought to be expanded to include the experiences of *all* those with maternal roles, who self-identify as mothers, affected by the CJS. By acquiring this knowledge, academics and practitioners might also be able to identify ways in which this trauma can be minimised, to better support women. As argued here, women's work is never done.

CHAPTER 7

'And Still I Rise'
Hope, Trauma and Imprisoned Women

Christy Pitfield and Anna Motz

In this chapter we describe the trajectories of women into the CJS, and the destructive power of re-enactments, often traumatic, that can include the impact of incarceration itself. How can we work with women in these situations to help imprisoned women to break out of these cycles of pain and address our own role as therapists and workers, enabling us to retain a sense of hope in the possibility of change? Can we address both the trauma within the lives of women in contact with the CJS and the traumatising aspects of imprisonment itself? As one life sentenced woman, Lily, put it, 'The system can mould you and shape you, but it can't break you.' We offer an anonymised clinical illustration of how one woman, whom we have called Maja, inspired by Maya Angelou, inscribed trauma on her body through self-harm, and describe how therapeutic work with her, and with the team around her, made change possible. The poem 'And Still I Rise' by Maya Angelou, herself a survivor of sexual trauma, evokes the possibility of change and growth despite the legacy of brutality she, and so many other women, carry. In the chapter we describe the impact of trauma-informed work on Lily and on the system within which she, and we, find ourselves. We outline the challenges that this presents throughout.

Women's routes into the CJS differ distinctly from men's (Corston, 2007). Women generally do not commit violent offences, but when they do, their targets are their intimate partners or children, family members, and their own bodies, rather than strangers (Motz, 2008). Men pose greater risk to members of the public than to intimates and are responsible for over 75% of violent crime according to the 2017 *British Crime Survey*. Despite these clear differences, criminalised women are often sentenced without consideration of their social, personal and family circumstances, or the mainly non-violent nature of their offences, and they often receive very short custodial sentences in a prison system designed essentially with men in mind (Baldwin and Epstein, 2017). As more women than men are primary carers for children, the impact of their imprisonment is significant and harmful; these short sentences disrupt the care of children, can jeopardise accommodation, and do not allow the women to engage in treatment programmes that address their complex difficulties and help reduce the risk of their re-offending (ibid).

Given the significance of trauma in the lives of most criminalised women, it is essential that all practice with women in prisons and at all stages in the CJS must be trauma-informed, that is, it must take account of the causes of offending behaviour and the deep levels of distress, abuse and victimisation that underpin it. Awareness of the traumatic trajectories of women's lives, and the risk of re-traumatising them and their children needs to underpin decision-making at all points in the women's journey into custody, and beyond. It is essential to consider women both in their social context, and with awareness of their emotional state, being mindful of their prior experiences and the traumatic roots of their offending. Such awareness should be evident from the point of arrest, sentencing and conviction, and, if in custody, in the daily regime of prisons, and, finally, in the pathways out of prison into the community.

Trauma-informed practice means seeing the ways that incarceration re-creates trauma and finding alternative ways of managing women's pathways. Following a lecture tour of the UK penal estate in 2017 by Stephanie Covington, a US-based clinical psychologist and pioneer of Trauma-informed Care and Practice (TICP), the *One Small Thing* 'trauma-informed' training package (supported and facilitated by prison philanthropist, Lady Edwina Grosvenor) was rolled-out to staff in women's prisons across England and Wales. This training has been undertaken in our prison, but it is not always possible for this complex, total institution to reflect on its own practices, and to highlight examples where, rather than help the women within it, instead and often unintentionally harm has been inflicted. There are five key components of trauma-informed care, that are:

- Safety
- Trustworthiness
- Choice
- Collaboration

- Empowerment (Harris and Fallot, 2001; Covington, 2012).

As a clinical psychologist, psychoanalytic psychotherapist and forensic psychotherapist Anna Motz also specialises in psychodynamic understanding of the women with most complexity in terms of their backgrounds and their offending history, as well as working with the staff teams in the women's networks. Christy Pitfield is clinical psychologist and a specialist in perinatal mental health and complex trauma. We are both trained in mentalisation based therapy, using an attachment-based model to understand and treat women's expressions of 'non-mentalising' — that is those occasions where thoughts cannot be processed and unbearable feelings are evacuated through action, often in the form of self-directed violence. We help the women and the staff to identify the wishes, feelings and beliefs that underlie behaviour, and to reflect on this.

In our work we use both a trauma-informed approach alongside a psychoanalytic one, in which the underlying meaning of a woman's behaviour and presentation is constantly borne in mind, and weight given to unconscious wishes, desires and intentions. In an example, Lily, who spoke of how she can resist the brutalising elements of prison may, at times, appear to push away those who reach out to her, and to seek solitude and isolation. We understand this as a defence against her underlying wish to make contact but a fear that history will repeat itself and she will once again be abandoned. Rather than take her request to be left alone at face value, we will persist in asking her to meet with us, and show dedication to the part of her that wants to relate to others, seeing her as defending herself against a fear she cannot yet articulate. Similarly, we use the forensic psychotherapy model to understand that the crimes for which she was charged may symbolise underlying pain or anger, so that, in this case, her crime of arson was not just an expression of rage, but a way of communicating that the home she set fire to was one where abuse was taking place. It had a meaning, that can, through working with her, be decoded and understood.

The trauma-informed approach is consistent with a psychoanalytic one, and insists that the criminalised woman is treated respectfully, sensitively and with a close eye on her mind and her relationships — she is not simply a body to be punished and confined to a restrictive environment. The role of relationships is central to both approaches, and the trauma-informed worker, like the psychoanalytically informed clinician, has to be aware of their own feelings and attitudes in the work, and the dangers of re-enacting earlier patterns of abuse and neglect with the criminalised women.

While some women in prisons display signs of psychosis, more will exhibit features of attachment difficulties and personality vulnerabilities, characterised by unstable relationships, intense, rapidly changing emotional responses, and intense dependency needs, alongside difficulty trusting others and a fragile sense of self (Ayiegbusi, 2020). Alongside higher rates of classifications of personality disorder compared to the general population, the women in these settings frequently share histories of multiple trauma and attachment disturbances, creating profound difficulties in relating to others, despite the women's own wish to engage. The rates of adverse childhood experiences (ACEs) are high in this population; a report found that 53% of women in prison experienced emotional, physical, or sexual abuse during childhood (Light, Grant and Hopkins, 2013; McKeown, 2010). A disproportionate number of women in prison have grown up in children's homes, in care and/or under the responsibility of the local authority at some point.

Clearly, vulnerable and traumatised women are not the exception in prisons. In 2019, 53% of women in prison reported having experienced emotional, physical or sexual abuse as a child and 49% of women in prison reported being a victim of domestic violence. Thirty one percent of women prisoners have spent time in care as children, compared to 24% of men, and perhaps most significantly, almost half of all women in prison (46%) have previously attempted to take their own lives (Prison Reform Trust, 2015).

Although presenting as 'offenders' the women we meet have suffered tremendous levels of trauma from an early age, which can often go unnoticed (Motz, Dennis and Aiyebusi, 2020). The perpetrators of this harm are often family members, who either inflicted physical, emotional or sexual abuse on the women, or allowed it to happen, through serious neglect. The trajectories that the women follow are ones that then create further risk, in turn exposing them to more trauma and pain, and requiring more savage forms of defence and self-protection (Fossey and Black 2016; Aiyegbusi, 2020). Sometimes this is in the form of withdrawal, emotional numbing, dis-engagement from schools, social services, foster homes, parental homes, peers, and from knowing about, articulating what was being done to them. At other times survival strategies can include manic forms of activity to distract from the underlying pain, including sexual risk-taking, either for masochistic pleasure, and the legacy of confusing being loved and cared for with being wanted sexually, or for material gain, or simply to survive. We know that selling sex can be used as a survival strategy for homeless women (Warburton, 2019). Another form of sanctuary is immersion in the world of substances, alcohol and risk-taking, Women may rely on these activities, not to harm others, but to feel that they are alive, numbed to pain and able to suppress underlying feelings of vulnerability and fear. The women oscillate between these defences, revealing the stark inconsistency and chaos of both their early lives and their current mental states. Nothing is constant, nothing can be trusted. How can one make sense of a world in which nothing and no-one can be trusted, least of all those who were tasked with protecting and loving us?

 Pause for Thought

- What conflicting emotions might occur if abused by someone 'meant' to love you?
- How might this experience impact on other relationships and/or one's life choices?
- How might a child make sense of the fact that the person they most trust in the world has lied to them and hurt them? How could this impact on future relationships?
- What are the dangers of using substances to 'cope' or to block out or numb feelings experienced as a result of trauma?

For women who have experienced abuse, survival, both psychological and physical, is imperative. One mode of psychic survival is to split off the hatred for the mother, and attack one's own physical body, emblematic as it is of the mother's body. In this way the internalised mother is externalised onto the flesh and so through cuts, burns, strangulations, starvation and the ingestion of toxic substances, that symbolic and literal representation of mother can be punished. The hated maternal object is attacked symbolically, through these assaults on the body she has created, in her own image. For this reason, the assaults on the reproductive organs, directly through mutilation of the breasts or vagina, or indirectly, through the starvation of anorexia, and the cessation of the menses (menstrual cycle) that can eventually result, can be seen as an attack on the bodily representation of the mother, and of the woman's own trajectory, especially her potential maternity (Welldon, 1998). Self-harm for women can offer a tremendous sense of relief, release and even euphoria, as they attempt to purify themselves from toxic feelings, and restore a state of peace (Walker and Towl, 2016). Self-harm reveals several underlying wishes: to sever the connection with the mother, to obliterate memory of trauma and abuse, to preserve in the flesh the wounds that would otherwise be invisible and to create a transcendent state of mind, one that hovers above the world of pain and feeling. However, its effects are only short-lived and so compulsions to act recur, as the woman enters an addictive state, in which the only perceived solution to emotional pain is to inflict physical pain, sometimes toying with death (Motz, 2020).

As the women seen within these settings have often had multiple experiences of betrayal and misunderstanding by those in authority, often starting with their parents, or carers, they are likely to be wary of engaging with professionals. From the outset those tasked to care for them have let them down, leaving them with a sense of distrust, hopelessness, and defensiveness. 'In their interactions with women, practitioners may be faced with anger, frustration, lack of trust, scepticism, and exhaustion' (Craissati, et al, 2015: 100). The women's feelings toward early carers can be transferred onto clinicians and custodial staff, with powerful results, including unconscious re-enactments of early trauma.

The traumatic experiences that women in prison have suffered are not confined to individual experiences of abuse and exploitation, but can also have a cultural and racial dimension, that is all too often overlooked. Women from black and minority ethnic communities are particularly vulnerable to being treated as though they are dangerous, as unconscious and conscious bias creates distorted perceptions, where their expressions of distress are reconfigured as acts of aggression (Prison Reform Trust, 2017). Aiyegbusi describes this powerfully when she states:

'Black girls and women are likely to attract particular projections associated with low status, invulnerability, precocious or exaggerated sexuality, violence and other forms of criminality. A social unconscious loaded with their historical devaluation and disavowed brutalisation in Europe and by the European diaspora over a number of centuries, brings to bear a particular type of racist imagery that is difficult not to internalise.' (Aiyebusi, 2020: 19)

The Lammy Review (2017) of the experience of black, Asian and minority ethnic (BAME) people in the British CJS identified an even greater disproportionality of black men and women in its prisons than in the USA, a country known for re-enacting the trauma of chattel slavery through its mass incarceration of black people. Additionally, the Corston Report (2007), a review of vulnerable women in British prisons, highlighted the doubly vulnerable status of black women. The joint publication by Women in Prison and Agenda (2017) describing the experiences of BAME women in the CJS entitled 'Double Disadvantage' reported that 8.8% of female prisoners are black, though just over 3.3% of women in the general population are black, demonstrating their overrepresentation in custody. Black women are approximately 25% more likely than white women to be sentenced to custody in the Crown Court. This disproportionality increases further in the case of drug offences where black women are about 125% more likely to receive a custodial sentence than are white women (Aiyegbusi, 2020; Motz, 2020).

Approximately two thirds of women in prison have backgrounds of extreme trauma and neglect from an early age. Many have substance misuse difficulties, histories of domestic violence and many have had their own children removed, for some as a result of coming into custody (Baldwin 2022a). Women can become caught in a vicious cycle between poor mental health, substance misuse and criminal behaviour (often to fund their 'addiction'). Our role as clinical psychologists is to assess and treat those most in need, often those presenting with complex trauma, and lives that from earliest childhood have experienced neglect, physical abuse, emotional and sexual harm.

The women we work with have often had major disruptions in their care, with a significant proportion having spent periods of time in the local authority care system, where they were known as 'looked after children' (Corston,

2007; Fitzpatrick, 2017).[25] As they developed into adolescence they may have used substances, alcohol and self-harm as ways of numbing themselves to the pain they suffered and been exploited by others sexually. If they were in contact with mental health services, they often attracted labels of personality disorder, or unspecified mental illnesses, which can be seen as crude labels for the constellation of behaviour the women display to express and communicate their distress (Hackett, 2015). Understanding this as the manifestation of complex trauma is more helpful, although the broad category 'personality disorders' has, at times, been useful in offering a framework for viewing the women as suffering from profound difficulties in regulating emotions and managing impulses as a result of the experiences they have gone through.

It is therefore essential to recognise that the trauma that these women have experienced in the past, and still battle, is not only overlooked in their sentencing and subsequent placement, but also often re-enacted within custodial settings and in the community (Motz et al, 2020). There are powerful intergenerational factors that perpetuate these cycles of offending and trauma re-enactment, that current sentencing practice overlooks. We are particularly interested in those aspects of the women's presentations and histories that are hidden or unseen; we want to reveal and attend to the invisible but indelible trauma that has shaped their lives.

The following anonymised clinical material outlines this attempt, in some detail, describing not just the work with individual women but also with the other professionals involved in their care, who often have little knowledge of complex trauma yet who are responsible for their day-to-day care, and setting out goals for their progress through the system. The staff can move quickly from being pulled into rescuing or punishing positions in relation to the women, and both extremes are potentially abusive, and unstable (Hamilton, 2010).

---

25. Fitzpatrick explores the issue of girls who have been in care, disproportionately represented in the CJS and cites an HMIP report that identified the following: 'a pattern of reoffending for girls who were Looked After by local authorities, many who were also extremely vulnerable' (p. 4). In addition: 'It was particularly concerning that, for those girls who had been 'Looked After' by the local authority before their sentence, links with their social workers were often weak. In such cases, local authorities were failing to meet their legal duties' (HMIP, 2014: 9). This fits with wider evidence on the neglected needs of care leavers in the CJS. The Corston Report (2007) also highlights how many women in prison were formerly in the care system. This does not mean that all care leavers enter prison, in fact it is only a small percentage who do, but that there is a large proportion of women in prison who have been in care, and even when they have not, that they have significantly more adverse life events and traumatic experiences than women in general.

▌▌ Pause for Thought

- What aspects of prison could appear dangerous or frightening to a woman who enters for the first time?
- How might she express her distress? What impact could this have on the staff?
- How might a traumatic past manifest in the prison?
- Please take a moment to view this short video providing the context for the death in custody of Sarah Reed — how might her trauma have been better responded to? YouTube: 'Sarah Reed dies at Holloway Prison' (2016, Channel 4) https://www.youtube.com/watch?v=P_E6oxc19Hs
- What could create a 'safe space' in a prison?
- What would prison staff need in order to be able to deal with trauma and the way it impacts on the women within custody?

Clinical Illustration

The following case study illustrates the impact of trauma, and the trajectory of the lives of many women who come into contact with the CJS. The case study is anonymised and based on our work within a female prison, a busy and often chaotic environment, where women are on remand for relatively minor offences, and others with long histories of violence. In it we outline Christy Pitfield's work with Maja, a young woman of 25, remanded in custody for burglary.

Maja

When I (CP) met Maja, she had been in and out of prison for two years, receiving very short sentences, which added to the chaos and instability in her life when in prison, she would lose accommodation and leave homeless. She was trapped in a cycle of trauma, addiction and offending. Her longstanding reliance on self-harm as a coping strategy continued in custody.

I first learnt about Maja when I was called to an emergency meeting following an incident where she had seriously harmed herself, by tying a ligature and cutting her arms. I remember being shocked and overwhelmed by how many other professionals were in the room: prison managers, prison officers and various others whose positions I didn't know, as if they had all been drawn there by an invisible force. The meeting was focused on the question of how we 'stop the self-harm'. As a clinical psychologist in the meeting, it was hoped I might have the answer to this. I asked various questions about Maja and found myself confused; there were so many people in the room, yet nobody knew why she harmed herself. Were they there because they were fearful her self-harm would become more serious? Did they want to rescue her? If so, what from? There was a sense of urgency and panic in the room, to find an answer, yet when I asked questions to understand the function of self-harm, staff began talking about their positive working relationship with her and their ideas of how she could be persuaded to stop self-harming, through incentives, that is, rewards for so-called good behaviour. I felt suffocated and wondered whether Maja might also feel this way when all of these faces turned up each day, desperate to rescue her (but less obviously desperate to understand her).

It became obvious to me in that moment, the staff working with Maja needed support and to understand her. A powerful feeling and sense of clarity came over me in that meeting and I was certain of the need for emotional containment of her distress, and that of the staff: I would complete an assessment and psychological formulation, but I felt it was essential that fewer staff should be involved with her in order for Maja to feel safer. The notion of containment is not one of external control and restriction but refers to the way that, in good enough parenting, the carer is able to take in the needs of the baby, including her anger, fear and sadness, and manage it so that the baby can feel safe, eventually returning it to the baby in a form that is bearable. This is a function that carers provide when things work reasonably well and they are able to bond with their infants, and the infant forms a secure attachment to them, but many women in the CJS have had highly disturbed early lives, characterised by disruption and uncertainty, with no secure and safe person into whom they can project their powerful feelings—no-one to act as a container for them. The result is often that when faced with strong and painful feelings, the women feel overwhelmed by them and want to convert the emotions into actions, evacuating pain through violence against themselves in self-harm, or blotting it out through alcohol or drugs. Part of the essential role of therapists is to offer an experience of emotional containment and not become overwhelmed by the feelings the women express or react punitively to them.

I needed to be able to offer Maja a protected space for the clinical work, and also attend to the environment and the professionals working with her, to help them to understand and support her. I hoped that 'less might be more'; by having a small, reliable, consistent group of professionals in her care, we would arrive at a position where Maja was receiving more of the right kind of support rather than being overstimulated and confused. Having so many different professionals working with one, vulnerable woman, could generate an incoherent and inconsistent approach. This would mirror Maja's early experiences of being moved around in the care system, spending time in foster placements with many carers, some of whom were abusive, others kind, but with no sense of stability or consistency.

I wondered what it was about Maja that staff wanted to rescue as I arrived to meet her for the first time, to begin my assessment, only to have her tell me quite forcefully that she didn't want to meet. She presented as neglected and exposed, with no make-up or façade to protect her, looking years younger than her actual age, like a girl living on-the-streets, defenceless. I encouraged her to come into a clinic room, away from the main area, to talk about why she didn't want to meet, but she remained on the prison landing among other residents. I wanted to ensure I did not push further for conversation in such a public forum. I wanted to create clear boundaries and so I let her know I would book a subsequent appointment at the same time the following week. She acknowledged this but did not commit to meeting with me.

I continued to hold meetings and discussions about her through the week and I became aware that the professionals in her now well-defined support system were repeatedly encouraging her to meet with me, suggesting on one occasion during a panicked call to me, that I go and see her immediately following another serious incident of self-harm. In this phone call I sensed the tremendous unmet need, both in Maja and those supporting her, and I felt the force of the wish for me to rescue her. I reflected on this and thought that rushing over to see her following an incident of self-harm would have been confusing for everyone involved, it would have taken me outside of my role, turning me into an emergency worker. I was concerned too that attending in this 'crisis' and showing such interest then, rather than at times she was calm and quiet, could reinforce Maja's use of self-harm in the longer-term. While I understood it as a form of communication, my aim was to help her develop a wider repertoire for self-expression and, where possible, to reduce her reliance on this alone as an urgent request for help. I wondered whether behind the prison officers' ostensible request for me to attend to support Maja there was a hidden wish for me to support them, to contain their emotional distress and hold them in mind. I realised that this too was essential, and that the staff needed to feel contained in the same way that I was helping Maja to be. I was offering her an experience of having her feelings safely held for her, lodged in my mind, and the staff also needed to have a sense of being heard, understood and responded to. This would allow them a far stronger position to support her by listening to her distress, thinking with her about the feelings that threatened to overwhelm her, and naming the triggers that reawakened past trauma. I did not attend to see her following this incident but arranged to meet with the staff who worked with her, to help them manage their sense of powerlessness and fear. This was received very well, and it was moving to see how prison staff, so often expected to be tough and unemotional, were able to express feelings of vulnerability, concern and care.

For the next few weeks, I saw Maja individually, and she alternated between attending our sessions and sitting on the floor with her back to me, or arriving and leaving after a few moments. She was a petite, childlike woman. She often looked unkempt and wore prison-issue clothing of grey tracksuit bottoms and tops, a sign in prison of a person having none of their own clothes or belongings, or family to provide these for them. At times she presented as agitated and hyperactive and at others she wept. I often felt forced into the role of mother, wanting to protect her and to give her the care she was so clearly craving. I recognised that the staff also felt this pull to help her, and to get drawn into trying to repair the damage of her past.

Maja gradually revealed some painful details about her early life and the significant trauma she had experienced from an early age. Her presentation in the room with me and how others felt around me led me to formulate that she had a severe attachment disorder. She seemed to rely, whether consciously or not, on various competing strategies to attract me, sometimes rejecting me and leaving the room, at other times asking me to take her home and asking about my personal life. The way in which she told her story was revealing of her insecure attachment style, describing a childhood so filled with insecurity and abandonment it had left her with an incoherent way of relating to others, characteristic of attachment disorders. She would share small insights into her early life, then withdraw, or recount memories that were fragmented, presenting timelines without any structure. The narrative was incoherent, fragmented and yet there was something in Maja that constantly evoked my care, and interest.

Maja had experienced an unstable upbringing with incidents of childhood sexual abuse, rejection and loss. She had tried to protect her siblings from being abused, which meant she suffered immensely. She was subjected to physical and emotional neglect that resulted in her being placed in foster care. Her siblings remained in the care of her mother, who she told me had hated her, that she believed she would have been happy if she died. She served the function of what Lloyd deMause (1990) calls a 'poison container'—the receptacle into which her mother poured unwanted aspects of herself, only then to attack her for being so 'bad'; in this way Maja contained the hated parts of her mother and could then be punished for this. As so often happens when children are misused in this way, Maja identified with those hated aspects of others and thought of herself as worthless, ugly, unwanted and bad; in a clear example of projective identification, she identified with the toxic projections put into her. When she was eleven, she had been taken into care, placed there by her mother. This further intensified her strong sense of being unwanted and unworthy.

Maja had struggled in the care system, her body primed to be frightened and hurt, having learnt the adults around her were abusive and untrustworthy. She once laughed as she told me she had over 100 placements in her teenage years, quickly blaming herself for being 'a nightmare'. She described being angry and aggressive towards others and said that all she had wanted was to be with her family. Her siblings had been left in her mother's care, signifying that they were wanted, while she was rejected, but she still longed to be part of this family unit. It became apparent that her family had offered little protection for her, and she had experienced further abuse in a care home, to which she had been exiled. Her education had been enormously impacted by moving around and she had rarely attended school. Maja's few memories of school were of her being told she was stupid, being singled out and humiliated when she did not understand something and being bullied by other children. Though Maja was clearly bright, she remained uneducated and filled with a sense of failure.

Unsurprisingly, Maja began drinking and using drugs when she was 14 and found comfort there. She formed relationships with others who were in similar circumstances, and this provided some of the sense of connection and care she had longed for. This period was short-lived and destructive as Maja began shoplifting to fund her drug use, a behaviour that was rewarded by her peers. She began by stealing food and clothes but over time she became more violent and was charged with robbery, having threatened a member of the public.

There are periods in which Maja was under the care of Child and Adolescent and Adult Community Mental Health Services, where professionals saw her as unwell and in need of assessment and treatment. She was often referred following serious self-harm, or suicide attempts, 'out of control behaviour', attention deficit hyperactivity disorder (ADHD) or depression and anxiety, all of which can be understood as her reactions to trauma. Maja engaged at times, with services, but these periods of engagement were punctuated in her mind by those professionals leaving or giving up on her. When she was 19 years of age, she gave up on seeking support, something that had taken courage and felt risky, given her history. She dropped out of treatment regularly to avoid painful feelings of loss and abandonment. Her clinical files make frequent reference to her 'poor engagement', and 'treatment failure', and it seemed that she had internalised these dismissing labels, leading her to feel little hope for support and treatment.

When she was 17 years old, Maja had fallen pregnant, during a period of time when there had been some stability in her life. She had her own flat, was enjoying studying at college and remembers being excited she would have a baby. The pregnancy was unplanned and she was not in contact with the father, with whom she had had a brief relationship She described a desperate wish to have been able to care for her daughter, Jana, but social services became involved when Jana was one year old and concluded that, Maja, known to them as a child in need herself, was not adequately able to care for Jana's needs. She had no support from her family and described being very alone during Jana's first year of life. Although Maja managed to feed and tend to her daughter, social services were concerned about emotional neglect, Maja's often frightening and erratic behaviour and ongoing substance misuse. When her daughter was a year old, she, like her mother had been before her, was placed in foster care due to these concerns. At this point Maja's mental health worsened (not least because of the additional stress, trauma and fear of losing her child), and she did not engage in any support and Jana was eventually placed for adoption. The care proceedings were clearly re-traumatising, reminding her of the ways she had been treated in care, and intensifying her sense that she was not allowed to have anything good for herself, and indeed, that she was not to be trusted. Her love for her daughter was evident, but as a young girl, with no internalised experience of good parenting herself, she had fallen back on the modes of survival with which she was familiar, and not attended to the needs of her baby. She clearly needed help and support but was not able to engage with the local authority, trusting no-one and seeking comfort where she could. Furthermore, as so often happens once a child has been removed, access to certain aspects of support is also removed (Baldwin, 2022a; Morris, 2018).

Maja's description of her pregnancy, the birth of Jana and her adoption were part of the hidden trauma that she held inside her, with shame and grief. I had known Maja for two years before she was able to speak of this trauma, without leaving the room. She felt paralysed by feelings of grief and shame, convinced she had let her daughter down and should be punished, but also unable to manage the intense sense of deprivation and injustice she felt about her removal from her care. At the same time there was part of her that felt relieved that her daughter might be offered the kind of secure home of which she herself had been deprived, as she feared that she would not be able to provide this herself, aware of how hard she had found it to care for her, much as she longed to. She felt guilty that she hadn't been able to offer it, and hoped the future could be different for her daughter, at times wishing that she too, had been fostered or adopted by a loving family. Strange as it may sound, she felt that some aspects of prison, and some of the staff who worked with her, could play this role for her. I wondered whether a placement in a mother and baby unit might have been a way to enable her to care for her own child, as this might have offered her the care and containment that she needed to be able to attend to the needs of another, but this had not been an option.

Maja's transition to motherhood and the subsequent loss of her baby harshly reawakened her own trauma, her longing to be cared for and her unmet emotional needs. After her daughter was removed, she described being more fearful of rejection, more vulnerable and experienced increased flashbacks and nightmares of her own childhood. In the absence of support, her drug use and offending worsened and she entered the CJS. Sadly, this cycle of trauma, missed and lost opportunities for support, child removal, additional maternal trauma, substance misuse to cope with the pain, and reoffending to fund an addiction, is a cycle many criminalised mothers find themselves in, particularly those who have used substances as a means of coping/blocking/dealing with trauma (Baldwin, 2022a).

▌▌ Pause for Thought

- Think about the missed and lost opportunities to support Maja. In an ideal world at what key points would intervention and support have occurred and how might that support have changed the outcomes?
- What are the barriers to support?
- How do you feel that mothers and children sometimes pay the ultimate price (separation) for the consequences of some of the barriers — especially those that are resource-led?
- What might Maja want to say but does not yet feel safe to?
- What events might trigger memories of her daughter, and the pain of separation?

The Therapeutic Relationship

My therapeutic relationship with Maja was now well-established enough for her to begin to explore the meaning and function of her self-harm with me. She described intense feelings of anxiety when she was alone, or in response to distressing flashbacks and nightmares to childhood sexual abuse, and the day her daughter was removed. She felt she had had no way of managing these experiences and said she would self-harm to 'stop' feeling. At other times she would try to ask for help, but she would struggle to verbalise how she was feeling and what she needed from professionals. This led her to feeling rejected, scared and alone. She was trapped in an impossible conflict where she needed help, but she was left feeling even worse when she asked for it. She manifested clear symptoms of PTSD, and we could name these as such. Maja was struggling to survive in prison, not only because of her pre-existing trauma and related issues, but now also with her additional 'maternal trauma' and maternal emotions—which, as is often the case, were not readily acknowledged or recognised by the prison system (Baldwin, 2022a). Day-to-day in the prison, Maja would be highly sensitive to approaches from staff asking how she was, as her expectation of care was that it would be abusive; in response to their expressions of concern she was often verbally aggressive or insulting, as if pushing them away. In turn, the staff around her would feel hurt and rejected by her, often leading to a more punitive approach and hostile communication.

Despite this, Maja remained attached to prison as if the environment helped her feel safe, again not an unusual experience for deeply traumatised women (O'Malley, 2018). She had professionals and peers who knew who she was. For Maja, it was the first time in her life she felt that anybody had cared for her. I understood now that staff working with her daily were in touch with this part of her and responding by wanting to rescue and take care of her, the helpless child in need of a parent. They were pulled into this role unconsciously, and yet could not sustain it, eventually abandoning or rejecting her (or at least it being perceived as such by Maja). The reality was such that staff changes, staff resources, and role boundaries meant that it was not always possible, practical or appropriate for prison staff to support Maja in the way she wanted (and needed). Nonetheless, it was in this way Maja's early life, and its trauma, was constantly being re-enacted in the prison setting. Maja's wishes for it to be different were disappointed time-and-again, leading to anger at the staff and towards herself, expressed through Maja's 'acting out', disengagement and self-harm.

Progress in Maja was often hard to see and define. While I knew that the therapeutic relationship was strong and thus a marker of progress in my mind, I also knew that this, at times, exposed her fears of being rejected by me. For her, there were personal 'risks' associated with allowing herself to form a relationship with me. Furthermore, the absence of tangible progress frustrated the prison staff whose primary goal (perhaps understandably) was to reduce Maja's self-harming. Their own terror that she would soon seriously harm herself or die continued to overwhelm their capacity to bear any small progress and positive steps in mind. While one of the main concerns of the institution was preventing a death in custody and reducing self-harm to demonstrate that the prison was safe, there was also a real fear for the staff involved with Maja that she would die, or seriously damage herself.

I was mindful of the first meeting with the network around Maja, where I had been tasked with reducing her self-harm. I realised that stopping self-harming was not something she always wanted and knew too that this provided her with a powerful tool to communicate her distress, as if this was a 'passport' to care, as well as an outlet for emotions she was unable at that time to express any other way. There is no doubt that for some women self-harm is not only a management strategy, but also an alternative to suicide (Walker and Towl, 2016). As Motz describes (2009) for many women, self-harm is a means to staying alive, and reflects a hope that the environment will recognise their need to relate to others and communicate their painful states of mind.

Maja's capacity to develop a narrative of her life was key; it was essential to help create a coherent story in her mind of how she got to this point, rather than have her resort to a kind of passive acceptance of her losses and pain, with her characteristic self-blaming statement 'It's all me'. Maja had a strong internal critic, believing she was pathetic and weak for having emotions and not being able to cope 'like everyone else'.

Through our therapeutic relationship, gradually, Maja began to understand herself better specifically in terms of what was going on it her own mind before she harmed herself. When she was able to identify clear triggers, we considered other ways she could regulate her feelings, often in a physical way.

A significant moment in the therapy occurred when Maja herself began to describe how the pattern of self-harm, substance misuse, and going to prison made her feel worse rather than contained by the external controls of the prison environment and soothed by receiving the punishment she felt she deserved. She was now experiencing depression. This realisation clearly catalysed change, and Maja began talking about taking responsibility, considering what she wanted for her life as an adult. Like so many traumatised women in Maja's position, at the point that this realisation took place Maja had endured several years of being 'told' she needed to do this, but with little understanding of what this actually meant. Taking responsibility meant taking a risk, what would she lose if she did not self-harm, or stopped coming to prison? In this period Maja developed some friendships in prison that were not based on the shared use of substances, and she took on a job. This began to help her develop an alternative identity to simply being a 'self-harmer'. Her support network remained heavily involved, to reassure her that she wouldn't lose everyone who cared for her as she started to progress. At times this became difficult, and Maja would revert back to the 'comfort' of self-harm and was subsequently harsher and more critical of herself for returning to 'old' ways of behaving or coping. The staff would then often become hopeless and despondent, and I was often struck by how difficult it was to get key professionals in a room. This was a marked difference to the initial meeting.

As Maja assumed a less dependent and childlike position, wanting to take on responsibility and exert her agency, difficult as this task was, she lost the care of those who seemed, unconsciously, to want to adopt a rescuing role and treat her as a collapsed and needy child, rather than adult woman. Thus, some staff were now feeling like Maja used self-harm as a means of manipulation and this led to some resenting her—because Maja's periods of abstinence meant to the staff that 'she could stop if she wanted to'. We had to work with these staff to help them see that Maja's self-harm was an attempt to communicate distress to them, and did not feel consciously chosen, but a desperate means to get unmet needs met, and to express feelings that were not yet possible to put into words. She felt she had no other choice but to mark her pain on her body, viewing it as both a safe place onto which to direct anger and despair, and a means of communicating this to others. It actually helped her to stay alive rather than being an attempt to die.

Motz (2009) writes about the many functions that self-harm serves, including the following:

- It reveals the significance of the earliest experiences of maternal care and the particular importance of the skin.
- It can symbolise traumatic breakdowns in early care that are unconsciously re-created in later assaults on the body.
- It can communicate distress, anger, protest and the hope that a real attempt will be made to relate to the person who self-harms.
- It can be seen as a suicidal gesture, but rather, as an attempt to preserve life, and to represent and contain unbearable states of minds.
- Self-harm can create a narrative and embody unbearable feelings and unspoken thoughts. It is seen as a form of self-expression and communication, both conscious and unconscious, which is not wholly destructive but has important hopeful and self-preservative aims.

- Marking the body can give form to inchoate despair and convert physical to psychological pain.

▐▐ Pause for Thought

- What are your feelings about self-harm?
- What activities do you think could be considered forms of self-harm?
- Can you see self-harming activities as lying on a continuum?
- What activities do you engage in that could be considered forms of self-harm?
- What functions does Maja's self-harm serve?
- How does someone using self-harm as a means of coping with their trauma make you feel?
- If you do see it as manipulation how might that view impact on your work and the women you work with?
- Can you re-frame that as a means to have unmet needs for care addressed?
- How does that change your feelings about the women with whom you work?
- How can you inform yourself about self-harm and how to respond to it?

It became ever clearer to me that the hour a week I met with Maja was not enough, and that the professionals working with her daily needed to be able to understand her self-harm, and their responses to her. This understanding from staff and increased appointments with me were key to enabling staff to maintain boundaries that ensured they would neither be punishing nor rescuing Maja, and importantly, to support her own effort to take responsibly for her life. Further, to assist Maja to regulate her feelings in other ways than through self-harming alone. She desperately needed a means of self-care, emotional regulation, and someone to keep her in mind. While I could serve that function to some extent, it was essential that we developed a 'team mind' that could be relied upon to know and care about her even when I was not present.

The therapy finished as Maja approached the end of her prison sentence. Following nearly two years of working with Maja and her support network, a more unified approach to her self-harm was evident. There were fewer professionals involved in her care, but those relationships were strong and consistent and trauma-informed. At times of crisis, when Maja self-harmed more often or more severely, the staff were still pulled in to re-enact her traumatic early life, displaying incoherent and inconsistent attitudes towards her and alternating between suffocating and abandoning her. The notion of a 'team mind' and 'less is more' was lost at these moments, showing clearly how Maja's attachment disorder developed, and was reinforced through these re-enactments. She would behave frantically to attempt to keep those she relied on near her, and would oscillate between angry outbursts, serious self-harm, withdrawal and tears. Although Maja continued to tie ligatures at times of crisis, these were less often, and she seemed more able to resist the urges. We continued to explore these impulses and their triggers in weekly therapy sessions, after a year, Maja sat in the room with me at a table, exploring these together for the full hour session. She neither left abruptly nor sat on the floor with her back to me. I now saw her as an adult and had watched her grow during therapy from an impulsive adolescent into a woman with pain and difficulties that she could describe and reflect on.

The ending of her prison sentence and impending freedom, so often celebrated in our environment was marked by intense feelings of loss and grief. The final sessions were painful for Maja, when I attempted to explore her feeling about ending the work she reverted back to leaving the room abruptly or became inconsolable. She was ambivalent about leaving and wondered if she would be safer in prison, an irony that many of us working in this setting often consider. I worried she might not manage the transition to the community and would find it too difficult to build supportive relationships there because of her past trauma and its effects. It was difficult for me to say goodbye. Whilst I was pleased with her progress, I knew the work we had done together was only the beginning, but I was hopeful that she had been able to internalise a good experience of care, and that this could be held inside her. Our aim was ultimately to replace the external controls of the prison walls with internal ones, but the years of damage, and difficulty trusting anyone, least of all herself, meant that this could only be achieved very slowly and that there would inevitably be times of collapse. Maja was able to reflect on this and wrote poetry to express her feelings of pride in the work we had done together and hope in the possibility of finding a different way of living.

Pause for Thought

- Why might Maja have felt safer in prison than outside?
- What does this tell us about our society and services 'outside'?
- Think about times you have withdrawn from your working relationships with individuals — or have changed job roles — have you /can you/ will you give thought to being able to do this in a trauma-informed way?
- What would the ideal trauma-informed withdrawal look like?

Concluding Thoughts

This work had not just been a one-to-one therapy with Maja but had involved thinking with the team, containing this team and also setting boundaries — a few rather than many professionals, clear structures and reasons for seeing her, responding less dramatically in crisis and attending to her needs at times when she was not self-harming, encouraging her to relate in ways that were constructive and built on her considerable resources — ordinary activities like jobs, giving her space and time to read, and write, and form friendships. I helped the staff to direct her to therapy to explore her grief and guilt about her daughter in a trauma-informed way, rather than discussing this all the time with anyone who would listen, as this was overwhelming for her, leaving her feeling like she was fragmenting, as various parts of her life would be 'lodged' in different staff members. What she needed was containment and understanding. In this way I acted in some ways like a parent who could think about their child rather than just react, and who helped others around her to reflect on her, rather than simply respond with punishment or attempts at rescue.

Maja remained at risk, particularly when leaving the prison and entering a community that had no place for her. Like so many young women in this situation the practical steps of obtaining housing, benefits, or a job, finding a way to structure her day and engaging with a network of people who could support her, were daunting. The organization Women in Prison offered a through the gate service, having also offered regular sessions with Maja in custody. They then met her on her day of release and accompanied her to the approved premises and to establish contacts with her general practitioner, benefits office and local church. All of this proved invaluable. The transition from an institution like a prison to the community is huge and can leave women feeling lost and unsteady. Trauma-informed practice takes this into consideration and ensures that transitions, into and out of custody, recognise the complexity of such a journey. It is a real attempt to address the complex needs of women in prison including self-harm, suicide, mental health difficulties, substance and alcohol misuse and to change the physical as well as psychological conditions for women.

For the prison system to truly operate in a trauma-informed way, it was not enough that individual clinicians offered Maja care and understanding, but the whole of the organization needed to understand the meaning of her self-harm, the impact of her past trauma on her current functioning and the power of staff's own responses to her. They could, unthinkingly and unknowingly, repeat the damage of the past, punishing her for being frightened or lonely, or showing her need for care the only way she had learned to — through the marks she made on her body. They could promise care and attention that was impossible to follow through with and repeat her earlier experiences of betrayal and deception. The staff were attachment figures for Maja, at all levels of the hierarchy, and unless we could help the whole staff team see this, and also generate a consistent plan for responding to her self-harm, we would be working in isolation, positioning ourselves as 'good objects' in a sea of 'bad objects' and this would help no-one, least of all Maja.

We developed a team mind, and this sense of care and consistency, alongside Dr Pitfield's individual work with her, enabled Maja to be able to reflect on her own mind. She relied less on her body to express her painful feelings.

In our work we are ever-mindful of the years of trauma that the women have endured, and need to keep the hope of recovery and change alive, despite their repeated experiences of loss, abandonment and grief. Additionally, we need to help contain the tremendous anxieties that the staff, both clinical and custodial, face when coming into contact with the women, and being confronted with their bodily expressions of grief and fear. The system itself can recreate trauma and introduce new forms of pain, humiliation and brutality. Perhaps the most important aspect of our care is not the skill of our psychotherapeutic techniques, or interventions, but our capacity to turn up reliably, week in and week out, to bear witness to the past and present suffering the women have endured and to help them to express their pain through their voices, their writing and their art, rather than on and through their bodies.

In telling Maja's story we hope to have shown something of the opportunity that custody can offer both women and clinicians to help women break out of destructive cycles, borne of their traumatic experiences. To do this requires care, sensitivity and willingness to bear the weight of past trauma, for the imprisoned women and the workers themselves, and is a complex but essential task. We aim to keep the hope alive for the women who all too often feel hopeless and undeserving of care, helping them to access the considerable resources within themselves to maintain lives outside of custody.

CHAPTER 8

Women's Experiences of Presenting as Homeless Post Domestic Abuse
Homelessness Policy and Domestic Abuse — The Changing Legislative Context

Kelly Henderson and Yoric Irving-Clarke

Figures from the Department for Levelling Up, Housing and Communities showed that 5,590 households were assessed as homeless because of domestic abuse in early 2021 (out of a total figure of 34,830 households). According to Jayanetti (*Guardian,* 30 October 2021) this was the highest 'since records began in 2018 — and a third higher than in the same period in 2019'.

Housing policy in the UK has a relatively short history with serious housing policy only beginning in the period post-World War One, and clearly after World War Two with the Beveridgean Welfare State. Nevertheless, there have been previous and concerted efforts to provide housing and support for those in poverty, although they have often been both neglectful and brutal, compared with the more supportive role we see today (Irving-Clarke, 2019).

This chapter looks at homelessness policy in the UK with reference to efforts to address domestic abuse (such as they have existed). It considers the subjective concept of vulnerability which has been a long-term problem in assessing homelessness as a result of domestic abuse, and the recent changing legislative landscape. Finally, it details some real-world examples of women's experiences of the homelessness system as they attempt to leave abusers with a particular focus on the experience of women presenting as homeless. In considering the real-world examples it ends by highlighting some of the emerging good practice which, as yet, is unfortunately not the norm. The chapter also highlights how the failures and lack of understanding and responsiveness in the system contribute to women's trauma, often re-traumatising them during the system processes and assessments.

The Poor Laws as the Foundation for What Became Homeless Policy

Dating back to the 16th century, the 'Poor Law' was a collection of local and national measures that attempted to provide a basic welfare safety net for the poor. These laws were a consequence of the social pressures of the time, e.g. the dissolution of the monasteries removing the relief they provided, or devaluation of the currency. They can be seen as a reaction to this poverty, designed to maintain the social order and stave off unrest (Fink, 1981). The Act for the Relief of the Poor 1597 (amended in 1601) established the first national framework for relieving poverty by establishing 'overseers of the poor' who were responsible for distributing food, money, and other essentials to those in poverty. The 1601 amendment enabled the creation of alms houses or poorhouses for the 'impotent poor', those who could not help themselves. Alms houses had been around for some years, running parallel to other measures to assist the poor. These were originally linked to monasteries and charitable donations from merchants, landowners, and other people of means (see Pannell and Thomas, 1999 for a further history of alms houses). Assistance from the State came at a price. The able-bodied poor were set to work in a 'house of industry' where materials were provided for the poor to work productively, the idle poor (presumably those who were deemed as refusing to work in a house of industry) were sent to a house of correction or even prison whilst pauper children would become apprentices. This system continued until the 19th century.

The system for assisting those in poverty was updated again by the Poor Law Amendment Act 1834 when provision was placed under a single system of administration (rather than the existing parish-based system). A Poor Law Commission was established to oversee the operation of the new system at a national level. Parishes were clustered into Poor Law Unions (each run by its own Poor Law Board), and Union Workhouses established to provide relief to the poor in the area covered by each union (Irving-Clarke, 2019). At this time, relief to the poor was provided both as 'outside relief', financial or charitable relief provided direct to the poor, and 'inside relief' — the workhouse. This was a place where the poor were provided with unpaid work, which covered their board and lodgings; during the 1840s the workhouse became the only avenue of relief to the poor (ibid). Workhouses did not distinguish between the circumstances of paupers and were designed to act as a deterrent to poverty through a reputation of brutality, but as Crowther (1981) notes, the reality was often more one of neglect and boredom. The poor law system continued well into the 20th century as homelessness policy failed to keep pace with positive changes to wider housing policy after World War One. For example, the Tudor-Walters report highlighted the shortage of good quality homes for men returning from the war and recommended a huge housebuilding programme as well as introducing space standards (Park, 2017). This was implemented via the Housing and Town Planning Act 1919 (the Addison Act).

At this time, provision for homeless people continued to consist of large, poor quality converted workhouses and resettlement units, known as 'spikes' with shared dormitories, they were predominantly associated with single, white, middle-aged 'men of the road' with alcohol problems (Neale, 1997). Despite the National Assistance Act 1948, hostel provision continued to be large and basic, some having up to 100 beds primarily used for emergencies and for those excluded from accessing other accommodation (Busch-Geertsema and Sahlin, 2007). These Acts focused on the poor as opposed to homelessness per se. Homelessness due to domestic abuse was not part of the conversation.

Duties Imposed and Updated

The first duty to set out specific actions to house homeless people was placed upon local authorities by the Housing (Homeless Persons) Act 1977. Those with a 'priority need', who were 'unintentionally homeless' and with a 'local connection' qualified for statutory rights and were, by law, provided with temporary hostel provision, whilst settled accommodation was sought (Jones and Pleace, 2010). Section 29(1) of the 1977 Act gave local authorities a duty to promote the welfare of:

> 'Persons aged 18 or over, who are blind, or dumb, or suffer from mental disorder of any description and other persons aged 18 or over who are substantially & permanently handicapped by illness, injury or congenital deformity or other such disabilities as may be prescribed by the minister.'

This was one of the first policies to define a specific group as 'vulnerable' and therefore entitled to State services. Readers will notice that those fleeing domestic abuse are not even close to being included in this definition. Indeed, until the late 1960s and 1970s, domestic abuse was hardly seen as a policy or public issue in the UK (Irving-Clarke and Henderson, 2021; 2022).

Before looking at domestic abuse specifically, in terms of general homelessness policy, the arrangements put in place by the Housing (Homeless Persons) Act 1977 persisted until 1996, when there was significant change. The Housing Act 1996 changed the requirements on local authorities, placing a duty upon them to make provision for individuals and families experiencing homelessness.

The statutory definition of homelessness was updated from that given above to include:

- pregnant women, or any person who resides with a pregnant woman;
- households with whom dependent children reside or might reasonably be expected to reside;
- all 16- and 17-year-olds, provided they are not a 'relevant child' (relevant children remained the responsibility of social services) or a child in need to whom a local authority owes a duty under section 20 of the Children Act 1989;
- all 18-to-20-year-olds (other than 'relevant students'), at any time after reaching the age of 16, but while still under 18, who are no longer looked after, accommodated or fostered;
- any person who has lost her/his accommodation as a result of an emergency such as flood, fire or other disaster.

Housing Act 1996 Part VII

The Act also mandated that people:

- of old age, mental illness or disability, physical disability or other special reason, or someone who lives with one of these categories of vulnerable person:
- who have been looked after, accommodated or fostered and are aged 21 or over (other than ' relevant students')
- who have been a member of Her Majesty's regular naval, military or air forces;

- have served a custodial sentence, been committed for contempt of court or similar offence, or been remanded in custody;
- who have had to leave accommodation because *of violence or threats of violence from another person that are likely to be carried out* (italics added).

The above must be accepted as in priority need provided that the authority is satisfied that they are *vulnerable because of being in one of these categories.* Being in priority need was significant as it meant that a household must be provided with interim accommodation whilst any investigations were ongoing, and permanent accommodation by the local authority, if it were determined they met the criteria. This was the first time that domestic abuse appeared in any homeless legislation.

The issue here in terms of domestic abuse as the cause of homelessness meant that vulnerability was not a given and those considering the cases of women presenting as homeless due to domestic abuse were not required to have specific or mandated training in terms of the understanding of vulnerability or trauma because of domestic abuse or indeed any training on domestic abuse per se.

The definition of homelessness underwent another overhaul by the Homelessness Act 2002, to include:

- a pregnant woman or a person with whom she resides or might reasonably be expected to reside;
- a person with whom dependent children reside, or might reasonably be expected to reside;
- a person who is vulnerable because of old age, mental illness or handicap or physical disability or other special reason, or with whom such a person resides or might reasonably be expected to reside;
- a person aged 16 or 17 who is not a 'relevant child' or a child in need to whom a local authority owes a duty under section 20 of the Children Act 1989;
- a person under 21 who was (but is no longer) looked after, accommodated, or fostered between the ages of 16 and 18 (except a person who is a 'relevant student');

- a person aged 21 or more who is vulnerable because of having been looked after, accommodated, or fostered (except a person who is a 'relevant student');
- a person who is vulnerable because of having been a member of Her Majesty's regular naval, military or air forces;
- a person who is vulnerable because of:
  - (a) having served a custodial sentence,
  - (b) having been committed for contempt of court or any other kindred offence, or
  - (c) having been remanded in custody.
- a person who is vulnerable because of ceasing to occupy accommodation because of violence from another person or threats of violence from another person which are likely to be carried out;
- a person who is vulnerable for any other special reason, or with whom such a person resides or might reasonably be expected to reside;
- a person who is homeless, or threatened with homelessness, because of an emergency such as flood, fire, or other disaster.

Once again, the 2002 Act did not see the person to be vulnerable because of domestic abuse per se — that vulnerability had to be demonstrated or proved and it continued to be down to those assessing homelessness to decide on that vulnerability.

Prevention and Relief

Based upon the recommendations of an expert, independent panel, the Homelessness Reduction Act 2017 (HRA) again updated duties on local authorities in addressing homelessness. Beginning as a Private Member's Bill introduced by Bob Blackman MP, it was subsequently supported by the Government and passed in 2016 (Homeless Link, 2018). The HRA introduced five key changes.

- The period for being 'threatened with homelessness' was doubled from 28 days to 56 days.[26]

---

26. Meaning you can approach your local authority for support and advice if you are threatened with homelessness within 56 days.

- Advisory duty — strengthening the duty on local authorities to provide advice and information.
- Duty to prevent and relieve homelessness.
- Duty to conduct a housing assessment and put in place 'personal housing plans'.
- A 'duty to refer' to encourage public bodies to work together on preventing homelessness. The public bodies include prisons, social service departments and Job Centre plus amongst others.

Defining and Proving Vulnerability

In terms of homelessness policy, as we have detailed earlier, domestic abuse did not factor in the legislation for many years. The Housing Act 1996 Part IV finally did make specific provision for applicants for homelessness assistance who were deemed 'vulnerable' and therefore in 'priority need', thus being owed a duty to be housed by the local authority. The Homelessness Act 2002 refined the definition, however applicants had to prove they were vulnerable 'because of' having to leave their home due to threats of abuse, rather than automatically being considered so, as some other groups were. Hall (2020) points to Burrows et al (1997) who highlight that housing is different to any other form of benefit or service in that the level of proof required before help can be offered is unprecedented. Placing the burden of 'proof' on people, most often women, who are already victims of domestic abuse is deeply troubling and fundamentally traumatising for women.

Crisis (2015) state that 'In depth interviews with the respondents from across Great Britain found that people were often given no assistance at all because the council did not perceive them to be vulnerable enough, that they had made themselves intentionally homeless or that they did not have a local connection' (ibid: 19). The definition of 'vulnerable' was the subject of some debate and considerable case law. Initially, in *Pereira v Camden Council*, the Court of Appeal held that a person should be considered 'vulnerable' if their circumstances were such that they would suffer more than the 'ordinary' homeless person and would suffer an injury or other detriment that the ordinary homeless person would not. Indeed, this became known as the Pereira test. This was updated by *Hotak v London Borough of Southwark* [27] which found that a duty may be owed (to investigate) if a person is more vulnerable than the ordinary person. This has been clarified by the Supreme Court which ruled that, firstly, a person's circumstances should be considered in their entirety when assessing their situation. Secondly, that vulnerability should be judged against an 'ordinary person' and *not* an 'ordinary homeless person' (see Irving-Clarke and Henderson, 2022).

The All-Party Parliamentary Group on Ending Homelessness (APPGEH) report 'A Safe Home — Breaking the Link Between Homelessness and Domestic Abuse (APPGEH, 2019) stated that the vulnerability test was an 'unnecessary and inappropriate barrier to survivors accessing settled accommodation' It reported that whilst we know that domestic abuse is often responsible for a person's homelessness, in 2017 only '2% of people accepted as homeless and in priority need were considered to be a priority because they were vulnerable as a result of domestic abuse' (ibid: 16).

This has now been rectified by the Domestic Abuse Act 2021, which has clarified in an important step forward that those persons fleeing domestic abuse must be considered vulnerable automatically, under the terms of homelessness legislation.

The Domestic Abuse Act 2021

As readers will have noted, the above definitions of statutory homelessness did not include those fleeing domestic abuse as being in 'priority need'. Although there was scope to deem them so if they are considered *vulnerable* because of *domestic abuse.* The 2021 Act rectifies this situation by deeming them so. Robert Jenrick MP, Secretary of State for Housing, Communities and Local Government stated:

'I can confirm that through the Domestic Abuse Act, the government will also be ensuring that victims of domestic violence get the "priority

---

27. *Hotak (Appellant) v London Borough of Southwark (Respondent)* [2015] UKSC 30.

need" status they need to access local housing services much more easily': Homelessness Policy Paper (Home Office, 2021).

The 2021 Act also:
- Enshrines a definition of domestic abuse in law.
- Enshrines the role of a Domestic Abuse Commissioner in law.
- Makes changes to the justice system to better serve victims of domestic abuse.
- Strengthens support for victims and their children provided by local authorities.

On housing and homelessness, the Government placed a statutory duty on Tier 1 local authorities (County Councils and Unitary Authorities) to provide accommodation and support to people fleeing domestic abuse. Local authorities are required to either create a new commissioning body for domestic abuse services or specify which existing body will take on the new responsibilities. Tier 2 (districts and boroughs) have a statutory duty to cooperate in delivering services to meet the new duty. Tier 1 authorities (above) have a statutory duty that frames the delivery of support to people experiencing domestic abuse.

There is now a duty on lead authorities to convene a multi-agency 'Local Domestic Abuse Partnership Board', which must perform certain specified functions, as outlined, and explained in statutory guidance. Interestingly, there are no specific requirements for housing providers of homeless authorities to be part of the boards despite Part 4 of the Act setting out that the boards must assess the need and demand for accommodation-based support for all victims, including those who require cross-border support. In addition, the partnership boards must also:
- Develop and publish strategies for the provision of support to cover the locality and diverse groups of victims.
- Make commissioning/de-commissioning decisions.
- Meet the support needs of victims.
- Monitor and evaluate local delivery.
- Report back to central government.

There is also a duty for lead authorities to have regard to statutory guidance in exercising these functions; and on Tier 2 district, borough and city councils and London boroughs to co-operate with the Local Domestic Abuse Partnership Boards. There will also be new mechanisms in place to measure value for money and service quality (Homeless Link, 2018).

The Government published the Tackling Domestic Abuse Plan (TDAP) (HM Government, 2022b) which sets out how it will invest over £230 million to deliver provisions within the Act. It highlights that research has identified four key problems that the TDAP seeks to address.

- **Problem One** — The stubbornly high prevalence of domestic abuse.
- **Problem Two** — The significant loss of life caused by domestic abuse.
- **Problem Three** — The negative health, emotional, economic, and social impact victims and survivors face during and following domestic abuse.
- **Problem Four** — An efficient system is necessary to allow us as a society to tackle domestic abuse.

In terms of domestic abuse and homelessness it can asserted that the issue fits particularly into problems three and four above and we welcome any positive movements to bring change so that those survivors homeless as a result of such abuse can access safe, affordable accommodation that meets their needs. The TDAP also states that as part of the Victims Funding Strategy the Ministry of Justice (MOJ) is considering the introduction of national commissioning standards across all victim support services and Department for Levelling Up, Housing and Communities Quality Standards for support in safe accommodation. This would result in the commissioning of support in safe accommodation for domestic abuse victims and survivors and their children being subject to the same standards as all victim support services.

The Government (at the time of writing) has two current consultations: one seeks responses and evidence on issues faced by victims and survivors in joint tenancies. It points out that victims and survivors can be threatened with homelessness by perpetrators if they are in a joint tenancy and being at risk of paying costs such as rent arrears. If the abuser does not pay despite being in a joint tenancy this can lead to eviction thereby causing issues accessing further housing as a result.

Currently, without agreement from their landlord, victims and survivors can only transfer a tenancy into their name solely through the courts. This leaves victims and survivors in an insecure position. The Government is currently seeking to explore solutions in those cases whereby it is the right option for those victims and survivors to remain in their own home.

The second Government consultation running at the time of writing is seeking responses in relation to regulation to prevent local authorities applying a local connection test for victims and survivors of domestic abuse who apply for social housing. The consultation highlights that some local authorities continue to exclude victims and survivors of domestic abuse from social housing if they do not have a local connection. The consultation will consider how this exemption can be better implemented.

Having detailed the homelessness legislation, we now go on to look at women's experiences within the homelessness system.

Women's Experiences

This section outlines women's experiences of presenting as homeless who are fleeing domestic abuse. We have set the backdrop and incremental approach in relation to homelessness legislation and the inclusion of domestic abuse (Crisis, 2019). Research shows this important step change is much needed (Irving-Clarke and Henderson, 2022; Henderson 2019). Women's Aid, in their Hidden Housing Crisis (Women's Aid, 2020) report examined the housing experiences of survivors of domestic abuse. This draws on evidence from the Women's Aid Survivor Voice Survey 2019 and case study interviews with survivors and a caseworker from Women's Aid's No Woman Turned Away team. Women experienced mixed responses when approaching their local housing team for emergency accommodation because of domestic abuse, indicating differences from area to area.

The Women's Aid Nowhere to Turn Project (2021) has since 2016 provided vital support for women and children unable to access refuge space. In its latest findings it stated that of the 166 women who were supported by the project:

'62 (37.3%) contacted a local housing team and at least 20 of these (32.3%) were prevented from making a valid homelessness application.'

Reasons given for this included:
- Housing teams ignored guidance which states that local connection rules do not apply in cases of domestic abuse.
- Suggestions by staff to return to the perpetrator(s).
- Recommendations to call the National Domestic Abuse Helpline instead.

A similar picture was found in Crisis's No One Turned Away (2016) research. They found many local authorities failed to assist those presenting as homeless due to domestic abuse and pointed to a lack of sensitivity when dealing with survivors. Some of the examples cited included survivors being asked to recount their experience in public, or alarmingly mirroring the Women's Aid findings, told to return to the perpetrator.

Henderson (2021) asked women in a refuge setting to describe their overall experience of presenting as homeless because of fleeing domestic abuse. The research included a questionnaire and in-depth interviews with women who had presented as homeless due to domestic abuse. Comments from the women completing the questionnaire included:

'I felt I was being a burden': Mindi

'I felt I was a statistic and not a person': Camille

'There was no empathy—some staff were snappy with me': Fiona

'I was made to feel worthless and embarrassed': Yasmin

'I didn't think I was taken seriously or listened to': Sarah

'I felt let down and unsafe [when placed in hostels]': Sue

The same research ascertained views from refuge workers as to what would improve things in their opinion and included in-depth interviews with women who detailed their experiences in presenting to the local authority as homeless as a result of domestic abuse. Angie talked about having a positive response from the local authority worker despite being nervous about approaching the council. She said:

'I was very nervous about approaching the council regarding finding a home when [I] was in a refuge. My previous experience at other councils had been very negative, so that is what I was expecting. I was given a key worker and I had her number so this meant I could speak directly to her, and she would keep in touch with me. I felt that she understood me and that made a difference. It was an informal process and not like my previous experiences with other councils.'

While she was in the refuge, Angie pointed out that the council worker looked for suitable properties for her and contacted her when she found a property that she thought might be suitable.

'After a few months of her looking for properties for me, I was offered a private rented property and it was the first offer and I took it. It was in a nice area, quiet and had trees. I couldn't quite believe it would be mine until I actually got the keys. I felt it could be taken away at any point.'

Angie went on to say that she had been worried about what she might be offered and talked about the relief she felt when the property was offered. She added that waiting to see what you might be offered was very stressful as, 'You must have a good reason to turn a property down'.

Mia had a different experience in presenting as homeless. When she did so she was advised by the council that she had to present to the local authority where she was from — despite the local connection rules not applying in cases of domestic abuse. It is important to note that many women would not be safe if housed in their local area — hence the reason why women are often housed in women's refuges away from their local area and their locations are kept secret. Mia stated:

'I have been told I need to move back to my area which is [names area]. This is fine but I cannot be back in the area of [names location] that my ex-partner is in. He would find me. Last time I did that and moved back to the area he found me and kicked the door in. The last property I was offered was actually just five bus stops away from where he lives so there was no way that I could accept it.'

In addition to the concerns about offers of property, its location and 'needing a good reason to turn it down', Natalya talked about the experience of viewing properties in some areas she didn't know which entailed travel costs. She said:

'I accessed help from the council myself, but I could have got help from refuge staff if I needed it. The first person at the council who was dealing with my case wasn't very helpful. I saw a number of flats which were all quite a distance away and I spent a lot of money going to see them with my baby, spending money on train fairs, etc. Some, for example were an hour by train.'

Natalya pointed out that she was a very capable person and that this was important as she had to be persistent in dealing with the local authority. She felt she didn't know what would have happened to her if she hadn't been so persistent. She said her experience finally improved when she spoke to someone else at the council who understood her, reflecting Angie's point in the importance of someone understanding. Natalya explained:

'I called every day for two months asking for a property. Things changed when I was passed to another person when the person that I had been dealing with was on holiday. The person was very understanding and understood me straight away—she told me "Don't worry we will find something suitable for you and your baby". In two weeks, she had found me something.'

In detailing their first contact with the housing authority, women talked about the negative and re-traumatising experiences in explaining to a stranger why they were homeless. Earlier research by Henderson (2019) found survivors spoke of the uncertainty of not knowing how much of their story to tell when presenting as homeless. This uncertainty of what to expect in the process was echoed by Emma who felt upset after re-telling her story. She said of her first visit to the council:

'I didn't understand the process or what was expected of me. I think the most upsetting thing was having to explain what happened to me and I remember feeling really upset afterwards. I felt I had to "prove" what I had been through. I felt the person assessing my case was undertaking a bit of a tick box exercise. But this was my life and the reliving to a stranger what I had been through was distressing.'

The distressing and traumatising process of disclosing why they were homeless was mirrored by Jackie who took a refuge worker to the local authority with her:

'It feels like a lonely process, telling someone about the worst experience of your life. You feel the person doesn't always get what you have been through. I was grateful I had the staff member from the refuge to support me as I am not sure I could have coped doing this on my own.'

As well as the process being a distressing experience, Mina outlined that it felt like a case of jumping through hoops to even tell her story and the feelings of uncertainty in what would follow. She outlined the impact of telling what she had experienced:

'I remember the first thing I had to do was to have a phone call to see even if I could get an appointment—that was the first hoop to jump through. I then had an appointment and had to say what had happened. I remember thinking I have already told police and others and there I was again telling another person what had happened to me. It is draining.'

Mirroring the experiences of Mia, she said:

'I think the scary bit was when they tell you there is a property and you are scared to say no as what else will they offer you, could it be even worse? It is a worry what to accept. You worry they are thinking well...is this it.'

In addition to the experiences of women, refuge workers were asked what would make things better. They responded with three key improvements that would make a difference to women's experiences. Their responses centred round the widening out of opportunities to seek help and for the person providing that advice and support to understand domestic abuse. The three improvements identified were:

1. **Using community venues to seek support and access homelessness advice**. This would remove some of the fear of presenting as homeless and allow women to seek advice earlier and could help their decision-making when they were ready to leave.
2. **A dedicated helpline for victims and survivors of domestic abuse.** To seek support which would again give survivors the confidence to seek housing advice and support in the knowledge that the person they would be speaking to would understand domestic abuse and therefore their situation.
3. **Ensure all staff working in a homelessness setting area are trained to understand domestic abuse.** For example, to undergo the Women's Aid Change That Lasts, Ask Me training which equips participants with an understanding of domestic abuse and how to respond to survivors.

The Homelessness Code of Guidance in Relation to Women Presenting as Homeless

The experiences of women presenting as homeless have been problematic as demonstrated, and amendments to the Homeless Code of Guidance (HCOG) in October 2021 on the back of the Domestic Abuse Act 2021 set out that local housing and social services authorities must have regard to the code when exercising their functions relating to people who are homeless or at risk of homelessness. It sets out several points relating to how local authorities should respond to domestic abuse stating:

'An important factor in ensuring that an authority develops a strong and appropriate response to domestic abuse is understanding what domestic abuse is, the context in which it takes place in and what the impacts are on victims; as well as how the impacts may be different on different groups of people.' (Section 21.11 HCOG)

The guidance also sets out that housing authorities 'seek to be flexible in their approach' recognising that in some cases it may not be safe for some to approach the housing authority directly. To counteract this, it stipulates those options available to victims of domestic abuse should be maximised to allow them to make a homelessness application. This was an issue highlighted by refuge workers, it will be interesting to see what efforts local authorities take to make this happen. It is important that local authorities enable access to homelessness assessments in other community venues and indeed refuges themselves.

It points out that specialist training for staff and managers will help them to provide a more sensitive response and housing authorities are strongly encouraged to provide risk-assessment training to support staff and managers with responsibility for assessing applications from victims of domestic abuse. It is disappointing that the HCOG does not clearly mandate and only strongly encourages housing authorities to do so.

We, the authors, would go further and argue that all housing staff and managers should receive trauma-informed training and trauma-informed policies and practice must be adopted.

Developing Good Practice

Whilst there is a myriad of examples of women being further traumatised when presenting as homeless as a result of domestic abuse there are also some examples of areas actively adhering to the code of guidance and making the process less traumatic for those presenting.

Cheshire East

Cheshire East local authority sets out that it takes a holistic and multi-faceted approach in relation to domestic abuse and housing needs. Crucially, their focus is on increasing skills and knowledge of staff working in the housing and homeless sector to identify potential domestic abuse earlier so that support can be offered sooner.

As well as increasing skills within the homeless sector they also have a focus on increasing skills and knowledge of specialist domestic abuse staff around housing related support options including options available from partner agencies.

The Next Chapter

The Next Chapter, a domestic abuse charity in Essex, has invested in developing their knowledge and skills in understanding housing and homeless legislation so they can support women accessing their services. The training has equipped staff to effectively work with housing providers and housing authorities to positively challenge their practices and advocate for women. This movement in practice represents an incremental change.

Conclusion

It is clear from the examples above that understanding the lived experience of women fleeing domestic abuse is key to positive change. Recognising and reducing the barriers women face when attempting to leave an abusive partner is essential to minimising the traumatising experiences women have described in this chapter.

For centuries (until the 1960s and 1970s), domestic abuse was not on the policy agenda of Governments, or even particularly in the public consciousness (Irving-Clarke and Henderson, 2022). Indeed, until relatively recently it was thought to be a private or domestic matter (Henderson, 2019). This was until, in the late 1960s and 1970s, feminist activists began to raise awareness of domestic abuse and 'women's fear' (Warrington, 2003). Marches, rallies, squatting, and lobbying were all used as mechanisms to raise awareness (ibid) with a view to assisting victims, challenging male violence and changing women's position within society (Dobash and Dobash, 1979).

From these efforts, and related to a housing crisis in the 1960s, some activists started what were the early domestic abuse refuges, often in squats, staffed by volunteers and run on shoestring budgets (Irving-Clarke and Henderson, 2022). These early refuges raised awareness of domestic abuse as an issue but also established it as an issue intrinsically linked to housing, and it has remained so ever since, even though this has often been far from explicit in homelessness policy. Challenges in funding make many of these refuges precarious, and they are able to assist only a small proportion of domestic abuse victims. Many women remain in their own homes in violent, sometimes life-threatening situations because the barriers to leaving feel unsurmountable. There are many barriers to leaving for women in domestically abusive situations and housing is but one factor — but it is a significant factor. Failing to understand, address and support the significance housing plays in relation to domestic abuse fails women and children and contributes to their vulnerability and safety.

The experiences of women detailed in this chapter point to the trauma encountered when presenting as homeless due to domestic abuse and the uncertainty of what to expect. Furthermore, the women's experiences in this chapter highlight the re traumatising impact on women when the 'system' fails them. The system must do all it can to reduce this barrier by recognising domestic abuse as a valid reason for housing/re-housing, and by making the process in this situation as painless as possible. Not least by ensuring all staff are given trauma-informed training in this area.

The Domestic Abuse Act 2021 and the updated Code of Guidance on Homelessness for Local Authorities now sets out clear expectations in terms of responding to homelessness because of domestic abuse, legislative remedies and guidance is a positive step. Positive and meaningful change can only occur if there is real commitment to really understanding women's lived experience. Policy and legislative change are welcome but it is the implementation of such changes that impacts women seeking housing support when attempting to escape domestic abuse. This must happen alongside a determination to avoid the re-traumatising of domestic abuse victims/survivors in their attempts to access support and accommodation.

CHAPTER 9

'There's Nothing Left, Nothing Left of You'
Criminalised Women and Trauma

Dr Nicola Harding

When a woman enters the Criminal Justice System (CJS), it is often the most recent catastrophic event in a life that has been punctuated by trauma. This chapter considers the social manifestation of trauma within a study co-produced with criminalised women as they navigate community punishment. Working together to tell their story, criminalised women produced visual research data, offered oral testimony, and allowed me to observe the social interactions between them and criminal justice practitioners that took place within the research environment. The chapter examines the presence of trauma within the individual and collective narratives offered by the women within this study, both before, during, and beyond criminalisation. Also how social responses to trauma are enacted by the women within the research space itself as they bore witness to each other's trauma narratives. The study found that criminalised women manage their trauma through the use of humour and telling their narratives through imagined others or focused on imagined elsewhere. However, these mechanisms for managing trauma are often misunderstood by criminal justice practitioners as being disingenuous, detached or failing to engage seriously in their punishment. This chapter invites those who work with women in criminal justice to understand a little more, enabling the creation of trauma-informed spaces that condemn a little less.

Introduction

'Psychological trauma is an affliction of the powerless. At the moment of trauma, the victim is rendered helpless by overwhelming force. When the force is that of nature, we speak of disasters. When the force is that of other human beings, we speak of atrocities' (Herman, 1992: 33).

When the force is that of punishment, we speak of justice. Whether receiving a prison or a community sentence, the process of arrest, attending court, and being sentenced to punishment is traumatic. This is because 'traumatic events overwhelm the ordinary systems of care that give people a sense of control, connection, and meaning' (ibid). The process of criminalisation—arrest, investigation, court appearance, labelling, sentencing, and punishment—dislocates individuals from wider society, removing any control they may have had in determining their own short-term and long-term futures, and strips an individual of their humanity. As such, the process of criminalising an individual should be understood as a trauma-producing process.

As already indicated the chapter considers the social manifestation of trauma within a group of criminalised women. Considering the oral testimony, they offered, visual and creative data produced during a participatory action research cycle, and observations of the social interactions that took place within the research environment, it examines the presence of trauma within the individual and collective narratives put forward. It also looks at how social responses to trauma are enacted by the women within the research space itself. Diverging from the notion of a practitioner as a 'witness', the chapter considers how co-produced and reciprocal trauma recovery can be exercised by women subject to punishment together, 'bearing witness' as a form of peer recovery from traumatic events, including criminalisation itself.

Co-produced Research with Criminalised Women

Working with 28 criminalised women, and four female criminal justice practitioners in the north-west of England, this study examined the lived experiences of women subject to community punishment. The study took a feminist, co-produced approach, utilising creative methods with the principles of a Participatory Action Research (PAR) framework (Harding, 2020b). At every stage there were criminalised women involved in the research process, including design, data collection, analysis and dissemination. This led to the production of 25 narrative maps, 18 letters titled 'Dear future me …', and 220 photographs that were then coded and organized into thematic groupings. One of the most prominent themes identified was the trauma associated with criminalisation which, for most of the women, formed part of a continuum of violence experienced across their life course.

Criminalisation as a Trauma Producing Process

While the process of criminalisation (in the UK at least) cannot be perceived as life-threatening, on a philosophical and psychological level, the criminalisation of women threatens every part of the life they are accustomed to through the loss of jobs, relationships, children, and sometimes liberty. As such, the process of events that create a criminalised woman fits Brison's (1999: 40) definition of a traumatic event being 'one in which a person feels utterly helpless in the face of a force that is perceived life-threatening'. On a more practical level, the extremely high prevalence of self-harm amongst female prisoners (Hawton et al, 2014), and the risks posed to women held in immigration detention centres, where they have often fled due to sexual violence on return to their home countries (Malloch and Stanley, 2005), build a case for the acceptance of criminalisation as a life-threatening process with very real psychological, physical, and social consequences.

> 'The immediate psychological responses to such trauma include terror, loss of control, and intense fear of annihilation. Long-term effects include the physiological responses of hypervigilance, heightened startle response, sleep disorders, and the more psychological, yet still involuntary, responses of depression, inability to concentrate, lack of interest in activities that used to give life meaning, and a sense of foreshortened future.' (Brison, 1999: 40)

All of the women in this study demonstrated many of the long-term effects of trauma, describing various diagnoses of post-traumatic stress disorder (PTSD), problems with sleeping, and the inability to concentrate. Small talk as the research room was being set up at the women's centre focused on the women's shared experience of being unable to sleep properly, being diagnosed with depression, and feelings of 'impending doom'. My research notes describe some of these conversations:

'Everyone is very aware of their mental health. Two women have just been comparing their prescriptions from their doctors for anxiety medications and beta-blockers to stop their heart racing. Another said she can't sleep on her own now and has her youngest daughter sleep in her bed. She says to other people it's because her daughter won't sleep without her, but her daughter is fine, "It's me" she said.'

Jessica, one of the peer mentors, discussed how she was struggling with certain aspects of her life that left her unable to concentrate:

'I can't concentrate on anything…I do apologise if I do look like I am staring at you blankly [but] I am listening…I struggle concentrating these days.'

Despite outwardly appearing to be doing very well — holding down a full-time job, volunteering as a peer mentor, and pursuing further education opportunities, Jessica struggled to concentrate during research sessions. As evidenced in the above quote, she would often acknowledge this and apologise. This would lead to a discussion of something that had triggered her to think about a traumatic event in her life. In this instance, it was a letter she had received that had summoned her to the welfare benefits office. At a later research day, she disclosed that it was not anything to worry about, just an administrative error as they had not realised that she was now in full-time employment. However, as Jessica's offence was related to the welfare benefits system, this letter was enough to trigger a traumatic response.

PTSD was originally described under the American Psychiatric Association (APA) diagnostic manual as 'outside the range of usual human experience' (APA, 1980: 236). However, as Herman (1992: 33) argues, and has since become readily accepted, traumatic events are not 'outside the range of human experience', particularly for women whose lives are often punctuated by different forms of abuse that constitute traumatic experiences.

Sarah, another of the peer mentors, described the role that her diagnosis of PTSD had played in her personal relationships and subsequent criminalisation:

'I ended up with a condition called post-traumatic stress disorder that made me…for a time, a much weaker person and put me in a position where I allowed the partner who I had when all of this happened, to be a bit more dominant over me.'

Sarah felt that her previous traumatic domestic violence relationships had played a role in how submissive she became with her partner. In later narratives, she described a period of sustained manipulation, verbal and emotional abuse and coercive control. It is within this context that the lawbreaking occurred that ultimately led to her criminalisation. By the time Sarah became criminalised, trauma had already punctuated her day-to-day life.

A distinct element of all punishment is the transition from arrest, to court (either magistrates' court or Crown Court), and then on to either prison, community punishment, and/or probation supervision. The women in this study detailed, with great pain, the experience of this transition from individual to part of a system that holds their immediate and long-term futures within its power. Trauma within the CJS has often been imagined as a side effect of imprisonment, with studies highlighting links between imprisonment and the production of trauma (Gelsthorpe, 2009; Segrave and Carlton, 2010). However, the women in this research that had spent time in prison identified the court process as feeling perhaps initially more traumatic than the daily reality of prison life.

Peer mentor Jessica described how she was told she would probably go to prison, and how it was the experience of the court process that impacted her life dramatically, and in different ways to receiving punishment:

'At the magistrates [court]…he [solicitor] said "You need to be looking at it today that you could be getting down for 12 months"…I remember walking out…for a cig, and like just that hurt, you know when it goes down your body into your legs, and you're thinking I'm not coming out for 12 months.'

Like Jessica, most of the women agreed that the process before punishment was an experience that they will never forget and are reluctant to relive, describing the process of sentencing as a particularly key traumatic point. Janine (unpaid work) recalled how difficult she found the process of attending court:

'You are in the dark. You don't know what's going to happen. Your solicitor gives you the worst scenario possible, and…that's the hard bit, because—and this sounds terrible—but when it doesn't happen, you are sort of left again, wondering well what do I do now? Because you have psyched yourself up to the worst possible scenario that's going to happen, you have built yourself up to it [and when] it doesn't happen…you have got to deal with that then.'

Janine was ultimately sentenced to unpaid work and community supervision. However, she had been told at the last moment that she may go to prison. What she describes is the CJS holding absolute, crushing power over her life during that time. She could not plan as she had no way of knowing what the future would hold. Shannon (unpaid work) echoed Janine's experiences:

'Numb, extremely numb. And again, scared about what's going to happen here. Because it's not explained to you…You are just told to turn up at such and such a time.'

The period before punishment was identified by all groups during analysis as a key period that impacted them negatively. The women grouped the images by producing photographs of places that were significant to them and where they felt they had had no power during arrest and sentencing (they included courts/probation or the justice centre and police stations). During analysis, the women identified these as places where they felt they had no power over their own lives or futures. In line with Brison's (1999) definition of trauma as overwhelming 'the ordinary systems of care that give people a sense of control', these are some of the institutional spaces where the women pinpoint a traumatising loss of control occurring during their experiences of criminalisation.

The images the women produced showed the court, where cases were examined and women sentenced to punishment; the police station, where women were brought after initial arrest and sometimes made to check in while on bail; and the 'justice' centre, where pre-sentence reports (PSRs) were made about them — but not by or with them (see again Harding 2020b). These were all spaces that the women felt deep emotional pain in physically revisiting. The difficulty in revisiting such spaces was reflected in the composition of the individual images. All images were taken from outside — the women took the photographs from across the road, outside the gates, and often with a barrier between them and the space.

When discussing the period between arrest and sentencing during analysis, the women repeatedly cited the court process as being the 'worst time' in their lives; often due to uncertainty over their future and becoming 'branded' criminal or a bad person. The trauma of this process, from initial criminalisation to the commencing of punishment, was deepened by the length of time that it took for 'justice' to be served. For Janine (unpaid work), the journey to court had taken a long time, with her spending 17 months on police bail. Here she describes the ebb and flow of emotions she felt in the build-up to court sessions:

'This should have all been sorted ten months ago, but because of the system, it just got dragged on and on and on. And nobody else seemed bothered. Let's just delay it five weeks. That is basically how I lived my life for 12 months was just five-week blocks…So, you have the build-up to knowing you're going to court, you went to court for the day, it gets kicked out and postponed again for another five weeks, so you have that big comedown.'

The women described these events as 'elongated' and 'drawn-out' processes that kept them in the dark. They felt that they may have been the subject of the proceedings, but that they were not part of the procedure — they held no power within this process. This meant that they had to put their trust in a process of 'justice' and rely on solicitors or barristers for information about their own futures. All the women described their lack of knowledge during this process through feelings of helplessness, leading to the production of trauma. This trauma was only made worse by the handling of knowledge by the women's legal teams, with very little knowledge given until the last minute, and then possibilities for punishment offered that played on the women's worst fears, often minutes before a hearing. For all the women, the court process was a period of suspension from 'normal life', whilst still going about their day-to-day activities, relationships, and responsibilities (all the women in this study were granted bail and remained within the community for the duration of the trial). However, 'normal' was suspended for all as they were no longer considered by themselves or others the same person. It is through this criminal justice process that the women were forced to face and accept the labels applied to them.

Labelling and Trauma

For the women in this study, up until this point, any deviance from societal norms had been temporary; for most of the women (25 out of 28) this was their first time through the CJS, and for those that did have previous convictions these were generally very minor which did not trigger full engagement with the CJS, or they had been dealt with in different jurisdictions many years before. It is the reaction of others to the initial deviance through processes of labelling that deviant identities become acknowledged (Chadwick and Little, 1987; Lemert, 1951; Muncie, 2008). It was in facing this societal reaction and coming to terms with the labelling that now applied to them that the women began to feel the pain of becoming labelled deviant:

> 'It's the feeling numb, and the guilt and the shame you have when coming out. Then it hit the papers, so you have to deal with people. I've never had anyone say anything to me. But you look at them and think, what are you thinking? What are you saying about me? They are probably not saying anything, but you have still got that in your head. What are you talking about? And that's the hardest thing to get past.' (Janine, unpaid work)

This labelling of women during the criminal justice process is a key part of criminalisation. However, becoming labelled is a social process that is about more than identifying lawbreakers. Labelling attaches moral judgement and stigma to the individual that goes beyond the lawbreaking act. As such acts that are not lawbreaking in one context become criminalised through the stigma and moral judgements attached to them in another. Chadwick and Little (1987) explain:

'Law-breaking refers to a violation of established legislation, for example exceeding the speed limit. Criminalisation refers to the behaviour seen to be deviant, but not necessarily lawbreaking, which then becomes criminalised.' (ibid: 255)

The most obvious form of labelling was the use of high visibility vests to identify the women who were completing community payback (unpaid work). It is legislated that all community payback should have a shaming element, as such vests identifying the individuals as 'offenders' have to be worn. When discussing having to wear the jackets Betty (unpaid work) said:

'That's what the courts say we have to wear…When we were out in the front, brushing up leaves and weeding, and other people can see, that is horrible…it's demeaning. I didn't like that.'

Betty asked me if I had heard the story about another woman being spat at outside the school gates in front of her children. When I asked Betty if she had experienced anything like this herself, she replied:

'I remember once, me and few others were around the side and a woman said to her daughter "Don't be looking there, that's where all the naughty women are"…One of the women really kicked off. They [the women completing unpaid work] had a right go at her.'

Betty was very keen to add:

'It wasn't that any of us didn't want to do the work. We were quite happy to. It was what was written on the back. People treated us differently. If you had a high visibility coat on without "Community Payback" nobody abused you.'

The women in this study considered themselves 'normal' women, who, on criminalisation had become outcasts, 'bad girls', and abnormal. This abnormality was shameful for them. Becoming labelled as such meant that they were being held up as examples of what a woman should not be and how a woman should not behave. It is the labels and stigma attached through criminalisation, and the practical ways in which these labels affect daily life, that produces trauma. Criminalisation is not merely a recognition of lawbreaking, but a collection of formal and informal communicative processes that seek to label and punish an individual.

Some of the women discussed how they dealt with the formal application of labelling by hiding the process as much as possible from their families.

> Claire: 'Mine don't know.'
> Abbey: 'No, mine don't know, my mum and dad don't know that I come here.'
> Nat (practitioner): 'But that's your choice.'
> Janine: 'It's not that I didn't want to tell my family. I just didn't want them to go through the hurt of what was happening.'
> Abbey: 'To protect our families, we didn't have a choice.'

Claire and Abbey managed to minimise the application of the deviant label applied to them through the court process by hiding their convictions from those close to them. They rationalised this by protecting their families from the harm of going through the process with them. More specifically, they felt they were protecting their families from negative labelling, and the shame and stigma that comes from having a daughter, sister, or mother who is considered criminal (Arditti, J, 2005).

> 'I have never felt so worthless in all my life, it was just hideous, and because my daughter was there as well. She was crying, I was crying, I was just so embarrassed for her sake more than mine because I thought … she is going to have this on her shoulders as well.' (Helen, unpaid work)

Helen explained how the weight of her conviction was not just her burden to carry, but one that was also felt by her daughter. Importantly, it was not the lawbreaking behaviour per se that was the burden, but the embarrassment and stigma of having a mother who is labelled criminal. Claire and Abbey were also not trying to protect their families from their lawbreaking behaviour, but from the negative labelling that comes with criminalisation. However, it is also possible they were doing this to protect themselves from further judgement and the stigmatising effects of labelling from their families and friends. This was a particular motivation for Sophie (unpaid work):

'I never told my nan I was here because she was quite old and judgemental, and very proper, and then she found out on my birthday.'

When she found out, Sophie's Nan did show her disapproval and reinforced some of the negative labels associated with criminalisation. This was unsurprising to Sophie and the other women, as they all agreed that the judgement from family was worse than that from strangers. The family, particularly older women within it, are agents of informal social control over younger girls and women (Schur, 1984; Heidensohn, 1985). It is older women who pass on the 'right' way to behave as a woman. The women's behaviour is a reflection on the older woman that she has not done her job of nurturing a respectable daughter or granddaughter properly.

Just like Sophie, many of the women were unable to hide their new 'deviant' label from their family, friends, and the wider community. Janine's trial was widely reported in the local press.

'I always knew it would go to the newspaper, but I thought it would go to the newspaper at the end [of the trial]…[Instead] it went [to the newspaper] halfway through the trial…and I had to carry on going to the court and through the system. And then at the end [of the trial], it went into the newspaper again, so I had that double whammy. Whereas if it had just gone in the paper at the end, I had prepared letters to my family, it was all written down, it was all explained to them how I wanted them to know about it, and not how some other person had written it in the newspaper. That wasn't my side [of things], and that was wrong.'

The open access of the courtroom through the public gallery meant that some of the bigger cases, particularly those that ended up in the Crown Court, were reported in local and national newspapers. The women indicated that this reporting was then posted and discussed in online spaces, such as social media sites, opening up new avenues for labelling of the women. Worried that there may have been stories published about her sentence, or rumours circulating about it, Amy (unpaid work) admitted to seeking out any formal labelling applied to her because of her conviction: 'I Googled my name, just to see if there was anything.'

Janine felt deeply troubled by how her case had been reported whilst the case was ongoing. Although she had been warned and expected the case to be publicly reported, she thought this would only be on sentencing. When the case was reported at an earlier stage in the process, Janine was unprepared and had not discussed what was happening with her family or friends before they read it in the newspaper or on Facebook. Janine found this a particularly hard time to recount; her recollection was punctuated by sobs, and tears fell from this otherwise stoic woman:

'It was put on Facebook when it initially came out in the paper. [The comments under the article said] she doesn't go by the name Susan; she goes by the name of Janine. So, it is out there.'

She demonstrated the impact labelling had had on her everyday life through disclosing that she has not been to the doctor's surgery in over two years. Her fear was attending somewhere where her name would be called, and her anonymity compromised, meaning that those who had read about her in the paper would remember her and she would be recognised as an 'offender'.

Therefore, she did not attend the doctors to receive medical help, the Job Centre to claim welfare benefits or places that were unknown to her as 'safe' spaces. As such, she was becoming increasingly reliant — practically and financially — on her husband. Her world had become her home and the weekly visits to the women's centre. Whilst discussing the impact of labelling on her behaviour, two more women identified that they also no longer go to the doctor's surgery for the same reason, including Helen (unpaid work) who added:

'Something as simple as going the doctors, you don't think when you are sitting there. I had forgotten, and I went to the doctors and they announce your name over the tannoy don't they? When you are to go in? Luckily for me there was only one person in there when I got up to walk out [but] I thought she's talking about me, she recognised the name.'

To which Sophie (unpaid work) replied: 'That has stopped me going the doctors that has.'

Nat, the practitioner, (inadvertently) validated these fears as a rational response to the way people respond to disclosures of ongoing cases and sentencing of women by local news sites on social media. She offered an anecdote about another woman who had identified herself as suicidal after reading the comments made about her conviction on social media.

> 'It was literally the things that had been put on, she was like "Nat just read it." I said do you know what love, I don't want to read it, and I was like "Do you know what? just delete it, block it, don't have it, don't have your Instagram, don't have your Snapchat".'

Nat then explained that this young woman did get signposted to, and did get help from, a mental health centre. However, she reflected on how the woman was not just commented on, but rather the comments had turned into harassment, stating that 'they absolutely tortured her'. Nat explained that this was a regular occurrence in the women's centre.

> 'The amount of women that I have to sit with who have been absolutely hung, strung, by social media sites—not by a judge who has sat there [but by] someone who is sat in their own house on that big pedestal, torturing someone.'

Being labelled criminal became a great source of internal stigma and shame that had an isolating effect (Rasmusen, 1996). The experience of criminalisation, through the application of the deviant label, extended beyond the administrative experience of attending court and receiving punishment. The implications of being labelled criminal offered immediate symbolic personal consequences and impacted on the women's abilities to complete 'normal' everyday tasks and maintain 'normal' relationships.

The labelling of the women in this study did not always negatively impact their relationships with family and/or friends. For example, a few of the women's immediate family rallied around to support them as, through the process of criminalisation, truths about their lives that they had concealed from family and friends were revealed. For all the women in this study, one such 'truth' was relationships that were steeped in domestic violence—through control, manipulation, physical and/or sexual violence—and for some histories of similar abuse beginning in childhood and extending throughout their lives. Those that supported the women during these periods of intense vulnerability overlooked the deviant labels applied to them as criminalised women and rather attended to them as victims. Whilst the process of criminalisation was universally experienced as a traumatic period in the lives of the women in this study, it was not the first traumatic event many of the women had experienced. Instead, it was a more formal and public version of trauma that had punctuated their lives. Trauma was a common feature of the women's daily activities, and for many, it contributed to the behaviour that led to them being criminalised.

Managing Trauma

As the women in this study testified, trauma from grief, abuse, and loss had punctuated their lives, with criminalisation often becoming the latest in a litany of traumatic events. To negotiate the effects of trauma, the women developed ways of removing themselves psychologically from the traumatic events/circumstances. The two mechanisms for psychological removal observed in this study were *humour* and *imagining an 'other' or elsewhere*.

Humour

> 'Perhaps I know best why it is man alone who laughs; he alone suffers so deeply that he had to invent laughter.' (Nietzsche, 1968: 52)

As she recounted the build-up to the day of her sentencing, a time that she described as 'traumatic', Jessica found the conversation diverted by a photograph that someone has taken of a miniature mobile phone next to a lighter to show size and scale. She then described an interaction with a neighbour on her estate the day before sentencing where she was offered an illegal miniature mobile phone:

Jessica: 'Someone offered me one the day before I got sent down.'
Frances: 'Did she?'
Jessica: 'Mmm [laughs], it's bad enough where I was going, he asked me if I wanted one to take in. I said, "Are you real?" That's what it's like living on my estate.' [All laugh]

Just before this exchange, Jessica had been wiping away tears from her blood-shot eyes after describing the terror she felt in being sentenced to imprisonment. However, within minutes she and the other women in the group were laughing. This laughter was the first, but certainly not the last, episode of 'inappropriate' or unexpected laughter experienced within this research. Despite group discussions covering traumatic events, including abuse, childhood trauma, and the lived experience of criminal justice processes and punishment, there were frequent bursts of laughter.

Practitioners often peered through adjoining windows with puzzled expressions as laughter punctuated the otherwise sombre and tear-filled sessions. To an outsider, this laughter may have seemed crass, proof enough to question the authenticity of the women's descriptions of this as a time of trauma; surely laughter means that the tears she is still wiping away are just 'crocodile tears', an act for the others in the room. Jacqueline A Bussie (2015) discusses laughter as 'ethical and theological resistance' in the face of oppression and dehumanisation. Drawing on excerpts from Nobel Peace Prize winner Leymah Gbowee's memoir, *Mighty Be Our Powers* (2011), Bussie (ibid) highlights how when laughter is used as a coping mechanism in response to a traumatic event, others label it, and those who are laughing, 'sick' or immoral.

'We all howled and choked. A Swedish boy who was working with the Manchester researchers looked at us in horror. "You people are sick!" he shouted and ran off. We almost killed ourselves laughing. You laugh instead of cry. You laugh because you survived and, in an hour, something else might threaten your life. What else can you do?' (Gbowee and Mithers, 2011, p. 213).

The narrative of 'If we don't laugh we will cry' was a common thread throughout the research, as women realised they were breaking the roles expected of them, where this laughing could be perceived as mocking the justice system, their punishment, and/or their victims. Bussie (2015) asks:

> 'Why are Gbowee and the oppressed men and women of Liberia laughing at their own oppression and suffering? Why does such laughter make many of us uncomfortable, like the Swedish boy in Gbowee's story?' (p. 171)

Pondering further why those suffering oppressions, and laughing about it, have been largely ignored by theologians, Bussie (ibid) argues that the lack of understanding of laughing during tragedy speaks to our inability to really listen and hear the most vulnerable. She theorises laughter as ethical and theological resistance to oppressive structures that produce trauma.

Herman (1992) suggests that 'the core experiences of psychological trauma are disempowerment and disconnection from others' (p. 133). Therefore, it is understandable how the collective activity of laughing during times of acute hardship, oppression, and psychological pain, may provide a way of resisting the trauma imposed by oppressive structures. Laughter can empower the survivor of trauma to recount the experience, re-narrating it in a way that makes sense of the trauma experienced (Herman, 1992). Laughter can also help forge new human connections.

The women in this study were not known to each other before punishment. The peer mentors were matched with people new to the process precisely to offer advice, guidance, and reassurance for women who, through criminalisation, had been disconnected from their usual wider social networks. However, despite not being known to each other, the women came together to support each other through the retelling of their stories.

During one of the map-drawing sessions, it was a summer day and so the windows were wide open. As the women and I drew maps and discussed what we were drawing, talking about the stories of our lives, music from a busker on the street below wafted through the window. As Christie talked us through the abusive relationships she had encountered throughout her life, from childhood to present, all the women had tears in their eyes. Christie sniffed and wiped a tear away from her cheek and said, 'Did you bloody pay him or what?', referring to the busker singing sad love songs over a makeshift loudspeaker. On saying this, the room erupted in laughter. Tears flowed but the laughter continued, with some of the women also breaking into song. The lyrics to the song then became ways to talk about the horrific abuse endured, with the narratives punctuated by laughter and tears. Laughter, however, was not only stimulated by situational factors, such as the music from the busker or conversations outside of the scope of the research, but by the products of the research itself.

While reflecting on the images produced during the data collection, Helen discussed the travelling she had done in her life, how she had worked in America for years before her offence, and how an abusive husband meant she had to leave and return home to the UK. Another abusive relationship led to the event of breaking the law. This was quite an emotional story for her to tell, as she felt that 'her wings [had] been clipped' by abusive men, and now by the punishment she was subject to. She then identified an important image to her, her car:

'That one's my car, and it's depressing because I can't use it anymore. And I have to walk past it every day to go and get the bus [laughs]...Well, it's going to have to be sold because by the time I get my licence back the insurance will go sky high, and financially I just can't.' (Helen, unpaid work)

The image was as symbolic as it is practical for Helen. By losing her driving licence and her car, she also lost independence, thereby making her more dependent on her friends and family; something she discussed with obvious discomfort. However, Helen and the whole group then made the sale of Helen's car to each other a running joke of the session, with Helen herself offering me 'a lift home with her' on the bus as we got up to leave.

Helen: 'This is a very definite punishment for me, yeah.'
Abbey: 'Whereas for me, I'm learning to drive, so I just look at that picture and only see a positive.'
Helen: 'Do you want to buy a car?'
Abbey: [Laughing] 'Depends how much!'
Shannon: 'Will you do her a good deal?'
Rachel: 'Will you do it for her on the weekly?' [All laughing]

Whilst appearing to be a big joke, the above exchange was looked on distastefully by the unpaid work practitioner, who pulled a disapproving face and quickly sought to calm the women by uttering 'Come on now'. The 'joke', however, was a way of processing the trauma Helen had felt throughout her traumatic relationships and the 'justice' process. It was not really about the car, but about defusing the other aspects of her narrative that she found traumatic. Independence was extremely important to her. Helen described how she had prided herself on the ability to get away from abusive relationships and protect her daughter. Walking past her car that she could no longer drive each day was not traumatic because she had to ride the bus, but because it was a symbolic representation of all that she had been through; losing her independence felt like a failure.

Abbey showed similar humour in a letter she produced titled 'Dear future me'. She detailed in her life map the significance of her past abusive relationships to her current criminalisation and punishment. She showed that she had experienced physical abuse within her relationship, to which she had retaliated. Whilst she had been too scared to involve the police previously when she physically attacked her partner during an episode of sustained physical and verbal abuse, he called the police, and she was arrested as a perpetrator of domestic abuse. When asked to think about the future, Abbey wrote 'Stop attracting knobhead men' to which she and the group laughed. Laughing about her relationships was a way of diffusing the trauma of the physical and emotional abuse she had endured, which ultimately led to her criminalisation.

Among each of the groups, there was a lot of laughter around the role of relationships in the lives of the women. As most of the women disclosed past or current experiences of domestic abuse, it is unsurprising that discussing anything related to relationships resulted in the use of humour to produce laughter as a way of processing the traumatic memory of these relationships. When examining the images, the women produced for analysis, the group of women subject to unpaid work spoke about an image that appeared to be a marriage certificate.

> Nicola (researcher): 'So, it looks like someone has put this image in this pile. What is it? A marriage certificate?'
> Abbey: 'That's a job in itself isn't it?'
> Shannon: 'I would have that as a punishment.'

Helen: 'I put that one as a hobby because some people do get married a few times don't they?' [All laughing]

Laughing at a horrific event when you are an 'innocent victim' such as Gbowee (2011) described may be viewed as 'sick' and not understandable as a reaction to trauma by a bystander. However, when the person laughing is a woman subject to punishment, and the bystander is the criminal justice worker, the implications are significant. Laughing is interpreted as a sign that the punishment is not being taken seriously, or that it is having a minimal impact; increasing the risk posed by the 'offender'. Laughing is determined to contradict the behaviour expected of those who are subject to punishment. Punishment is meant to be painful, and if those subject to it are laughing then the pain of punishment must not be felt in significant enough measure.

Humour and laughter are not the only ways in which the criminalised women in this study navigated the traumatic events of their lives and criminalisation. In response to the trauma experienced during criminalisation, women used laughter as a way of reconnecting with others, and they used imaginary others and an imaginary elsewhere as a way of reconnecting with their self.

Imaginary other

Herman (1992) describes reconnecting with oneself as a key stage in recovery from traumatic events, recognising that imagination plays a key part in this process. As the traumatised individual moves away from re-living the traumatic present, unable to remember or think to the future, she begins to reconstruct a new self, both in real and imaginary terms. She can remember the best parts of herself from her life before the trauma occurring. In revisiting old desires, she constructs a fantasy of how life can be, based on her life before the traumatic event(s) and, within a therapeutic environment, can make the link between fantasy and actions towards that goal (Herman, 1992). The women in this study did this in two distinct ways. Firstly, they distanced themselves from the negative aspects of their life before criminalisation by discussing the images produced through an imagined 'other'. Secondly, they imagined futures free from a criminalised label in imaginary places away from their current lives.

During a session discussing the images they produced, the women still subject to community punishment discussed the meanings behind an image of a betting shop. The discussion that occurred was strange when contrasted to the peer mentor group's discussion. Whilst the peer mentor group all took ownership of their images, discussing each as belonging to them, the unpaid work group all discussed the images from the perspective of another, using phrases such as 'It could mean this…' or 'Maybe she took it because…'.

> Tracy: 'Gambling? They could be addicted to gambling…'
> Shannon: 'That could be how they got into trouble in the first place.'
> Helen: 'Yeah, the betting shop, spending all their money in there and then having to go out robbing.'
> Tracy: 'Or someone that they know.' [All laugh]
> Shannon: 'It's true though isn't it?' [Laughs]

One of the women (not in the previous exchange) had taken the photograph, but she did not want to explain the reason through ownership of the photograph. Instead, she distanced herself offering a possible suggestion rather than a definitive answer. All the women on unpaid work—bar one or two exceptions—discussed the images from the perspective of an imagined other. They offered explanations that were dislocated and abstract from their narrative, whilst simultaneously being informed by their day-to-day experiences. Discussing the images in this way served a significant purpose. Utilising an imaginary other rather than taking ownership of the day-to-day experiences of criminalisation dislocated the criminal label away from the criminalised women and onto the imagined other instead. By doing so, it allowed them to reimagine and reconstruct themselves without the labels attached to criminalisation.

Imagined elsewhere

Whilst the imagined other permitted a reformation of the past self, it was through picturing the future in an imagined elsewhere that this reformation of the self could become actualised. Helen, for example, was one of the few exceptions on unpaid work that felt able to take ownership of her photographs. However, the narrative she assigned to the images she produced represented an imaginary elsewhere, rather than an imagined other. Helen shared multiple images of collages and mood boards she had created and displayed in her home. The images were predominantly made up of pictures of New York City. Helen made a collage of images and displayed them in her living room, she called her collage her 'American Dream'. These were displayed in what appeared almost like a shrine, with candles and other precious objects arrayed in front of them. When holding this image, Helen discussed emigrating to America with her daughter when her punishment is over.

Moving to New York is now no longer a possibility for Helen, as the likelihood of obtaining an American visa with a criminal conviction is extremely low. Despite this, she clings to the idea of moving there to start a new life with her daughter. This imagined future elsewhere is an extremely important part of Helen managing her everyday life during punishment. The theme of futures in far off places was common, with imagined places by the sea or in the countryside popular. These imagined spaces were often drawn from early childhood memories, with visits to the seaside or country holding happy memories that are dislocated from the traumatic present. Sophie wrote about being near the sea within her letters to her future self. When discussed, all the women agreed that their overall aim would be to get away from the current urban environment to somewhere that was more natural, laidback, and accepting.

Conclusion

Gender-based oppression within a patriarchal society means that trauma punctuates the everyday lives of women. For women subject to community punishment and probation supervision the process of becoming criminalised — arrest, processing through the court system, receiving a sentence, being named in newspapers, and attending the women's centre for punishment — combine to produce yet another separate traumatic event within their already traumatic lives.

The research outlined in this chapter shows that during the process of punishment and supervision within the community, women are expected to visibly manage their trauma. The management of trauma, concerning criminal justice processes, is the measurable engagement with treatment programmes that address various factors responsible for the production of trauma; such as domestic violence awareness courses. However, criminal justice practitioners are continually recording and assessing behaviours to manage risk.

The management of trauma during community punishment and supervision manifests in the use of humour, and the use of the imaginary other/imagined elsewhere. The use of the imaginary other and imagined elsewhere are key in the process of managing trauma. The imaginary other serves as a way of discussing the painful realities of life without imposing these negative images and narratives on themselves. This is eventually phased out as punishment ends, with those no longer subject to the traumatic effects of initial criminalisation able to take ownership of their experiences, separating the traumatic experience from the self.

The imagined elsewhere serves as a mechanism to survive the trauma of criminalisation, by imagining space and time where the oppression of punishment and negative labelling implicit with criminalisation is no longer applied to them. During community punishment, the experiences of punishment and criminalisation are so entwined with their day-to-day lives that the only way for the women to think about it ending is through imagining a complete change to their day-to-day lives. The trauma is entwined with the experience of criminalisation, yet the ability to manage trauma is a key aspect of enduring punishment within the community.

CHAPTER 10

'It's Not a Joke — It's My Life'

Lucy Baldwin, Abigay Green and Melanie Brown[28]

'We delight in the beauty of the butterfly, but rarely admit the changes it has gone through to achieve its beauty': Maya Angelou

This co-produced chapter, written with two women with lived experience of the Criminal Justice System (CJS), highlights the direct relationship between trauma and criminalisation. It represents a collaborative partnership in which criminalised women have a voice, and highlights how and why this is of importance in ethical research with women. It goes on to argue for the 'factoring in' of maternal trauma in work with criminalised women in order to achieve a truly trauma-informed and gendered response. Abigay's and Melanie's histories and experiences are shared by many women in the CJS, yet so few women have a voice in academic spaces (Bozkurt and Aresti, 2018; Baldwin, 2021b). Thus, the chapter combines and applies an academic context and discussion with/to the lived experience narratives of Abigay and Melanie (written in their own words), to demonstrate the often direct relationship between maternal trauma, maternal identity and desistance.

Melanie Brown

Melanie is the mother of one daughter. She was sentenced to 12 months in custody for fraud for her first offence and first ever time 'in trouble'. Melanie, an ex-professional with mental health issues (bipolar disorder), had experienced domestic abuse and sexual abuse as a child. She was experiencing a

---

28. Abigay Green and Melanie Brown are pseudonyms as are their children's names (chosen by them). Participants in research they remained in contact with Lucy Baldwin and expressed a wish to co-produce this chapter. Ethical approval for the original study was granted by De Montfort University's Faculty Research Ethics Committee (FREC), including for publication.

severe depressive episode at the time of her offence. Melanie had not expected a custodial sentence, it was a complete shock to her. She went to prison not knowing who would pick up her child from school that day. Her ex-partner controlled her access to and contact with her child during her sentence. Melanie is now volunteering at a women's centre and is hoping to work there full time eventually. Melanie and her daughter are now finally very close, and she is no longer affected by her ex-partner, she is now in a loving and safe relationship.

Abigay Green

Abigay is a mother-of-four and grandmother of two. She describes having a long history of addiction, relating to alcohol and drugs. Her substance reliant issues were born out of significant trauma in her childhood. Abigay experienced and survived incest, rape, and domestic abuse. She describes her relationship with their children now as 'complicated', but is forging ahead in her close and loving relationships with her grandchildren. She is now 'clean and sober'. Abigay now supports women in the CJS and feels she is able to use her negative experiences 'for good'. She loves to paint and writes poetry.

Ethical Research with Criminalised Women

Quinlan, Baldwin and Booth (2022) highlight the all too often present power imbalance between researchers and 'participants', and argue that 'tangible steps must be taken to actively reduce any power imbalance as far as possible, and further, to apply significant means of addressing that power imbalance'. They go on to say that this can be partially achieved at least by adopting what they call an 'Ethic of Empathy' model. The model highlights the significance of compassionate, thoughtful and inclusive research methods, but also the importance of a 'rolling reflexivity' of the researcher (ibid; see also Baldwin, 2022a). Rolling reflexivity (ibid) asks that the researcher is reflexive and responsive throughout the life of the study and beyond and not simply at the end of it, or included as a couple of statements focusing on what the researcher has 'learned'. The reflective thoughts and actions must focus on the participants of the study as well as the researcher. This is especially key in the early phases when planning and applying for ethical approval, and in considering how the investigation could be potentially re-traumatising of women participants in criminological research, not least because of re-traumatisation based on powerlessness (Quinlan, Baldwin and Booth, 2022). Thus, the Ethic of Empathy model, highlights the importance of inclusivity and visibility in research with those affected by the CJS.

Booth and Harriot (2021) highlight that although women who have experienced the CJS, and are 'much sought after as research participants', there remains a dearth of co-authored or co-produced literature, which they argue is neglectful, irresponsible and lacking in integrity. Booth and Harriott are both women with lived experience of the CJS and state that they have themselves felt 'exploited' and used by researchers in the past. In their chapter 'Service Users Being Used; Thoughts to the Research Community' (in Masson, Baldwin and Booth, 2021: 199), they raise questions about the reflexivity of researchers who are not thoughtful, compassionate and inclusive in their research methods, delivery and dissemination. Booth and Harriott describe how when they were research participants they sometimes felt excluded from the broader theoretical and contextual discussions about the purpose of the research, which retrospectively they believe is required in order to give the true 'informed consent' required in ethical research. They describe how it 'mattered' to them on the occasions they were included in such discussions, describing how this then empowered them to feel part of the intended 'change' or impact of the research. This discussion provides an important backdrop to this chapter, as do the longstanding and multiple discussions between its authors.

Abigay and Melanie were participants in the lead author, LB's research. Baldwin's matricentric feminist study (2022a) advocated strongly for the women to have a presence in her research and also to ensure that 'participants' were included in the design, and dissemination of, the research, as well as in the process of policy and practice change that occurred throughout it. The Mothers[29] in that study were at the centre of the study, and Baldwin states that one of her 'great joys' of undertaking that study occurred when a friend reading the research said 'It … feels like a joint effort between you and the women and its very much about them and by them' (Charlie) (Baldwin 2022a: 314). LB remained in contact with many of the

---

29. Where the Mothers in that study are designated using an upper case M.

research participants (if they wished to), and has co-presented/co-delivered teaching, and co-authored with several participants from her research. Thus, it wasn't a stretch to ask Abigay and Melanie to contribute to this chapter with aspects of their narratives and lived experience. Abigay and Melanie were supported by the lead author of this chapter and each other through this writing project.

Melanie

I was glad to be asked to write this—and as an ex-professional woman, now limited in my employment opportunities, it was a good excuse to be able to use my brain again. Given the themes of the book I thought I'd include some references to trauma and how that interacted with my life and my journey to prison. I am going to reflect backwards because I'm some years out now—but the trauma and the triggers never leave me. Triggers can come from silly things—like at New Year's Eve we didn't have party poppers because I worried they are classed as explosives and come under firearms. Little things like that remind you that you are a convicted criminal all the time. I think the same if I get a parking ticket or a speeding fine—will I get recalled?

My road to prison was a long one really but it started … the original sin if you like, with abuse, it was traumatic and it has stayed. I was abused in my family as a little girl. No-one believed me or if they did they decided to ignore it, and I genuinely believe that sealed my fate. Repressing the memories, dealing with my family who seemed blind to my pain meant my mental health slowly but surely disintegrated and I ended up using alcohol to numb the pain and block out my feelings.

At first this was manageable, well I thought it was, but then people at work noticed I was drinking a lot. Someone reported me for smelling of alcohol in the mornings. I was given a warning and watched. No-one asked if I was OK, no-one asked why I was drinking. I could feel my anxiety rising and my mental health getting worse, but I couldn't seem to do anything to stop it. I didn't feel like I could ask for help. I had a daughter. I was a mum—if I told people I was struggling and drinking I was afraid my ex, who was fighting me for custody, would take my daughter. So, I kept it to myself. My daughter knew, of course she did—which just made the guilt worse.

I tried to take my life. Even after I was admitted to a psychiatric unit after a suicide attempt my family would just shout at me and tell me to get a grip. It's no surprise I ended up in a coercive and controlling relationship was it with them for family? I was away in a psych ward, but I felt safe. Even though my daughter was desperate to see me I dreaded coming home. I feel so much guilt remembering that. I had convinced myself she was better off without me. I can't imagine what a mum trying to kill herself does to a child — how unimportant I must have made her feel. The guilt was awful, but I couldn't talk about it to anyone. I was diagnosed with bipolar — which explained a lot. But things don't just get magically better overnight because you know what's wrong with you.

Then I was convicted of drink driving with her in the car. Because I was arrested, they had to contact my ex to take my daughter. I'd given him a gift. He immediately applied for a residence order and got it. I was distraught and desperate. Once I lost my daughter I lost hope. I couldn't see the point in anything. My alcohol use spiralled. I lost my job. I was drinking everyday and sometimes I couldn't remember where I was or how I got there. Then I was raped on my way home drunk, by a taxi driver — I never reported it. Why would I? For everyone to tell me it was my fault and to be fair in a way it was. I know that's all trauma I know it is logically. Then I was arrested for being drunk and disorderly, shoplifting alcohol, resisting arrest and assaulting a PC. I can't even remember any of it I was so drunk at the time.

I did not expect a custodial sentence, apart from my driving offence it was my first time in trouble — I wasn't a risk to anyone, my solicitor didn't think I'd get a custodial sentence either. I hadn't told my ex I was in court, and my court date was on the first time my ex had let me see my daughter. She had stayed overnight, and I took her to school telling her I'd pick her up later. But I didn't pick her up. I was sent to prison.

> One of the prison officers who had, I dunno, noticed my nice clothes and nice accent and previous professional status asked 'How does a nice girl like you get to somewhere like this?' When I was telling the prison officer about my 'catalogue of errors' before I came to prison and how it had happened, he laughed, he actually laughed and said 'Oh wow that's quite a fall from grace' or something like that. I was so upset I said to him why the hell are you laughing, 'It's not a joke ... It's my life'!!
>
> Being apart from my daughter was so traumatic. My ex was furious, he said I was a disgrace, and he wouldn't let me speak to my daughter for six weeks, and only then as long as I told her I was a bad person, and I was ashamed, and I was a terrible mother. He said if I didn't say all of that he would just never let me speak to her again or give her back ever or let me have contact when I got out. It was the worst time of my life. I tried again to take my life in prison. I just couldn't see the point in living. Without my daughter life felt pointless and hopeless. I couldn't see how I'd ever get the strength to get and stay sober or get some kind of responsible or respectable life back. I was broken.

Missed and Lost Opportunities

Melanie's story highlights how, long before most mothers enter prison, there have often been multiple missed opportunities to support mothers differently. This is not uncommon. In many instances, had the mothers been appropriately supported much earlier, they might never have gone to prison at all. These missed and lost opportunities were often about responses to trauma (sometimes as far back as childhood), mental health, abuse, and addictions, but significantly also around motherhood (Baldwin, 2022a). Mothers in my (LB's) research often spoke of how their maternal experiences were intertwined with their offending and criminalisation, particularly those mothers who were using substances. Many of the mothers in the study were living in what I have termed a 'Circle of Circumstance' (see Figure 1) which included poverty, surviving trauma, mental ill-health, ongoing/past abuse, and damaging relationships. For several of the mothers in my study, becoming/being a mother was a positive for them, sometimes the only positive in their lives. However, mothering in the context of addiction, of past or ongoing abuse, and/or in poverty is challenging, and—as described by many of the mothers — stressful and guilt-inducing. Mothers in these circumstances are no less than the rest of us, subject to the influence of the widely held beliefs and expectations about motherhood. Beliefs about how a mother should, or importantly should not, behave. For criminalised mothers particularly, this perceived 'failure' to live up to these ideals of motherhood, and the subsequent internalised shame and blame can lead to a feeling of being a 'failed' mother (Baldwin, 2015; 2022a; 2022b).

As the Circle of Circumstance model (Figure 1) illustrates, many criminalised mothers use substances as a means of coping or blocking out pain from an original trauma. As previously stated, this might be childhood or early adult abuse (or both). Substance misuse, which somewhat inevitably goes hand-in-hand with an offending lifestyle (to fund the addiction), can then become a pattern, a habit. In reality, it is often women's only perceived available means of dealing with or responding to trauma that they are forced to live with. The circle of circumstance in which many criminalised women live means that they are often in already challenging and compounding circumstances (poverty, housing and food insecurity, domestic abuse, mental health issues and discrimination). Cuts in support services, like drug and alcohol services and primary social care services mean that even if support were available to mothers, access to services is often significantly delayed.

Substance-using pregnant women and mothers are sometimes already subject to increased surveillance and may face arrest, prosecution, conviction and/or child removal (Banwell and Bammer, 2006; Stone, 2015) if they seek help and support. Something women have described as a very real fear and a reason for not 'asking for help' (Baldwin, 2022a; 2022b). We know that women of colour and women in lower socioeconomic brackets are particularly overrepresented in such circumstances (Thomas, 2022).

Thus, it is often at a point of crisis when mothers come into contact with the CJS. That crisis point may be an arrest/contact with criminal justice/imprisonment. This can result in child removal and/or imprisonment. Tragically any support mothers might have been receiving from social services at the point of the crisis is often withdrawn once the child is removed (Barnes in Baldwin, 2015). As Morriss observed this is sudden and impactful to both children and mothers and any priority they might have had in terms of access to services is lost: '...once care proceedings end, the mothers are effectively abandoned by the state. Children's Services do not remain involved as there is no longer a child of concern, and the Court does not monitor the provision of any of the services, be these mental health or drugs related services, recommended during the proceedings' (Morriss, 2018: 818).

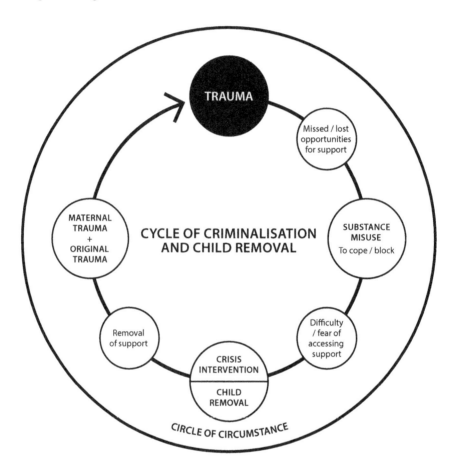

Figure 1: Circle of Criminalisation and Child
Removal. Reproduced from Baldwin, 2022b.

As illustrated in the model above, the mother is now left to deal with the trauma and loss of a child on her own. On top of the original trauma women already dealing with the new layer of maternal trauma find it is often too much for mothers to bear. Resulting in some mothers feeling they have no alternative but to revert to their previous coping strategies of blocking out or dealing with/ managing their pain by using substances. Which subsequently can drag mothers back into an offending lifestyle; not least because they are now dealing with the pain and shame of having a child removed, of feeling like a failed mother, and being without any therapeutic support (Baldwin, 2022a; Morriss, 2018).

Furthermore, mothers who have lost the care of children can often lose access to benefits or housing and thus the material as well as emotional consequences of child removal are vast. It is worth noting that it is mostly working-class mothers whose children are removed into local authority care. Morris (2018: 820) describes poverty as 'the elephant on the room' when it comes to child neglect. There is a long known association between children's chances of being subject to abuse or neglect and the socio-economic circumstances of their birth families, and yet rarely is child removal framed as a public issue and a matter of avoidable social inequality, instead it is regarded as an individual fault and responsibility (mostly of the mother), which provides a further source of shame and pressure on already disadvantaged families and mothers (see Bywaters at al, 2016: 6).

As is also demonstrated in the model, and also a recognised response to the loss of a child, especially through forced child removal (Stewart, 2015), a mother may seek to repair and heal her maternal trauma through replacement, i.e. she will become pregnant again; and so the cycle repeats. With every child removal there is an ever-more deepening reluctance on the mother's part to ask for help or engage with services because of a fear of losing her children; 'Why would I tell them I was struggling? Why … so they can take my kids again, no way' (Shanice) (Baldwin, 2022b: 18). Thus, a new 'crisis' point is reached again and the cycle and resulting trauma is repeated and layered.

The cycle illustrated above can be related to mothers at all stages of their criminal justice journey as they can be/are 'trapped' in the cycle both before and after prison. Moreover, with every child removal the risk of losing future children to the childcare system increases, not least because historical child removal is all too often used as a primary indicator of 'risk' with future pregnancies (Barnes, 2015; Morriss, 2018). Consequently, many mothers end up losing multiple children to the care system, whilst the same societal and multi-agency failures and inequalities persist. As the cycle plays out, maternal trauma adds to the original trauma and pre-existing addiction issues, and yet maternal trauma has, historically, rarely factored into the care of criminalised or imprisoned women — not even into gendered and trauma-informed responses (Baldwin, 2022a).

Most women experience pressure to adhere to commonly held beliefs and the strict rules of a 'good mother' model, precisely to avoid being seen as a 'bad mother' (Arendell, 2000), something Baldwin calls the Mothers Code of Conduct. Mothers who use substances or engage in criminal behaviour experience strong social and internal stigma, as 'good mothers are not supposed to engage in such things' (Couvrette et al, 2016: 293). As painfully described above by Melanie, mothers who lose their children to the care system can feel they 'have nothing else to lose' and as though there is 'no point' in 'even trying' to abstain from substances or desist from offending behaviour because they have already 'failed' so badly (Baldwin, 2022a; 2022b). For some mothers these feelings have the effect of setting them firmly on a path of destruction and/or incarceration/ re-incarceration. Thus, highlighting how for many women their motherhood is inextricably linked to their engagement, rehabilitation and desistance. Abigay's story as she tells it below further illustrates this phenomenon.

Abigay

If I could turn back time, I'd never pick up a fag, a spliff or a drug — they were the cause of the ruin of my life. The ruin of my motherhood and my time with my kids. I know it were my life experiences that led to me taking drugs, but you know what? I don't think they alone would have been the finish of me. I'm strong. I would have got through that stuff anyway. You can eventually heal a past to an extent, you can move on you can come to terms with it, all of those things would have been possible and would have happened, I'm sure. Maybe with support, that's essential. But it can be done. But you can't win against drugs. They take your life; they rob you of decency and emotion — they make you a horrible, horrible selfish person.

My childhood was awful I can't lie, there was so much abuse going on in my family that for a long time I thought it was normal, like everyone's life was like it. My sisters and I were all abused by my grandad and an uncle, but we all also knew our mam had been too. Violence, alcohol and seeing our mam battered was pretty normal and regular too. Our mam drank and we grew up just knowing that drinking made things better for mam. So, in some ways we were all always going to at least be drinkers. As you get older and you realise that life, the abuse and the drinking, it's not normal; but that almost messes you up more. Ignorance was bliss in a way. But honestly realising other people had lovely lives, that other people, other children, were loved, properly like, not like how I was loved, well it just made my life seem so seedy. I was ashamed of it, ashamed of me. I felt dirty.

When I started seeing boys I dunno how it happened really, but I never had one that was not violent — it's like I had a sign on my head. I don't know how they find you and how they just seem to know you'll put up with it. I went to hospital so many times — they must have thought I lived in a house that only had stairs and cupboard doors in it! It was honestly almost routine. I felt like I'd had a break if I managed not to go to hospital one weekend. But because they knew I drank I don't think they cared. But then I got pregnant and that was worse. He actually raped me when I was pregnant, Jamal's dad did, how disgusting is that? It was like I was reduced, made smaller every time he did it after that — and he did it a lot. I had my son then another one close after. I was drinking so much they had a syndrome, FASD they call it[30] I'm not sure how it affected them really though because as babies they seemed alright to me. Anyway the next few years passed in a bit of a blur really, the nursery knew I drank, school knew I drank, the social knew I drank, obviously the doctors knew I drank — but same as Mel no-one ever asked us why. If they had I might have been able to open up — but all they saw was drunk me, an alki, not a person , not someone being battered or in pain or who could do with a hand.

---

30. Foetal Alcohol Spectrum Disorder (FASD) can happen when alcohol in the mother's blood passes to her baby through the placenta. It can cause delayed development, learning disabilities, and physical challenges. It is irreversible but can be managed and supported to ensure FASD children reach their full potential.

My friend got me to go to Citizens Advice and they put me in touch with this drink and drugs support place and they tried to help me they really did, but it wasn't enough. I didn't know what I needed but I know I needed more.

Anyway by then I was stealing to fund my drink and I had started using a bit of weed at first, then speed to keep me comps mentas — it seemed to keep me sober. My fella eventually left me. Man I still feel aggrieved that it was him that left me, he was battering me and he left me telling me I was a drunk and he couldn't cope anymore. He couldn't cope!! I hadn't realised it but I suppose he had helped with the kids. So when he left they missed a lot of nursery and school and that brought the social down on me and before I knew it they was gone. They didn't offer me chance or support, just ultimatums to stop drinking — which I couldn't just do. I can't really go into that time in detail, it's too painful. But I will never forget them being taken. Screaming for me they were, they literally dragged them off me — police cars everything. The kids didn't want to go. They loved me and I loved them. I can see now years later that maybe I wasn't the best parent then and maybe they did have to go in care for a little bit — but not forever they didn't have to keep them — they could have given me a chance. If they'd have helped me I could have at least of tried to get better.

The next few years are a blur you know, I'm surprised I lived through it — I genuinely didn't care if I lived or died without the kids. I would get absolutely paralytic drunk, then get done, then get locked up, then get let out and drink again and it went on like that for literally years. I tried to have more kids, but I kept losing them — my body was wrecked from the drink I think, and I literally just couldn't stay pregnant. That made me feel even more of a failure, as a person but especially as a mum — I saw it as like God telling me I wasn't good enough to be blessed with any more kids. One of my lost babies, a girl, Kenise I called her, was quite late, she was nearly due and that one nearly killed me. I was on probation at the time, and I remember the officer getting on at me for missing appointments, telling me I was being recalled, and I'd lost my little girl — I couldn't believe it.

What did probation mean to me at that time — nothing, she didn't even say sorry for your loss when she found out either that officer you know. I got more sympathy and understanding from the girls in prison once I was back in than I got from any service worker. To be fair to her I hadn't told her myself — I couldn't talk about it and I knew she wouldn't be bothered anyway so I never told her — my mate who she was seeing as well told her. But apparently it was 'too late' and I still got recalled anyway but I was glad actually. I don't think I'd be alive if I hadn't — sad you have to go prison to save your life ain it!

For whatever reason that sentence was different — I think after Kenise died I wanted to be better. I had some hope that maybe I would have been able to get my boys back. I got out, I thought I'm gonna get them back — they were in long-term foster care by now but I was determined. I was clean I was sober for the first time in years. I had one tiny relapse when my sister died but that was enough. I failed one piss test and social services decided that was my last chance and they were going to apply for the boys to be adopted. Which they did and won. I was devastated. I had one last visit with Jamal and Jaxon but I wasn't allowed to tell them it would be the last time I would see them. Can you imagine that I had to try to stay strong and not be emotional. Afterwards I just literally broke down, on my knees, everything. You know what no-one from social services even checked I was OK, not even a are you OK do you have someone. It was cold man. I'm not proud of it but I left the contact centre and I got off my face. After months and months of being clean — but I just had no way of dealing with it — I couldn't deal with it. How can you — your children gone, gone maybe forever but definitely until they are grown men — and there is nothing, nothing you can do. I wasn't a mother anymore, what was the point in anything — that's how I felt. It was so much worse because I knew it was down to me. It was my fault. If I'd got it together sooner I might not have lost them. I hated the world, I hated the system, but most of all I hated myself. I felt lost and on my own.

The next few months were a total blur, I got pregnant — I'm ashamed to say I don't even know who by, and I didn't realise I was pregnant — I wasn't switched on enough to notice, I saw no-one about it and I honestly don't know if somewhere in me I knew and blocked it out or not — but I never felt the baby move that I remember. I didn't really show no sickness nothing — but I was being sick from the drugs anyway. Then one day I collapsed in the street in pain and someone in Marks & Spencer's called an ambulance. When I got to hospital, and they told me I was in labour I couldn't believe it. The baby came, Karis, she was beautiful, but she was really, really early and she only lived a couple of hours. I know social services would have taken her immediately anyway because at that point I was well on the drink and some drugs — but I was still devastated. I felt robbed — robbed of her robbed of even knowing I was pregnant and robbed again of being a mum. If anyone asks though I still say I'm a mum of four, 'cos I am though aint I? Two angel babies and two boys, well men now.

Again there weren't no support for me and after Karis I just went back to clocking out my pain. What else could I do!? Eventually I got into bother again but this time the judge listened, he'd read something about me that someone wrote — I don't even know who, probation I suppose, and he said I was suffering trauma and needed support. That was the first time I felt like anyone had given me a chance. He didn't send me to jail but made me go to a women's centre and honestly it was the best place on earth. It was surprising how many of us in there had similar stories, how many of us had lost kids, we all supported each other. There was a psychologist there and an art therapist and they really helped me to deal with my emotions and my trauma — from being a mum, from the past everything and I got proper help, for the first time really. Anyway, to cut a long story short that was the start of my better life, I was clean and have been ever since, not a single relapse. Someone said to me that one day my boys might find me, that one day I might be a Gramma and that some people got second chances. She must have been a psychic because that's exactly what happened.

My sons found me about six years ago now, obviously they are men now and we have missed so much, but we are getting there. They were adopted by white families, so it was important to them to know me, they wanted they said to feel 'black' to know where they came from. They both already had one child each, so I got to know them, but they have also both had another one and for those babies I've been in their lives since they were born — which I feel truly, truly blessed and grateful for. I love those babies like they are my own and I know I will never ever let my kids or my grandkids down again. I got there in the end.

When I meet women like I was, who are still in the thick of it — I show them pictures of me with my grandkids and I tell — it's never too late. I think that's a good place to stop.

Motherhood and Desistance

The creation, and importantly support, of a new pro-social identity is central to the desistance process of many ex-offenders or people who have come into contact with the CJS (Maruna et al, 2012; McNeill, 2006). While individual *choices* and *decisions* to desist have been shown to be a factor, and often an important one, there is most often more to desistance than simply willing it, not least structural inequality, disadvantage and discrimination.

Desistance is a complicated, often not linear process that is difficult to measure, as well as define. It is often thought of as the permanent cessation of 'offending behaviour', when in reality it can also be understood as a more fluid process in which episodic offending or relapse may occur. The pursuit and securing of long-term abstinence from crime is no doubt beneficial to criminalised individuals, their families, and ergo to society in general. However, arguably and especially in the case of women and mothers, there is often not enough attention paid to how best to support desistance. Thus, the reoffending rates remain high.

Every desistance journey is different, but most tend to involve both external support from others and internal change and self-discovery. Maruna et al (2016) found that to desist from crime, people need to develop 'a coherent, pro-social identity for themselves.' This mostly happens when people see themselves in control of their futures and have a clear sense of purpose and meaning in their lives. Abigay's story painfully but powerfully demonstrates how inter-connected motherhood and maternal trauma, and a positive maternal identity, can be to rehabilitation and desistance (Baldwin, 2022a; Bachman et al, 2016; Michalsen, 2020). It is easy to see how in Abigay's case her 'purpose' and 'control' (as highlighted by Maruna) are limited, challenged and impacted, specifically in relation to motherhood/maternal identity. Abigay felt she had little control over her life, especially in relation to her role as a mother, and as she herself stated, once her children were gone she felt her hope and purpose was too. Baldwin's research powerfully and convincingly demonstrates that this remains the case whether mothers' maternal role has been maintained or not, i.e. maternal identity is still a factor in mothers who have lost the care of their children (Baldwin 2017, 2018, 2020). Both Melanie's and Abigay's narratives demonstrate the often-complicated relationship motherhood and maternal emotion can have with offending/desistance. Moreover, they underscore how important it is for maternal trauma to be factored in when we are thinking about a trauma-informed approach with criminalised women. To fail to factor in motherhood and maternal trauma is to fail the women.

When women feel spoiled as mothers it can permeate their whole sense of self, as shown by Melanie and Abigay. And, consequently, this can be directly related to substance misuse and offending (Baldwin, 2022a). For some mothers once they felt they had 'failed' at motherhood they felt they 'had nothing to go straight for', revealing that the long-term impact of child removal is perhaps not always appreciated. As demonstrated earlier in Figure 1, circumstances such as those described above can result in mothers seeking to 'replace' their 'lost' child with another. However, without the support to address the mothers often complex issues (which is frequently withdrawn alongside the removal of the previous child), the cycle of removal persists.

The narratives of both Melanie and Abigay demonstrate powerfully that once they felt they had lost their roles as mothers, and their maternal identities were so badly spoiled, there was 'no point' in them seeking support or desisting from offending. Yet equally powerful are the points in both narratives where their motherhood *became* a significant factor in their motivation and determination to avoid further criminalisation.

Pause for Thought

- Looking at both Melanie's and Abigay's stories — where do you think the missed and lost opportunities were?
- What would good support have looked like and what might have been the alternative outcomes had they existed?
- What impact might that have had on the children's lives?
- And what are the long-term impacts of those missed and lost opportunities?

The lead author (LB's) research found that despite the importance mothers themselves attached to their maternal identity, 'structural barriers' and external as well as impossibly high personal standards complicate mothers' efforts to maintain or resume their maternal role. Stone (2016: 959) identifies that particularly in the case of mothers who misuse substances the 'powerful and stigmatising master narrative' of addict challenges mother's abilities to release themselves from their offending pasts and move successfully into a non-offending future. O'Malley and Devaney (2018) and Baldwin et al (2015), found that in relation to addicted mothers, the 'shame' of their perceived previously 'failed' motherhood compounded the trauma that led to the addiction in the first instance. In short, they felt 'to blame'. This contributed to mothers' ability (or inability) to abstain from drugs and/or alcohol and ergo from the offending undertaken to fund their addiction (and often the addictions of male partners).

Contemporary social work, partly fuelled by knee jerk reactions to high profile child deaths, and in line with political paradigms, places child protection, rightly so, as a priority. However, sometimes this can result in already stretched resources being focused on child removal rather than on supporting mothers and children to stay together (Barnes, 2015; Morriss, 2018). All too often sustained support for vulnerable or criminalised mothers has not been forthcoming. This is due to cuts in services and limited resources, but also because mothers were too afraid to ask for support, afraid of being judged bad mothers, seen as 'not coping', and/or ultimately, the fear of losing their children (Baldwin, 2022c). Maternal trauma has historically been ignored by the criminal justice agencies. The failures of society to meet the needs of mothers, or to address the poverty and trauma which so often taint the lives of criminalised mothers are rarely called into question in the courts or in the media, only the failures of the mother. The mother is held solely responsible, not society for its failings. Agents of criminal justice Baldwin has spoken to in the course of her research, until very recently, especially probation officers, have often said of their charges' maternal status, 'I just never thought to ask'.

Impact and Outcomes of this Underpinning Research

Understanding and recognising the significance of maternal expectation and maternal emotion, of the relationship between trauma, and mothering in, and through, adversity is key to working effectively with criminalised women, and must be done in a space of emotional and physical safety. It is only there that criminalised mothers will be able to explore openly and honestly their feelings and experiences and trauma, not 'just' as women, but as mothers. However, for criminalised mothers this is often not an option, either because of failure to recognise their needs, or as previously stated fear of unwanted intervention, or the mothers themselves not wanting to initiate conversations that for them are so painful. In 'Motherhood Disrupted', Baldwin (2018) reveals how the mothers in prison often refrain from speaking openly about their maternal emotions and their maternal role, experiences and emotions, despite them actually being a primary concern and focus. Importantly this is equally true for mothers who have lost the care of their children. The environment, regimes and structure of the prison play a role in this, as do their interactions and relationships with staff. Baldwin's research demonstrates definitively that maternal needs (concerning maternal loss, maternal emotions, maternal role and maternal identity), have been neglected in prison and that this has an enduring and profound impact on mothers and their children and grandchildren.

Similarly in probation work, mothers have historically been afraid to speak about their maternal emotions, despite them often being their primary concern — at least because of the fear of unwanted intervention (like social services), or that their worries and concerns would be dismissed as irrelevant to their probation supervision. Baldwin's (2022a), research highlights how mothers under probation supervision often felt 'surveilled rather than supported'. This means that often fundamental issues on which they needed support and emotional challenges that were (as previously described) relevant and mothers desistance/coping, were left under-investigated and most importantly under-supported.

However, for the first time in a long time, and certainly since *Mothering Justice* was published in 2015 (then, we believe, the first UK book to take motherhood and criminal justice as a sole focus), far more attention is being paid to motherhood and criminal justice. Organization like Level Up, Birth Companions, Women in Prison and Trevi House[31] enjoy an increased visibility and influence in relation to policy and practice change in this specific arena.

Baldwin has produced guidance for probation officers which is now available to all officers involved in the supervision of mothers and which can be found on the National Probation Service intranet.[32] Furthermore, specific working tools (again produced by Baldwin) to assist officers in their engagement with mothers under supervision are now present in the newly launched national toolkit for working with women. Meaning that, for the first time, motherhood and maternal needs will be factored into supervision and that opportunities for supporting criminalised mothers more effectively should be maximised.

Partnership work and discussions with Morley and Rushton (*Chapter 2*) as area women's leads are also ongoing. This work is committed to ensuring that all women who come into contact with the Probation Service have all of their needs, including maternal needs, responded to in a gendered trauma-informed way. Many probation officers, social workers and prison officers have benefitted from Baldwin's 'Mothering Justice' training—with more planned on a national scale.

Minson has produced information for mothers, sentencers and criminal justice practitioners that is widely available, this alongside revised and brand new national MOJ policy and practice guidance for pregnant and new mothers in prison.[33] Furthermore, other scholars like Booth, Masson, Epstein, O'Malley,

---

31. See https://trevi.org.uk/about-trevi/
32. An internal resource that can be accessed by NPS personnel but not the general public.
33. See https://www.sentencingcouncil.org.uk/overarching-guides/magistrates-court/item/general-guideline-overarching-principles/#Step%202%20Aggravating%20and%20mitigating%20factors The council's General Guideline: Overarching Principles has been published by the Sentencing Council following a period of consultation, to be used where 'there is no offence specific sentencing guideline, and in conjunction with offence specific sentencing guidelines'. The guideline includes an expanded explanation of the mitigating factor 'sole or primary carer for dependent relatives' which gives clarity to how sentencers should consider dependent children when sentencing mothers, fathers and sole carers. This is a significant step forward, and one that was recommended by the Joint Committee on Human Rights (JCHR) in their report of 9 September 2019: see https://shonaminson.com/2019/09/08/report-of-the-joint-committee-on-human-rights/

Powell, Pitman and Lockwood, to name but a few have all produced research and publications focused on maternal imprisonment, all of which has improved the understanding of the impact of maternal imprisonment, in some cases directly influencing policy and practice in the CJS.

Baldwin is working closely with the MOJ and other key partners like Sodexo (especially Bev Stephens — Women's Policy Lead) to produce a Motherhood Charter — which will provide a set of 'minimum standards' that prisons will have to adhere to/strive for in relation to meeting the needs of mothers in their care. The plan is to embed the standards deeply into the national infrastructure and for prisons to be accountable in relation to the care, support and wellbeing of mothers in prison.

Baldwin co-designed and piloted a Mothering programme with the Prison Advice and Care Trust (PACT) that is now licensed and accredited. PACT delivers it across the public sector female estate. In addition, Baldwin designed and delivered a similar programme, 'Mothering Justice', which has been adopted by Sodexo. This will be run in the future by Sodexo's Family Matters team, with guidance and quality assurance provided by Baldwin. These programmes provide invaluable and safe spaces for mothers to explore their maternal needs and coping, to assist them in maintaining and understanding their relationships with their children, and to prepare for release. Some of the mothers described these courses as 'lifesaving'.

Acting on recommendations from Baldwin and other scholars (like Raikes, Rees and O'Malley), a pilot to embed social workers into female prisons has begun, and plans are already underway to expand the provision. Much of the focus of this role is to support imprisoned mothers and early reviews and evaluations. Baldwin, Parent and Wray (2022) and Rees, Bezeczky and Waits (2022) provide irrefutable evidence of its success and necessity.

Thus there is a cautious optimism that a sea change, at least in part, is coming. It perhaps goes without saying that effective criminal justice is not possible without social justice, and much must be done to address the complexities, inequalities and challenges women face every day in our society. It is only in this context that women can avoid becoming criminalised and imprisoned for poverty and trauma as they are now.

It is vital to note that the very last thing we need is more women's prisons. Most women should not be in prison in the first instance (Corston, 2007).

Instead those dedicated funds should be diverted to supporting and developing community-based alternatives to custody. More than that, there must be a resourced and sustained commitment to supporting communities and services for women and mothers in our communities, not least to ensure they are safe and able to reach their full potential.

❚❚ Pause for Thought

- What are the barriers to supporting mothers and their desistance in your organization?
- What is needed to correct this?
- What can you do to challenge/support current provision?
- What one thing will you commit to doing in relation to criminalised mothers from hereon in?

CHAPTER 11

'We Are the Ones': Joining Forces and Creating New Tools for Change
Challenges for Academia, Charities and Practitioners

Kate Paradine

This chapter argues that if academics, charities and practitioners are to maximise our impact and finally create a sea change in the imprisonment of women, we need to focus on three areas for collective change:

- Strengthening the case for feminist prison abolition and building a vision for the future (whilst focusing on the 'long game' of the incremental victories that are needed);
- Speaking out for change together, amplifying our collective voices; and finally
- Sharing power and creating new collaborative tools for change.

Since the publication of Baroness Jean Corston's report in 2007 there has been cross-party and multi-disciplinary support for transforming women's justice and radically reducing the number of women sent to prison. The efforts of academics, practitioners and campaigners means that very few questions about the case for change remain unanswered. The evidence base is strong and has consistently shown that community alternatives to women's imprisonment are more appropriate and more effective at addressing the root causes of offending.

The Government's strategy for criminalised women, published in 2018, appeared to mark the end of plans to build five new women's prisons and set out the Government's intention to reduce the women's prison population by investing in community-based alternatives, particularly women's centres. This stated intent was a response to years of reports from the likes of Parliament's Justice Committee (2018; 2019) recommending radical change. It led to a refreshed ministerial Advisory Board on Female Offenders (ABFO) bringing together specialists across Government and academia with campaigning and service providing charities to advise on the delivery of the Women's Strategy.

The strategy reflected years of evidence providing answers to key questions that will be depressingly well-known to many readers of this book. The vast majority of women in prison have faced multiple disadvantages, often since childhood, including domestic abuse and other trauma and a third have experienced the care system (Motz, Dennis and Aiyegbusi, 2020; see also *Chapters 1, 2* and *4* in particular). As with men, racism in the CJS, means that black and minoritised women are disproportionately affected by imprisonment (see *Chapter 5* by Monica Thomas and Sinem Bozkurt; Prison Reform Trust, 2022; Agenda and Women in Prison, 2018; Petrillo, 2017). Most imprisoned women are sentenced for minor offences, often theft, serving short sentences which are still long enough to negatively impact the lives of women, their children and their families (Baldwin and Epstein, 2017; Booth, 2020b).

Commonly offences are linked to the offending of another (with domestic abuse a common causal factor), poverty, trauma, substance use or mental ill-health (Prison Reform Trust (PRT), 2022). Imprisonment, even of a few weeks, can mean losing home, job and children and the trauma of imprisonment can be long-lasting, often compounding and extending previous harm of abuse and neglect (Baldwin and Epstein, 2017). Chris Tchaikovsky, founder of the charity Women in Prison, summed it up,

> 'Taking the most hurt people out of society and punishing them in order to teach them how to live within society is futile. Whatever else a prisoner knows, she knows everything there is to know about punishment because that is exactly what she has grown up with. Whether it's childhood sexual abuse, indifference, neglect, punishment is most familiar to her.'[34]

Due to the fact that women are more likely than men to be primary carers, in 95% of cases when a mother goes to prison, her children will have to leave their home to go into the care system or to live with relatives (Caddle and Crisp, 1997; Minson, 2020; PRT, 2022). Again, the harm can last a lifetime, ricocheting through the family and the generations (Baldwin, 2015; 2020; 2021b; 2022a).

---

34. See https://womeninprison.org.uk/about/our-story

Amidst all this is the neglected issue, not of women as victims (which is more often the focus in recent years of the 'story' of women and prison), but of agency and the power and potential of women affected by the CJS to survive deep and multiple hardship and trauma and, with the right support, to thrive (see *Chapter 4* by Charlotte Barlow; Baldwin 2020; 2021c; 2022a); Booth and Harriott, 2021). The position of women as carers in families (of children and others, including older relatives) means that women often survive prison whilst trying to keep their families afloat from afar (Booth, 2020a). The resourcefulness and talent in prisons is an untold story for the whole system of imprisonment which, sadly, results too often in tragic waste of human potential and a focus on people in prison as perpetrators of crime or victims of life, rather than agents of change (Maguire, 2021).

There is a growing body of critique from women with lived experience of prison about this infantilisation and 'misuse' of women's voices (Booth and Harriott, 2021; Harding, 2021). Women in Prison came into being as a result of Chris Tchaikovsky's time in prison, her activism, leadership and partnership with Professor Pat Carlen. WIP is drawing itself back to those roots now with a self-critical analysis of power and focus on how women's voices and agency can be centred in every aspect of the organization. Similarly, some academics are taking a more self-critical approach to research activism and how power is shared ethically with people previously considered 'research subjects' (Harding, ibid; Quinlan, Baldwin and Booth, 2022). There has never been a time that real change has, on paper, been so close to hand.

So Near and Yet So Far

In the space of justice reform the issue of women in prison should, in theory, stand as a beacon of hope that change can happen. There has been progress. The Covid-19 pandemic has accelerated a reduction in the prison population. In March 2020 there were 3,623 women in prison, then in March 2021 this had reduced to 3,116, moving up to 3,211 by December 2021. This means that the women's prison population decreased by 14% from before the pandemic (February 2020) to December 2021 (the latest population figures available at the time of writing). In terms of the numbers of first receptions over the time periods specified, from April 2019 to March 2020, 6,852 women were received into prison as compared to 4,525 in the year April 2020 to March 2021 — a 34% decrease.

Sadly, the pandemic had a devastating impact on all people in prisons, with virtual solitary confinement for many, locked up 23 hours a day, and the harm of long-term separation from children and families when visits were stopped. There are now record rates of self-harm by women in prison revealing a continuing deterioration of mental health. In 2021 the MOJ released figures which revealed a 47% increase in incidents of self-harm on the women's prison estate from June of that year on the previous quarter. In 2022 Her Majesty's Inspectorate of Prisons and the Independent Monitoring Board have confirmed this deeply concerning picture. The tragic stories of deaths of women in prison documented by the charity INQUEST (INQUEST, 2018/2019) continue to result in the now, almost inevitable question, 'What was she even doing in prison in the first place?'

Since 2019, three babies have died during their mothers' imprisonment. One baby was stillborn in the mother's prison cell, another baby was stillborn in a toilet, and the third baby stillborn in an ambulance en route to hospital. Research has shown that cell births are not unusual and that pregnant mothers in prison do not consistently receive good quality ante natal care or services (Baldwin and Abbott, forthcoming 2023; Abbott, 2021; Prison and Probation Ombudsman (PPO), 2021; 2022). There is widespread evidence and argument for community alternatives to sentencing women to imprisonment, but especially concerning pregnant women (Epstein and Brown, 2022). The nature of prison, in terms of limitations on access to fresh air, exercise, balanced diet, healthcare and support networks means that it will never be a safe space for pregnant mothers and the PPO has confirmed that every pregnancy in prison is high risk (PPO, 2021).

In some communities, women's centres have become established as a specialist element of provision for women, and in the wake of privatisation (and recently re-nationalisation) the Probation Service has managed to retain the foundations, at least, of its commitment to a distinct trauma-informed approach to women, which is separate to that for men. In the new arrangements for support services alongside the delivery of the Probation Service, specialist women's services have a strong role to play (see *Chapter 2* by Claire Morley and Claire

Rushton). However, this can only be fully delivered if such services can emerge from the 'dead hand' of overly bureaucratic competitive tendering and obsession with 'contract management', whilst retaining the core values of being women-led and trauma-informed.

This needs to happen whilst taking on board the critique and learning about the real dangers of coming 'too close' to counterproductive controlling and punitive measures (Harding, 2020b). The privatisation of Probation Services in 2015 impacted negatively on women and women's services, including women's centres—resulting in lost funding, reducing services, closure or becoming much more removed from Probation Service referral pathways. Unification of the Probation Service and the increased understanding of the importance of trauma-informed practice are opportunities to tailor services in a way that responds to women's specific needs (see again *Chapter 2*). This will only happen if there is a commitment to the key tenets of such practice relating to real choice, consent and the need for systems and services that enable women to take control of their own lives.

Unfortunately, progress on implementation of the Government's 2018 strategy took a backwards step in January 2021 with the surprise announcement of £150 million to be spent on 500 new women's prison places (now £200 million according to a newer report from the National Audit Office in 2022). The plan was met with widespread condemnation, bewilderment and ridicule. This outcry included many members of the Minister's own Advisory Board who had not been consulted on this decision and were informed of it on the same day as the information was released to the press (despite the Advisory Board meeting formally the previous day).

There are many questions still to be answered about this unfortunate turn of events, not least about the strategic drivers and evidence for decisions about significant public expenditure and the role of independent advisors to government across disciplines and professional groups. The circumstances surrounding this development challenges the very existence of Advisory Boards and is one example of the risks of an autocratic patriarchal top-down approach of Government departments, and dysfunctional relationships between civil servants and other professionals. These issues are for exploring elsewhere, but an important backdrop to discuss options of where we go from here.

'We' Not 'They'

This chapter focuses on a different place to the Whitehall corridors of power: on the 'we' not the 'they' of Ministers and officials driving and implementing Government decisions, including who influences policy and choices about where precious financial resources are deployed. By the 'we', I mean the charities, practitioners and academics who imagine and pursue a different future, and advocate to end the harm of current criminal justice approaches (including the use of prison for women). Alongside these are the people with lived experience, their families and funders—the trusts and foundations that drive the campaigning, services and research activity that also shines light on both the current harm and future possibilities in pursuing active positive change.

So much of the energy of those researching, campaigning and trying to change the system goes on influencing (and sometimes battling with) the 'they'—those seen to be in power, usually Ministers and officials working with them. It is the Ministers driving the policy decisions and choosing how to spend public money; what to legislate on; directly influencing the civil servants who run our Prisons and Probation Service and the broader CJS, alongside prison governors, prison and probation officers, police officers, magistrates, judges and others.

In recent years many of these individuals and professional groups have been making their decisions in the context of public strategies and outwardly facing expressions of views that *they* 'get it', that *they* want to radically reduce the women's prison population and recognise that support services and community sentences are more effective for women. Yet, the decision to build 500 new prison places for women in response to perceived operational opportunity and availability of funds rather than in service of genuine need and strategy is a classic example of 'words not deeds'. The very clear message given by this action is that *'they'* will continue to send women to prison despite the overwhelming evidence for the case against.

The rationale given by the Government for building new women's prison places was that funding has been provided for more police officers, therefore more crimes will be detected, therefore more prison spaces will be required. The poor use of data and perceived inevitability of this outcome is an abdication of responsibility to address the broader systemic context of trauma and injustice in which women's criminalisation occurs. It also fails to take account the potential impact of the Government's own strategy. Ironically, the decision to invest so heavily in women's prison places undermines the much greater challenge of cross-government and multi-agency 'buy in' and financial commitment to an evidence-based strategy focused on community-based solutions where every part of the system plays — and pays — its part.

Whilst there has been a high turnover of Ministers leading on this area over the last decade, there have been gradual steps forward. As he handed over to the new Justice Minister Edward Argar, Minister Phillip Lee ensured publication of the women's strategy and a formal end in 2018 to previous plans (announced in 2017) to build five women's prisons. Both invested in listening to charities and academics working in the field and seemed 'converted' during their time in office to the belief that this could be a public policy area where progress was possible. Following broader acceptance of the evidence of the harm of prison across the MOJ at ministerial level, there briefly seemed real hope that an end to short prison sentences could be in sight, not just for women, but momentum was lost when these and other Ministers, including Secretary of State for Justice, David Gauke, and Prisons Minister, Rory Stewart, left office.

Despite decades of published evidence about the negative impact, ineffectiveness and inappropriateness of imprisonment, alongside a stated commitment to a Women's Strategy that had widespread stakeholder support, the perverse policy decisions continue. It must now be time to look somewhere else for the answers to change. As Einstein said: 'Insanity: doing the same thing over and over again and expecting different results'.

The focus of the remainder of this chapter is on what 'we' are doing, including charities campaigning and providing services for women affected by the CJS, academics and practitioners who have been building up such powerful evidence for change.

Failure

For all the talk of 'learning lessons' and reflective practice, remarkably little time is spent on questions like — 'Where are we going wrong?' and 'What have we learned from failure?'. As CEO of Women in Prison, working at the frontline of charity service provision and campaigning, I have seen first-hand how 'stuck' things can feel. On the tenth anniversary of the Corston Report in 2017, WIP published a summary of the lack of progress on the recommendations of the report (Women in Prison, 2017). It is argued here that reasons for this are, at least in part, because women's needs in the CJS tend to be subsumed under the shadow of the perceived lives of men caught up in the CJS (the 'invisible women' problem, Criado Perez, 2020), the patriarchal legacy and continuing influence of a 'prison works' narrative, where punishment and control reign supreme.

This chapter argues that the legacy of a patriarchally governed CJS, obsessed with punishment and designed by men in power (Carlen, 1985), drives the decisions and priorities of policy-makers and Government. It is a sad fact that, one way or another, there always appears to be space created in prison for more prisoners (by building more prisons and overcrowding the existing ones) yet interestingly, not in residential 'rehab' or mental health care (including that needed for pregnant women and mothers). Traditionally our focus has been on where Government and policy-makers are going wrong, and not on the role that 'we' have in this persistent failure to follow facts about what works and what doesn't.

Working at the frontline of leadership in the service delivery and campaigning charity sector I understand why self-reflection on failure is so difficult. The competitive arena for funding delivers a punishing schedule, and there is barely time to take breath before the next funding bid or quarterly report is needed (often requiring news of outcomes and achievements). This hamster wheel of securing funding feels like battle piling on exhausting battle and requires a focus on selling the things that work (or look like they do!) — not reflecting on and learning from the things that don't. What look like 'wins', such as some funding secured, can come with unintended consequences (including in relation to values and diluting attention on systems change) which can feel like hollow victories.

In the wake of the Covid-19 pandemic and the shocking announcement of building an additional 500 women's prison places there appears to be a feeling of collective learned helplessness and fatigue, a loss of hope, including in key Government departments like the MOJ. The consequences of this difficult time are many, but one of the most devastating is the sense of a potential retreat into siloes, of 'heads down', doing what needs to be done to get through the battle of the day and on to the next. This can result in the long-term visions and goal being lost or postponed. I've seen this most clearly in terms of service provision in the criminal justice space, but fear it will undermine progress in campaigning too, especially as resources become more scarce, and the political environment more openly hostile to the change that we need to actively pursue.

❚❚ Pause for Thought

- As charity leaders and academics, are spaces for reflection — individual, in teams and in partnerships — being built into our practice?
- Are we routinely looking critically at ourselves and the role we have in change, or just looking outside at the roles of others?
- Are we interrogating failure as a matter of routine, especially in how our messaging is landing, how we are sharing learning and the impact we are having?

Here, I argue that if academics, charities and practitioners are to maximise our impact and create a sea change in the imprisonment of women, focusing on the three areas for change set out at the head of this chapter.

Prison Abolition and 'Small Victories'

In Davis, Dent, Meiners and Richie (2022), *Abolition. Feminism. Now,* contemporary abolitionism is described as seeking, 'the dismantling of all systems of oppression, from white supremacy to the patriarchy':

'It demands that we invest in people not power; in communities not coercion; in healthcare, housing, education and social services, not prisons, detention centres and police forces. And it does so through a feminist lens, recognising that gender and sexual violence are encouraged and enabled by these same systems of oppression.'

In her article on abolition, Sarah Lamble (2020) starts with the words of the abolitionist organizer Ruth Wilson Gilmore,

> 'Abolition is not *absence*, it is *presence*. What the world will become already exists in fragments and pieces, experiments and possibilities. So those who feel in their gut deep anxiety that abolition means knock it all down, scorch the earth and start something new, let that go. Abolition is building the future from the present, in all of the ways we can.'

Lamble and others, like David Scott (2020) set out the possibilities of the abolition process or mindset in the context of the way that prisons and criminal justice responses perpetuate harm, violence and inequality:

> 'Abolition is about abolishing the conditions under which prison became the solution to problems, rather than abolishing the buildings we call prisons.' (Gilmore and Murakawa, 2020)

Lamble (2020) describes 'everyday abolition' as a collective everyday approach to social change, requiring us to dismantle dysfunctional structures, institutions while building up systems of care, well-being, and support that enable communities to flourish. The punitive carceral habits and logics that trap us equate justice with punishment. This includes the individualisation of problems, which actively utilises exclusion and public shaming and divides the 'us' from the 'them'; as opposed to building infrastructures focused on healing, connection, safety, collective skills and capacity to do things differently.

Prison abolition is about an end to the institution of the prison as a place of punishment, effectively warehouses where, in the words of Angela Davis, 'people are disappeared' not the problems that brought them there. This vision of abolition is that such institutions would no longer be needed and that the tiny number of people (the vast majority men) whose offending would lead to incarceration would happen in small therapeutic communities. This needs to be part of a totally reimagined justice system where structured community support, interventions and opportunities to 'give back' are the 'go to' not prison. Everything would need to be in place from birth so that problems could be 'nipped in the bud' and the social and economic conditions would require a

Welfare State ensuring the basics for survival and an end to the need for the likes of food banks.

There is an important parallel argument for better conditions for those imprisoned whilst this change happens, but this has to be made in the context of radically reducing the capacity of prisons, otherwise prison expansion will continue to dilute progress towards the end goal. The argument that 500 new 'improved' prison spaces for women could result in closure of 500 of the older less suitable cells might have a sliver of credibility if it was accompanied with a plan for this to happen and the data to guide it. As it stands there is neither. In any event all the evidence, such as that summarised over many consecutive years in the Prison Reform Trust Bromley Briefings, shows that whilst more prisons have been built, the crisis in prison has deepened, outcomes worsened and the prison population continued to grow.

A favourite quote of Chris Tchaikovsky was Joan Baez's, 'Small victories, big defeats' — the idea that to survive in a world of constant battle for systemic change (the 'big defeat'), we have to focus on the small victories that will help us reach our vision. In some ways those of us campaigning and researching for systems change have focused on small victories, but these have often resulted in too much time spent on 'group think' of the social media echo chamber, 'think pieces' published in places, again where the likely audiences probably share similar views to the author (a bit like this one!) and letters to the same newspapers, again read by people who are often already outraged by the injustice they see (Moore et al, 2017).

The reality is that there has been very little coordinated action focused on the harder to influence audiences, or collaborative planning identifying ingredients for success and converting the small victories into the long game of change. The victories I am thinking of are not those of 'prison reform', but towards the bigger prize of prison abolition. There has certainly been positive reform in prisons with more focus on education and trauma-informed practice, yet the crisis in prisons continues to deepen. It is a really positive development that largely as a result of the Black Lives Matter movement, abolition is entering the mainstream so that its hope and vision is no longer seen as the delusion of disconnected dreamers. We need to see the big vision of prison abolition in the context of its multiple battles on so many fronts, which are inevitably different to the (arguably more straightforward) battles of prison reform.

For the focus on the small victories to have impact, we need to develop a sophisticated incremental 'movement building' approach to the changing of hearts and minds. Since exploring the evidence on reframing from the Frameworks Institute and others,[35] I recognise that too often the messaging of those of us campaigning, providing services and building the evidence base is just 'off', or worse, counterproductive. The evidence and my fear is that the focus on the seemingly endless 'revolving door' cycle of harm and trauma is not just ineffective in changing public opinion but can also entrench hopelessness and despair when the opposite is needed.

The 'broken system' style messages (which I know I have been guilty of myself) can have an impact in the echo-chamber of social media, in conference seminars and on the broadsheet letters pages and might feel like powerful messaging, but for the change we need it is the court of public opinion and the unconverted 'non-believers' where we need to focus. One group whose influence is key is that of sentencers, whose evidence-based judicial independence could bring real change. Those in power tend not to frame this independence as an opportunity, but as a barrier to influencing and holding decision-makers accountable. Challenging, disrupting and restructuring sentencing, and the way sentencers make their decisions, is key to the long game of abolition. Part of this is how we 'sell' alternatives and disrupt the punitive 'someone must pay' mindset which centres punishment over other goals.

Hough et al (2013) found that punitive attitudes of the general public can be converted to more progressive thinking through education and understanding, highlighting the need to reach and inform wider audiences. However, a particular problem when framing the case in a gendered context, i.e. specifically arguing against imprisonment for women, is that it can be perceived as unfair, because it can be misinterpreted as a call to treat men and women differently. The message can backfire, leading the public to support uniform (rather than individually responsive) sentencing. It is not always understood or appreciated that fair and equal, doesn't always mean 'same'. Focusing on common sense changes and shared goals makes people more supportive of a range of progressive reforms—including eliminating racial disparities in the system. When arguing for an amendment to the Bill that became the Police, Crime, Sentencing

---

35. https://www.frameworksinstitute.org/publication/
talking-justice-reform-and-public-safety-a-frameworks-message-memo/

and Courts and Act 2022, Women in Prison and others lobbied for change by focusing on primary carers and the impact on children. This was in order to highlight the far-reaching implication of maternal imprisonment whilst avoiding the 'kickback' of 'why should she get special treatment?' and ultimately to secure the results needed. A campaign like this might not succeed at first but the groundwork laid, arguments won and key targets influenced can mean a win for the next time.

Practical issues like the imprisonment of primary carers lend themselves well to the value of pragmatism on people's attitudes towards criminal justice reform, and focus on this is proven to elevate support for reform (Hough et al, 2013). One of the problems we face is there is so much evidence that the system is failing on all fronts that too often we are presenting multiple unframed facts and evidence about the CJS without an accompanying value or influencing strategy, producing minimal or counter-productive effects. Carefully framing information about the real impact of imprisonment to focus on changing deep-seated and harmful attitudes are vital elements of the strategy to end mass imprisonment to focus on replacing the prison system with community-based change. The more the public know about community options and their effectiveness, the more likely they are to accept them as valid alternatives to imprisonment.

▌▌ Pause for Thought

- Are we thinking in terms of incremental steps towards a big vision or are we 'head down' to the next battle?
- Are we celebrating the 'small victories' and do we even share a view on what these are?
- Do we have a strategic and evidence-based approach to our use of language and key messages?

'Your silence will not protect you'

If we are to make the small victories work for us all and bring us closer to the big prize (abolition), those in traditional leadership roles and working in professions (academia, probation, policing) need to be routinely stepping back and sharing messages and messaging platforms with those with direct experience of the CJS. In reality, there are very few people who speak publicly on justice reform—the vast majority look and sound far too similar (I am including myself in this group). Sometimes silence is needed and stepping back and letting other voices be heard. Some brilliant people have given evidence to Parliamentary committees recently, but the most powerful I have seen in a long time were women from Revolving Doors with lived experience of prison. The strongest messages from coverage of the reports of the tragic deaths of babies born to pregnant women in prison has come from women themselves speaking about their experiences (Epstein and Brown, 2022).

Audre Lorde said 'Your silence will not protect you'—a warning the truth of which has reverberated across charities throughout the Transforming Rehabilitation (TR) years.

The silence of charities, especially the largest ones, remains a significant issue, driven by the fear of 'gagging clauses' which prevent critical public comment by service providers and fear of punishment by exclusion from campaigning and advocacy charities. Organizations working in and with prisons face a special form of silencing when their access to the space is effectively in the gift of governors and other officials. Arguably, the greatest threat of all is that of extinction, which alongside the obsession with competitive tendering has created a deeply unhealthy addiction to the pursuit of ever-larger contracts meaning some charities become just 'too big to fail'—or to speak out.

Many charities, especially the largest, have kept their counsel through the disastrous TR, with some consumed by the addiction and need for repeated or ongoing contracts that holds back so much real change. Smaller specialist charities, including Women in Prison, have had their 'fingers burnt' with undeliverable contracts, or having to end delivery due to issues relating to values clashes. On the ground I have seen the damage of privatisation and dysfunctional public sector commissioning as a core element of systems failure, yet it has received remarkably little attention in the world of academia or in the press. The words 'procurement', 'commissioning', 'public finances' don't give the promise of much of an endorphin rush of injustice and ethereal desire for change, nor do they feature heavily in driving research activity.

Interestingly, where academia is heavily aligned with practice—such as the *Probation Journal,* critique of the disconnect between policy, strategy and practice has been loud and consistent. Baldwin (2021c) argues that research and activism must go together, but that it is more likely to be found in the work of those academics whose backgrounds lie in practice.

There appears to be a certain 'snobbery' in academia in that practice focused academia (and academics?) are perhaps not always seen as 'real' academics (ibid). Thus, there are schools of academics who do not pursue the impact of research as the golden thread it needs to be if anything is to change. Initiatives such as the College of Policing Research Map are signs of hope that we could start to see research as a jigsaw puzzle for real world change. My experience from the front line is that service providing charities are routinely approached to facilitate researchers (often unrealistic and late notice requests for access to research participants), but are rarely asked 'What do you need to know?', 'How can we help you?' or 'Can we work together to publicise this research and reinforce your key messages?'

Imagine if every academic article, quote in the press, evidence given to Parliamentary Committees and speech in Parliament focused on the small victories of incremental winning over of hearts and minds. A sea change by us all is required and probably some difficult conversations need to be had about the respective roles and power we have. It may mean a decision not to support a well-meaning but poorly messaged campaign for change, or a piece of research with clunky 'doom spiralling' messaging and instead properly investing in collective framing of training and collaborative partnerships, and agreeing communication strategies across sectors and organizations.

We need to instil collective, reflexive discipline to let each other know when we get it wrong (although not the current fashion for performative 'calling out' in public) and, if necessary, pull back from reinforcing counterproductive messaging—by researchers and charities.

> ▌▌ **Pause for Thought**
>
> Are we:
> - sharing or giving up platforms of power or hoarding them?
> - choosing silence for fear of losing power (including funding)?
> - routinely asking (1) about all forums ?; (2) 'Who is going to get the message over best?'; (3) 'Is it my organization or my university department or do I know in my heart that the message is likely to land better if delivered by someone else?'
> - What stops us inviting others to the platforms of power?

It will mean 'push back' to journalists who get this wrong and sometimes saying no. All publicity is not good publicity. Sometimes it will mean Professor X or Chief Executive Y sharing or giving up the platforms which give us our power. It is this issue of power which is the third front of change to which I now turn.

Power and the 'Master's Tools'

Charity leaders working at the coal face, and other professionals including researchers, know that if we really want to get to the heart of systems failure we need to 'follow the money'. Despite the best collective intentions to pursue and achieve our organizational or individual goals, some of the competitive processes to secure funding can serve to entrench the harm of the dysfunctional system. Sometimes it is difficult to see this until it is too late, which is why reflective practice and examination of failure is so important. I am intimately familiar with the justifications we use, 'It's not ideal, but the alternative is worse'; 'It was this funding or nothing'; 'It's better we do it than someone else' or the variation of 'Women prefer it is us doing this than someone else'; 'We have to be in the system to change it'. Sometimes it feels like the only options are to 'follow the money' or do nothing at all — but we know from experience that this is not the case.

When the Government had plans to build five new women's prisons, some argued to end the campaign against them because 'we need to make the new prisons as good as they can be'. The same argument is sometimes applied to the 'residential women's centres' proposal in the Women's Strategy, despite the longstanding questions about the practical implementation of such a model. The proposals remain (although in reality with little evidence of the financial commitment to deliver) in the context of overwhelming evidence for an alternative approach—one that centres sustainably funded day services alongside long-term housing options.

There was a similar argument for charity provider engagement and involvement in changes like the Probation Service privatisation fiasco as part of the new probation delivery arrangements (including the 'Dynamic Purchasing Framework').

Being caught up in the world of commercial competition has many consequences of which silence can be just one. I believe it is possible to work within a system towards reform whilst pursuing the bigger goal of abolition, but this has to be done consciously to avoid diluted integrity and becoming lost down 'false alleys' of change. This requires constant reflection and analysis of power.

Audre Lorde said, 'The Master's tools will never dismantle the master's house'. A theme that runs through all the challenges, barriers and false starts that I have outlined is a lack of coordination, collaboration and collective action. Competition and the 'master's tools' of funding and illusory search for the Holy Grail of 'evidence' looking to satisfy the 'they', have dominated the energies of many of those of us needed in service of the bigger vision for change. Maureen Mansfield's Ted Talk on the funding of the women's sector sets out this problem with great power. Imagine if we acted collectively not just in our messages and who delivers them, but on the timing and nature of our game aiming constantly, in Mansfield's words, for 'the world we want, not the one we think we can get'.

Initiatives like the College of Policing Research Map could be used as a more proactive means of academics connecting to front line providers with a view to filling their evidence gaps. Academics publishing evidence could maximise impact by using an annual calendar of events with a view to targeting audiences that are less well-informed, as opposed to the traditional dissemination to the likeminded. Campaigning charities could 'divide up' their 'unconverted' targets to build relationships of trust and influence that isn't about their individual fundraising or influencing reach but instead, about 'our' campaign for change — aiming for the small incremental victories towards the big vision of abolition. The most powerful 'master's tool' deployed against researchers and charities alike has been the age old 'divide and conquer', gaining and maintaining power by breaking up larger concentrations of power into pieces that individually have less power than the one implementing the strategy and maintaining supremacy over your opponents by encouraging dissent between them, preventing them from uniting against a common enemy.

Research activism (Baldwin, 2021c; Baldwin et al, 2021) requires that academics and researchers have a responsibility for their work to count — to be active in the pursuit of change not just the pursuit of academic splendour, glory and reputation. The same has to be true of charities too. Research and knowledge for its own sake is an important principle of academia, and charities sometimes campaign on issues not because they think they will 'win' but because their values drive them to speak out. However, this should sit alongside the power of applied research and the need to focus consciously and collectively on the work that 'makes a difference', and that has impact.

It is striking how pervasive and effective the simple 'divide and rule' tactic has proved to be. When the decision was made not to consult the ABFO on the building of the proposed new prison places for women, the unyielding united front and persistence of the disparate membership seemed unexpected. Thus, a decision was, by officials and the Minister, to 'refresh the membership of the ABFO and existing members were asked to reapply for a seat at the table. However, and ironically, it is unlikely that officials anticipated that some of the original members would step back to make way for potentially even more challenging voices, and to encourage and practically support others to apply.

Current procurement practice assumes a lack of collaboration between providers — an assumption completely undermined by the local and regional women's sector providers of services partnership approach to commissioning women's services in the new probation delivery arrangements. The year leading up to this saw small charities helping each other with the skills and knowledge to qualify on the 'dynamic purchasing framework', with larger women's charities stepping up to enable smaller charities to 'bid' in partnership. There were also examples of officials responding to the systems changes needed to ensure a mixed economy of provision which built on local delivery, including co-commissioning of services in London and Manchester.

New approaches to locally-driven co-production and trust-based commissioning are springing up across the country. We don't need to always just imagine how things could work, we are seeing it happen. As such, in cases where we see impact, power is being surrendered. This includes the power of commissioners who 'know best', and of larger charities whose 'bid writing teams' know how to play the game, and even of smaller charities who were starting to be sucked into a competitive tendering; which ultimately disconnects them from their grassroots value base and the people they serve.

It is the undermining of 'divide and conquer' and building the united front that needs to be our collective focus. Alice Walker said, 'The most common way people give up their power is by thinking they don't have any.' We have to rediscover our power together and take our shared place in the battle for change. A starting point needs to be in reflectively accepting that responsibility for the failure to really progress change lies with ourselves as well as with others—and that the answer to the key challenges about making real change happen lies with all of us doing things differently—new activism tools for building a new house.

‖ Pause for Thought

- Are there any campaigns or academic research messages that you know are counterproductive but have supported anyway?
- Where are there new tools being deployed and how are they working?
- What power do you or your organization need to surrender or share, and who to/with?
- Who should be centred in the change?

Building a New House

There are three things I think we could do differently to rebuild hope that radical change is possible. Firstly, we need a clear and unwavering focus on the big vision of prison abolition to replace the dominant and failed narrative of prison reform. This means the 'long game' of building the case which centres the lifeline and anchor of specialist community-based support, like that from women's centres—a multi-generational vision. We need the discipline and processes that mean that every one of us is signed up to this battle and we need to frame every message from research and campaigns in a way that sells this vision.

Secondly, we need to address the complex issue of silence and silencing to speak out collaboratively, recognising the complexity of power and privilege within which many larger charities, established researchers and other leaders (including charity leaders like myself) may have become too comfortable. This will mean lifting up the voices of others who have been heard so rarely and committing to a collaborative long-term campaign focused on the incremental building of 'small victories'. In some cases that will mean some of us speaking less. It will also require a changed relationship between researchers and charities and Government departments, so that funding follows 'truth to power' not the 'careful' findings of researchers and service providers considered 'safe' by those in power.

The third thing we need to do differently is the most challenging of all—developing new tools of collaborative leadership and action crossing disciplines and sectors with academic researchers working alongside campaigning and service providing charities and women with direct experience of prison, with power genuinely shared in service of the big vision. Initiatives like the Women, Family, Crime and Justice Network illustrate how the multi-disciplinary sharing of power and voice can make a difference. Other younger partnerships like the National Women's Justice Coalition (which brings together women's service providing charities with a focus on women caught up in the CJS) have an opportunity to model this new collaborative style of feminist leadership.

There is hope. We can change things, we know it and there are the small victories which prove we have started, but the real lasting systems change will only happen if *we* change. In the words of the Jamaican American poet, playwright and essayist June Jordan, 'We are the ones we have been waiting for'. It all starts with us.

CHAPTER 12

Afterword, Summary and Closing Thoughts

Lucy Baldwin

This collection written by academic experts, practitioners, policy influencers and women with lived experience has robustly presented evidence and argument for gendered responses to women affected by the CJS. It has powerfully, and at times painfully, revealed the trauma that underpins the lives of many (if not most) criminalised women. It is hard to imagine that effective criminal justice can be achieved without improvements in social justice. We absolutely need the Criminal Justice System (CJS) to be more trauma-informed, but more than that we also need to ensure that it does not cause additional harm, additional trauma to people who come into contact with its services.

The trauma people with lived experience of prison are left with, specifically triggered by or originating from the prison experience, is a relatively new and emerging area of research (Piper and Berle, 2019). Research investigating the relationship between trauma and the prison experience tends to focus on potentially traumatic events (PTEs) that might occur in prison such as prison rape, witnessing violence or witnessing suicide. Rather than the trauma of separation from children or the prison experience itself.

Piper and Berle (2019) undertook a systematic review exploring the relationship between prison experienced trauma, PTEs and post-traumatic stress disorder (PTSD) outcomes, finding that experiencing prison can lead directly to PTSD. Similarly, Moore and Scraton (2014) explicitly argue that incarceration is a traumatising experience for women, one that is often experienced as 'destructive and debilitating', however how that translates post-release is not explicitly examined. Baldwin (2022a) found in her research with post released mothers; that traumatic effects (and in some cases diagnosed PTSD), was evident in mothers who had been involved in the CJS and ultimately prison, sometimes many decades after release. Traumatic experiences can shape many aspects of a person's life, their life chances and life choices

Traumatic life experiences are widespread, long lasting and damaging, exacting a huge cost in human suffering and the associated social, economic, and legal consequences of untreated and unresolved trauma in people's lives. Traumatic life experiences require the expenditure of considerable social and economic resources in the healthcare and child welfare systems, mental health and addiction programmes, social programmes, homelessness and housing services, and, too often, in family law, the CJS, and other legal areas. Trauma and law/justice are inextricably interconnected.

Trauma is not always obvious, or even out in the open, especially in relation to domestic abuse and coercive control. It is creeping, insidious, sometimes deeply buried, deliberately hidden or concealed — but nonetheless doing great harm as it evolves or becomes embedded in the psyche of those affected. Thus, meaning that compassion, caution and sensitivity is vital in all work with women.[36] Great care and mindfulness must exist to ensure that women's services are able to provide an environment of 'emotional safety' (Baldwin, 2015), in which truly trauma-informed, gendered support can be provided.

The trauma-informed services described in this collection have required a deep knowledge of the ways in which individuals may have perceived, adjusted to, and responded to their traumatic experiences and a commitment to modify organizational practices that may unintentionally trigger reminders of the traumatic event or the feelings of helplessness they experienced. By doing so everyone from front-line staff to professionals and administrators will be more likely to project a common organizational message: that the person affected by past trauma possesses valuable expertise and knowledge about their own 'problems'. 'Working collaboratively to facilitate the individual's sense of control and to maximise their autonomy and choices throughout the engagement process is crucial in trauma-informed services (Kubiak et al, 2017). As is recognising the person's own definitions of their trauma and what constitutes trauma for them (for example maternal trauma).

Trauma responses are often viewed as negative, criminal even — when often in fact they should arguably instead be viewed as adaptations a person has had

---

36. Obviously not all victims of coercive control or domestic abuse are women, but the book describes the context for women and is specifically gendered — hence the use of the term women.

to make, in order to cope with life's circumstances. Recognising and understanding trauma necessarily involves focusing on harms, and the ways in which traumatic events and responses interfere with and can compromise both early development (for traumas in childhood) and very often affect everyday functioning in adult life, sometimes even in ways that are not necessarily evident to the traumatised person. Recognition of trauma and its effects on a person's life, however, does not preclude a simultaneous focus on their resilience and strengths. Indeed, it would be a mistake to fail to acknowledge these. In fact, whilst it is important to recognise and understand the effects of trauma, it is equally necessary to recognise, understand and work with the concept of wellness and resilience, and how these are achieved, supported and maintained. This is a task the CJS must take seriously.

Resilience can be described as a person's capacity to deal with adversity. Given what we 'know' about the adversity of most people who come into contact with the CJS, it is imperative that building, supporting and facilitating resilience is part of our criminal justice response and rehabilitation. We must support, in the context of this book, women to be able to integrate and process overwhelming experiences so as not to become caught in them, destabilised or dysregulated by them in an ongoing way. Supporting and facilitating resilience should facilitate learning, understanding, coping and action.

Summary of the Collection

Chapter 2, argues for the adoption of a 'gendered whole systems approach', incorporating a specialist women's team model as a response to criminalised women. The authors provide a historical and personal reflection which gives a sound evidence-based justification for their argument. They reiterate the importance of a women centred approach in a women centred environment and where relationships and consistency are recognised as important and are valued. The chapter contains a convincing argument for a gendered approach, concluding that the core values of trauma-informed practice, namely *safety, trustworthiness, choice, collaboration* and *empowerment,* must underpin all work with women in the CJS. Taking up the baton, the authors in *Chapter 3* examine how criminalised women are made individually responsible for their crime and their circumstance. The chapter highlights how the lived experience and context of women's 'offending' is ignored and unaccounted for in criminal justice responses. The authors help us to understand how stigma, shame and societal expectations of women interact with desistance and how criminalised women experience the CJS and its responses. It concludes with a rallying call for criminal justice services to adopt a truly gendered and trauma-informed response to criminalised women and to challenge the current failings in social justice for women. Continuing the theme of the significance of the broader context, *Chapter 4,* highlights the not insignificant, not infrequent, relationship between women's criminalisation and domestic violence and abuse. The author argues that criminalised women have all too often 'offended' in the context of 'fear' and 'control', but that this is not accounted for in criminal justice responses to women. The author exposes the blurred lines between 'offender' and 'victim' in relation to criminalised women, arguing that only through a gendered and trauma-informed lens can we adequately respond and, importantly, support women who are criminalised in this context. The chapter concludes with the argument that such a response would rightly divert women away from the CJS and facilitate the provision of more appropriate and compassionate responses—which the author states would 'facilitate more positive outcomes'.

The authors of *Chapter 5* call for the cessation of the use of the term 'BAME', arguing that it is in itself problematic and exclusionary, advocating for the term 'racially minoritised' to be used instead. They argue that the CJS currently fails to fully recognise, understand or respond to its perpetuating racism; that without validating the pain caused by racism, 'trauma-informed' approaches and other strategies for support continue to centre white women's experiences whilst further marginalising women positioned as racially *other.* The authors conclude that without recognition or acknowledgement racism still has a presence and a traumatic impact in criminal justice, meaning it will not be possible to provide a truly trauma-informed response to racially minoritised women.

Chapters 6 to *10* focus on the individual experiences of women. The authors of *Chapter 6* set out a powerful account of the experiences of mothers, grandmothers and mother figures when a loved one is remanded in custody. The chapter reveals the secondary, but impactful and long lasting trauma felt by this often invisible band of women and highlights the lack of support for women in these circumstances. The authors provide a convincing argument for the need to improve on the availability of support for families affected by imprisonment and for the impact on the family (often women and children) to be factored in at the point of sentence — and that failure to do so is a failure to recognise the full reach of trauma of imprisonment/remand.

Continuing the theme of entering and experiencing prison, *Chapter 7* delves deeper into the pre-prison trauma experiences of women in prison, whilst importantly paying attention to the traumatising effects of being imprisoned. The authors reflect on their therapeutic work and demonstrate the necessity of factoring in trauma experiences in rehabilitative processes. Whilst the chapter advocates strongly for diversion from prison where possible, the authors also highlight the importance of a sensitive, gendered trauma-informed, therapeutic approach, which they argue assists in the breaking of destructive cycles — triggered by trauma. They conclude that this response must be underpinned by 'hope' in the women and of course in practice and rehabilitation processes. *Chapter 8* echoes previous chapters in relation to the significance of trauma triggers and highlights how various traumatic experiences can have far-reaching consequences in terms of women and their homes. The chapter vividly demonstrates the traumatising effects of being homeless, which for many women is then compounded by a dispassionate and non-trauma-informed response from services and system processes, especially for women escaping domestic abuse. The authors conclude with a demand that services become more trauma-informed concerning women and housing, making it clear that no service should re-traumatise women, particularly domestic abuse victims/survivors in their attempts to access support and accommodation.

In *Chapter 9*, the author continues to explore the individual experience and presentation of trauma in relation to women navigating community punishment. She highlights the resilience of traumatised women, the support women provide to each other and the humour that women use as a means of coping. In reminding us that manifestations of trauma are individual and varied, the author calls for patience, sensitivity, compassion, understanding and above all acceptance and a non-judgemental approach to how women cope with trauma. In a similar vein, *Chapter 10,* provides additional insight into the personal manifestation and impact of trauma. Hosting the voices of Abigay and Melanie, two women with the lived experience of trauma and the CJS, the chapter presents unique insight into the impact of 'missed and lost opportunities' for support—which for Abigay and Melanie, had they been acted upon, may well have changed the course of their and their children's lives. Certainly, it might have prevented them becoming criminalised or imprisoned. The chapter concludes with a call for maternal trauma to be factored in, both on an individual and structural basis. If we truly seek a just, safe, equitable and effectively functioning society, then we have to do better by women and children, especially at their most vulnerable points.

Chapter 11 rounds off the collection with a critical exploration of why 'we' (academics, practitioners, charities and policy-makers) have been calling for the same changes for women for many decades, yet with little progress. It would be too easy to say that this is because we live in a patriarchal society, where the male gender is more fully supported and enabled to succeed because of long held beliefs and practices that are so deeply embedded in our society, that they are not always recognised. This is of course true, but the chapter author argues more than that 'we' need a radical, concerted and determined pursuit of more ambitious goals—like abolition. In order to achieve this the author calls for a uniting of the collective 'we', and a commitment to create stronger working partnerships and 'collaborative leadership' across the sectors and within services. This 'sea change' must be directly and inclusively informed by the voices of those affected, and their views must be part of the shaping of new services and a more hopeful future.

Concluding Thoughts

The ever-widening gap between the 'haves' and 'have nots', and the cost of living crisis and its impact, makes the need for change more important than ever. However, the blatant political disregard for the most vulnerable and challenged in our society makes improvements in social justice feel unlikely. The tone-deaf announcement of another 500 prison spaces for women and the huge increase in the male prison estate seems to indicate a desire to lock away people rather than address the issues that often led to the offending in the first place. We, especially in the case of women, continue to criminalise poverty and trauma, yet we are only just recognising the responsibility of the CJS to tackle and respond to these issues more broadly.

We have to do better: for women, for their children and families and for society in general. Quite simply the consequences are too damning and damaging if we do not. Recommendations held in the arguments of the chapters of this book, if implemented, would see a reduction in the number of women going to prison, a reduction in the number of women entering or coming into contact with the CJS at all—but if and when women do enter it or have such contact, this collection provides convincing arguments for the adoption of gendered, culturally sensitive, trauma-informed responses to their criminalisation.

- Government must resource the changes required;
- policy-makers must take heed and take action; and
- practitioners must think about how to challenge and improve on existing failing services.

Importantly, practitioners must be supported strategically, professionally and personally in their mission to undertake genuine gendered trauma-informed work. We all have the ability to make some changes, to challenge the inadequacies of any current failings.

At the end of the previous chapter, its author Kate Paradine quotes June Jordan, who powerfully stated, 'We are the ones we have been waiting for' saying that it all starts with us. Let us make a difference—we are stronger together.

References and Bibliography

Adebisi, F. (2019), The Only Accurate Part of 'BAME' is the 'And': https://folukeafrica.com/the-only-acceptable-part-of-bame-is-the-and/ (Accessed 10 June 2021).

Agenda (2018), Tackling Double Disadvantage: Ending Inequality for Black, Asian, Minoritised and Migrant Women in the CJS, a 10-Point Action Plan for Change, Tackling Double Disadvantage—Agenda (weareagenda.org).

Aiyebusi, A. (2020), 'What Happened'? An Attachment Based Understanding of Detained Women with Offending Histories, Extreme Self-harm and Diagnosis of Personality Disorder in A. Motz, M. Dennis and A. Aiyebusi (2020), *Invisible Trauma: Women Difference and the CJS*, London: Routledge, 153–167.

All Party Parliamentary Group on Ending Homelessness (APPGEH) (2019), *A Safe Home: Breaking the Link Between Homelessness and Domestic Abuse*, London: APPGEH.

Allen, K. and Wozniak, D. (2011), The Language of Healing: Women's Voices in Healing and Recovering from Domestic Violence, *Social Work in Mental Health*, 9(1), 37–55.

American Psychiatric Association (1980), *Diagnostic and Statistical Manual of Psychiatric Disorders*, APA: Washington DC.

Annison, J. (2013a), Innovation in Probation Practice: Past, Present and Future, *Probation Journal*, 60(3), 227–241.

(2013b), Change and the Probation Service in England and Wales: A Gendered Lens, *European Journal of Probation,* 5(1), 44–64.

Annison, J., Brayford, J. and Deering, J. (2015), *Women and Criminal Justice: From the Corston Report to Transforming Rehabilitation*, Bristol: Policy Press.

Arditti, J. A. (2005), Families and Incarceration: An Ecological Approach, *Families in Society: The Journal of Contemporary Social Services*, 86(2), 251–261.

Aspinall, P. (2020), Ethnic/Racial Terminology as a Form of Representation: A Critical Review of the Lexicon of Collective and Specific Terms in Use in Britain, *Genealogy* 4(87), 1–14.

(2021), BAME (Black, Asian and Minority Ethnic): The 'New Normal' in Collective Terminology, *Epidemiol Community Health,* 75(2), 107.

Atkinson, K., Barr, Ú., Monk, H. and Tucker, K. (eds.) (2022), *Feminist Responses to Injustices of the State and its Institutions: Politics, Intervention, Resistance,* Bristol: Bristol University Press.

Aymer, S. R. (2016), 'I can't breathe': A Case Study — Helping Black Men Cope with Race-related Trauma Stemming from Police Killing and Brutality, *Journal of Human Behaviour in the Social Environment,* 26, 365–376.

Bachman, R., Kerrison, E. M., Paternoster, R., Smith, L. and O'Connell, D. (2016), The Complex Relationship Between Motherhood and Desistance, *Women & Criminal Justice,* 26(3), 212–231.

Bailey, M. and Trudy (2018), On Misogynoir: Citation, Erasure, and Plagiarism, *Feminist Media Studies,* 18(4), 262–768.

Baldwin, L. (ed.) (2015), *Mothering Justice: Working with Mothers in Criminal and Social Justice Settings,* Sherfield on Loddon: Waterside Press.

Baldwin, L. (2015), Summary, Conclusion Proposals and Best Hopes in Baldwin, L., *Mothering Justice: Working with Mothers in Criminal and Social Justice Settings,* Sherfield on Loddon: Waterside Press, 263–281.

(2015), Why Motherhood? Setting the Scene. A Personal and Professional Reflection in L. Baldwin (ed.), *Mothering Justice: Working with Mothers in Criminal and Social Justice Settings,* Sherfield on Loddon: Waterside Press, 19–42.

(2017), Tainted Love: The Impact of Prison on Maternal Identity, Explored by Post Prison Reflections, *Prison Service Journal,* 233, 28–34.

(2018), Motherhood Disrupted: Reflections of Post-prison Mothers, *Emotion, Space and Society,* 26, 49–56. https://www.sciencedirect.com/science/article/abs/pii/S1755458616300500

(2020), 'A Life Sentence': The Long-Term Impact of Maternal Imprisonment in K. Lockwood (ed.), *Mothering and Imprisonment,* Bingley: Emerald Publishing.

(2021a), Motherhood Challenged: A matricentric feminist study exploring the persisting impact of maternal imprisonment on maternal identity and role, doctoral thesis, De Montfort University. https://dora.dmu.ac.uk/bitstream/handle/2086/20813/Baldwin%20L.%20Final%20Thesis%20published%20%281%29%20%281%29.pdf?sequence=1&isAllowed=y Executive summary and full text: https://dora.dmu.ac.uk/bitstream/handle/2086/21372/Executive%20 Summary%20PhD%20LBaldwin%20PDF.pdf

(2021b), Grandmothering in the Context of Criminal Justice; Grandmothers in Prison and Grandmothers as Carers When a Parent is in Prison' in K. Mantas (ed.), *Weaving Creative and Scholarly Perspectives in Honour of Our Women Elders*, Canada: Demeter Press.

(2021c), Presence, Voice and Reflexivity in Feminist and Creative Research: A Personal and Professional Reflection in I. Masson, L. Baldwin and N. Booth (eds.), *Critical Reflections from the Women, Families, Crime and Justice Research Network,* Bristol: Policy Press.

(2022a), *Motherhood In and After Prison: The Impact of Maternal Incarceration.* Sherfield on Loddon, Waterside Press.

(2022b), Missed and Lost Opportunities: The Importance of Recognising maternal Trauma in Probation Supervision, *Probation Quarterly,* 23, 16–20 (doi. org/10.54006/TDRY6231).

Baldwin, L. and Abbott, L. (forthcoming 2023), *Pregnancy and New Motherhood in Prison*, Policy Press.

Baldwin, L., Elwood, M. and Brown, C. (2022c), Criminal Mothers: The Persisting Pains of Maternal Imprisonment in *Criminal Women: Gender Matters, Co-Authored by the Criminal Women Voice, Justice and Recognition Network* (CWVJR), Bristol: Bristol University Press, 107–131.

Baldwin, L. and Epstein, R. (2017), *Short But Not Sweet: A Study of the Impact of Short Sentences on Mothers and Their Children*, Oakdale Trust, Leicester: De Montfort University: https://dora.dmu.ac.uk/handle/2086/14301 (Accessed 11 October 2021).

Baldwin, L., Masson, I. and Booth, N. (2021), Continuing the Conversation: Reflections from the Women, Family, Crime and Justice network in I. Masson, L. Baldwin and N. Booth, *Critical Reflections on Women, Family, Crime and Justice*, Bristol: Bristol University Press, 219.

Baldwin, L. and Mitchell, S. (2022), 'Maternal Imprisonment: The Enduring Impact of Imprisonment on Mothers and Their Children' in I. Masson and N. Booth (eds.), *Handbook of Women's Experiences of Criminal Justice*, Abingdon: Routledge.

Baldwin, L., Parent, K, Wray, B. and Mulcahy, J. (2022), 'Out of Sight, Out of Mind' Arguing the Case for Social Workers in Women's Prisons, *Prison Service*

Journal (December), 263, 48–54. https://www.crimeandjustice.org.uk/sites/crimeandjustice.org.uk/files/PSJ%20263%2C%20Out%20of%20sight.pdf

Ballantine, C. (2020), Imogen Tyler, Stigma: The Machinery of Inequality, *Irish Journal of Sociology,* 29(2), 257–261.

Ballinger, A. (2000), *Dead Woman Walking,* Aldershot: Ashgate.

Ballinger, A. (2012), A Muted Voice from the Past: The 'Silent Silencing' of Ruth Ellis, *Social and Legal Studies,* 21, 445–467.

Barlow, C. (2019), Women as Co-offenders: Pathways into Crime and Offending Motivations, *Howard Journal of Criminal Justice,* 58(1), 86–103.

  (2016), *Coercion and Women Co-Offenders: A Gendered Pathway Into Crime,* Bristol: Policy Press.

Barlow, C. and Weare, S. (2018), Women as Co-offenders: Pathways into Crime and Offending Motivations, *Howard Journal of Criminal Justice,* 58(1), 86–103.

Barlow C. and Walklate S. (2022), *Coercive Control,* Routledge.

Barr, Ú. (2018), Gendered Assisted Desistance: A Decade from Corston, *Safer Communities,* 17, 81–93.

  (2019), *Desisting Sisters: Gender, Power and Desistance in the Criminal (In)Justice System,* London: Palgrave Macmillan.

Barr, Ú. and Christian, N. (2019), A Qualitative Investigation into the Impact of Domestic Abuse on Women's Desistance, *Probation Journal,* 66, 416–433.

Barr, Ú. and Hart, E. L. (2022), Constructing a Feminist Desistance: Resisting Responsibilisation in K. Atkinson, Ú. Barr, H. Monk and K. Tucker (eds.), *Feminist Responses to Injustices of the State and its Institutions: Politics, Intervention, Resistance,* Bristol: Bristol University Press.

Barry, M. and McIvor, G. (2010), Professional Decision Making and Women Offenders: Containing the Chaos?, *Probation Journal,* 57(1), 27–41.

Batchelor, S. (2005), 'Prove Me the Bam!': Victimization and Agency in the Lives of Young Women Who Commit Violent Offences, *Probation Journal,* 52(4), 358–375.

Becker, S. and McCorkel, J. A. (2011), The Gender of Criminal Opportunity: The Impact of Male Co-Offenders on Women's Crime, *Feminist Criminology,* 6, 79–110.

Beeble, M. L., Bybee, D., Sullivan, C. M. and Adams, A. E. (2009), Main, Mediating, and Moderating Effects of Social Support on the Well-being of

Survivors of Intimate Partner Violence Across Two Years, *Journal of Consulting and Clinical Psychology*, 77(4), 718–729.

Belknap, J. and Holsinger, K. (2006), The Gendered Nature of Risk Factors for Delinquency, *Feminist Criminology*, 1(1), 48–71.

Bettinson, V. (2019), Aligning Partial Defences to Murder with the Offence of Coercive or Controlling Behaviour, *Journal of Criminal Law*, 83(1), 71–86.

Bimpson, E., Green, H. and Reeve, K. (2021), *Women, Homelessness and Violence: What Works?*, Centre for Homelessness Impact.

Binney, V., Harkell, G. and Nixon, J. (1981), *Leaving Violent Men: A Study of Refuges and Housing for Abused Women* (reprinted 1988), Bristol: Women's Aid Federation England (Reprinted by National Association For Social Work).

Bloom, B., Owen, B. and Covington, S. (2004), Women Offenders and the Gendered Effects of Public Policy 1, *Review of Policy Research*, 21(1), 31–48.

Boachie, V. (2021), A Guide to Understanding Racial Trauma. https://sparkandco. co.uk/blog/guide-understanding-racial-trauma (Accessed 23 July 2021).

Bocknek, E. L., Sanderson, J. and Britner, P. A. (2009), Ambiguous Loss and Posttraumatic Stress in School-Age Children of Prisoners, *Journal of Childhood and Family Studies*, 18, 323–333.

Booth, N. (2020a), *Maternal Imprisonment and Family Life: From the Caregiver's Perspective*, Bristol: Policy Press.

(2020b), Maintaining Family Ties: How Family Practices are Renegotiated to Promote Mother-child Contact in K. Lockwood (ed.), *Mothering From the Inside: Research on Motherhood and Imprisonment*, Bingley: Emerald Press, 31–48.

Booth, M. and Harriott, P. (2021), Service Users Being Used: Thoughts to the Research Community in I. Masson, L. Baldwin and N. Booth (eds.) *Critical Reflections from the Women, Families, Crime and Justice Research Network*, Bristol: Policy Press, 199.

Booth, N. and Masson, I. (2021), Loved Ones of Remand Prisoners: The Hidden Victims of COVID-19, *Prison Service Journal*, 253.

(forthcoming), The Carceral Clawback of the Golden Thread: The Penal Punishment Journey Experienced by Loved Ones of Remanded Prisoners, Publisher/Journal to be announced.

Booth, N., Masson, I. and Baldwin, L. (2018), Promises, Promises: Can the Female Offender Strategy Deliver?, *Probation Journal*, 65(4), 429–438.

Booth, N. and Masson, I. with Dakri, F. (2022), (Wo)men in the Middle: The Gendered Job of Supporting Prisoners in Masson, I. and Booth, N. (eds.), *Handbook of Women's Experiences of Criminal Justice*, Abingdon: Routledge.

Bottoms, A. E. (1995), The Philosophy and Politics of Punishment and Sentencing in C. Clarkson and R. Morgan (eds.), *The Politics of Sentencing Reform*, Oxford: Clarendon Press.

Bozkurt, S. and Aresti, A. (2018), Experiencing Prison Life from Both Sides of the Fence: A Turkish Females Perspective, *Journal of Prisoners on Prisons*, 27(2), 17–35.

Bradley, A. (2021), Viewing Her Majesty's Prison Service Through a Trauma-informed Lens, *Prison Service Journal* (255), 4–11.

Bradley, R. G. and Davino, K. M. (2002), Women's Perceptions of the Prison Environment: When Prison is 'The Safest Place I've Ever Been', *Psychology of Women Quarterly*, 26(4), 351–359.

Braithwaite, J. (1989), *Crime, Shame and Reintegration*, Cambridge: Cambridge University Press.

Bramley, G. and Fitzpatrick, S. (2018), Homelessness in the UK: Who is Most at Risk?, *Housing Studies Journal*, 33, 96–116.

Braun, V. and Clarke, V. (2006), Using Thematic Analysis in Psychology, Qualitative Research, *Psychology*, 3, 77–101.

Brison, S. J. (1999), Trauma Narratives and the Remaking of the Self in M. Bal, J. V. Crewe and L. Spitzer (eds.), *Acts of Memory: Cultural Recall in the Present.* Dartmouth College, 39–54.

British Broadcasting Corporation (BBC) News (2019), If you want unsolicited advice, get pregnant. https://www.bbc.co.uk/news/world-us-canada-49235623 (Accessed 11 October 2021).

   (2018), Quarter of mums made 'uncomfortable' breastfeeding in public. https://www.bbc.co.uk/news/uk-scotland-43143510 (Accessed 11 October 2021).

Brunton-Smith, I. and McCarthy, D. J. (2017), The Effects of Prisoner Attachment to Family on Re-entry Outcomes: A Longitudinal Assessment, *British Journal of Criminology*, 57, 463–482.

Burke, L., Collett, S. and McNeill, F. (2019), *Reimagining Rehabilitation: Beyond the Individual*, London: Routledge.

Burke, L., Taylor, S., Canton, R. and Dominey, J. (2020), Punishment and Care Reappraised, *Spaces of Care*, 15.

Burman, M. and Batchelor, S. (2009), Between Two Stools? Responding to Young Women Who Offend, *Youth Justice*, 9 (3), 270–285.

Busch-Geertseema, V. and Sahlin, I. (2007), The Role of Hostels and Temporary Accommodation, *European Journal of Homelessness*, 1, 67–93.

Bussie, J. A. (2015), Laughter as Ethical and Theological Resistance: Leymah Gbowee, Sarah, and the Hidden Transcript, *Interpretation: A Journal of Bible and Theology*, 69(2), 169–182 (doi: 10.1177/0020964314564843).

Cabinet Office (1999), Modernising Government, HMSO.

Caddle, D. and Crisp, D. (1997), *Imprisoned Women and Mothers*, London: Home Office.

Campbell, M. and Troyer, L. (2007), The Implications of Racial Misclassification by Observers, *American Sociological Review*, 72(5), 750–765.

Canton, R. and Dominey, J. (2017), *Probation* (2nd ed.), Abingdon: Routledge.

Cardale, E. Edgar, K. and Swaine, K. (2017), *Counted Out: Black, Asian and Minority Ethnic Women in the CJS*, London: Prison Reform Trust.

Carlen, P. (1988), *Women, Crime and Poverty*, Milton Keynes: Open University Press.
  (1994), Why Study Women's Imprisonment? or Anyone Else's? An Indefinite Article in R. D. King and M. Maguire (Eds), *Prisons in Context*, Clarendon Press, 131–40.

Carlen, P., Christina, D., O'Dwyer, J., Hicks, J. and Tchaikovsky, C. (1985), *Criminal Women: Autobiographical Accounts*, London: Polity Press.

Carlen P. and Worrall, A. (2004), *Analysing Women's Imprisonment*, Routledge.

Carline, A. (2005), Women Who Kill Their Abusive Partners: From Sameness to Gender Construction, *Liverpool Law Review*, 26, 13–44.

Carter, R. (2007), Racism and Psychological and Emotional Injury: Recognising and Assessing Race-based Traumatic Stress, *The Counselling Psychologist*, 35(1), 13–105.

Carter, R. and Pieterse, A. (2020), *Measuring the Effects of Racism: Guidelines for the Assessment and Treatment of Race-based Traumatic Stress Injury*, New York: Columbia University Press.

Cederstrom, C. and Spicer, A. (2015), *The Wellness Syndrome*, Cambridge: Polity Press.

Centre for Social Justice (2018), *A Woman-Centred Approach: Freeing Vulnerable Women from the Revolving Door of Crime,* London: Centre for Social Justice.

Charles, N. (1994), Domestic Violence, Homelessness and Housing: The Response of Housing Providers in Wales, *Critical Social Policy*, 14(41), 36–52.

Chigwada-Bailey, R. (2003), *Black Women's Experiences of Criminal Justice: A Discourse on Disadvantage*, Sherfield on Loddon: Waterside Press.

Christie, N. (1986), 'The Ideal Victim' in Ezzat A. Fattah (ed.), *From Crime Policy to Victim Policy*, Basingstoke: Macmillan.

Chui, W. H. (2010), 'Pains of Imprisonment': Narratives of the Women Partners and Children of the Incarcerated, *Child and Family Social Work*, 15(2), 196–205.

Clarke, B. and Chadwick, K. (2018), From Troubled Women to Failing Institutions: The Necessary Narrative Shift for the Decarceration of Women Post Corston in L. Moore, P. Scraton, P. and A. Wahidin (2018), *Women's Imprisonment and the Case for Abolition: Critical Reflections of Corston Ten Years On*, London: Routledge.

Codd, H. (2008) *In the Shadow of Prison: Families, Imprisonment and Criminal Justice*, Abingdon: Routledge.

Comas-Diaz, L. Hall, G. and Neville, H. (2019), Racial Trauma: Theory, Research and Healing: Introduction to the Special Issue, *American Psychologist* 74(1), 1–5.

Comfort, M. (2008), *Doing Time Together: Love and Family in the Shadow of the Prison,* Chicago: University of Chicago Press.

Condry, R. (2007), *Families Shamed: The Consequences of Crime for Relatives of Serious Offenders*, Cullumpton: Willan Publishing.

Corston, J. (2007), *The Corston Report: A Report by Baroness Jean Corston of A Review of Women With Particular Vulnerabilities in the CJS,* London: Home Office.

Covington, S. S. (2007), Women and the CJS, *Women's Health Issues*, 17(4), 180–182.

Cox, J. and Sacks-Jones, K. (2017), *'Double Disadvantage': The Experience of Black, Asian and Minority Ethnic Women in the CJS*, London: Agenda.

Craissati, J., Joseph, N. and Skett, S. (eds.) (2015), *Working With Offenders With Personality Disorder: A Practitioners Guide*. London: Department of Health.

Crenshaw, K. (1989), Demarginalizing the Intersection of Race and Sex: A Black Feminist Critique of Antidiscrimination Doctrine, *Feminist Theory and Antiracist Politics*, University of Chigaco Forum, 139–168.

Crewe, B., Hulley, S. and Wright, S. (2017), The Gendered Pains of Life Imprisonment, *British Journal of Criminology*, 57(6), 1359–1378.

Criado Perez, C. (2020), *Invisible Women: Exposing Data Bias in a World Designed for Men,* Vintage (1st published as Perez, C. C. (2019), *Invisible Women: Exposing Data Bias in a World Designed for Men*, Random House).

Crowther, M. (1991), *The Workhouse System, 1834–1929: The History of an English Social Institution,* Methuen: London.

Daly, K. (1994), *Gender, Crime and Punishment*, New Haven, CT: Yale University Press.

Davis, A. Y., Dent, G., Meiners, E. R. and Richie, B. E. (2022), *Abolition. Feminism. Now,* Hamish Hamilton.

DeMause, L. (1990), The History of Child Assault, *Journal of Psychohistory*, 18(1), 1–29.

De Haan, W. and Loader, L. (2002), On the Emotions of Crime, Punishment and Social Control. *Theoretical Criminology*, 6(3), 243–253.

Devitt, K. (2020), *Resilience, Wellbeing and Sustainability in Women-Lead Probation Service Delivery.* Kent, Surrey and Sussex Criminal Research and Policy Unit.

Dobash, R. and Dobash, R. (1979), *Violence Against Wives: A Case Against the Patriarchy*, New York: Free Press.

Dominey, J. and Gelsthorpe, L. (2020), Resettlement and the Case for Women, *Probation Journal*, 67(4), 393–409.

Eaton, M. (1993), *Women After Prison*, Buckingham: Open University Press.

Elfleet, H. (2021), Neoliberal Feminised Governmentality: The Role and Function of a Post Corston Report (2007), Women's Centre in the North-West of England, *British Journal of Community Justice*, 16(2), 1–22.

Enos, S. (2001), *Mothering From the Inside: Parenting in A Women's Prison,* New York: State University of New York Press.

Epstein, R. and Brown, G. (2022), *Why Are Pregnant Women in Prison?,* Coventry University.

Fahmy, E., Williamson, E. and Pantazis, C. (2016), *Evidence and Policy Review: Domestic Violence and Poverty*, Joseph Rowntree Foundation: University of Bristol.

Faith, K. (2011), *Unruly Women: The Politics of Confinement and Resistance,* New York: Seven Stories Press.

Farmer, L. (2017) (First report), *The Importance of Strengthening Prisoners' Family Ties to Prevent Reoffending and Reduce Intergenerational Crime*, Ministry of Justice.

https://assets.publishing.service.gov.uk/government/uploads/system/uploads/attachment_data/file/809467/farmer-review-women.PDF

(2019) (Second report), *The Importance of Strengthening Female Offenders' Family and other Relationships to Prevent Reoffending and Reduce Intergenerational Crime*, London: Ministry of Justice.

Fawcett Commission on Women and the CJS and United Kingdom (2007), Women and Justice: The Third Annual Review of the Commission on Women and the CJS.

Fawcett Society (2004), *Women and the Criminal Justice System*, London: Fawcett Society.

Feinman, C. (1994), *Women in the CJS* (3rd Ed), USA: Preager Publishers.

Fink, H. (1981), *Social Philosophy*, London: Methuen and Co.

Fitzpatrick, C. (2017), What Do We Know About Girls in the Care and Criminal Justice Systems?, *Safer Communities*, 16(3), 134–143. https://doi.org/10.1108/SC-03-2017-0011

Fitzpatrick, S. and Stephens, M. (2007), *An International Review of Homelessness and Social Housing Policy*, London: Communities and Local Government.

Fleetwood, J. (2013), Keeping Out of Trouble: Female Crack Cocaine Dealers in England, *European Journal of Criminology*, 11(1), 91–109.

Fleetwood, J. (2015), A Narrative Approach to Women's Lawbreaking, *Feminist Criminology*, 10(4), 368–388 (doi: 10.1177/1557085115591998).

Frazer-Carroll, M. (2019), The Death of Annabella Landsberg Shows Why Vulnerable Black Women Should Not Be Sent to Prison: https://gal-dem.com/annabella-landsberg-black-women-should-not-be-sent-to-prison/ (Accessed 13 August 2021).

Gålnander, R. (2020), Desistance From Crime — to What? Exploring Future Aspirations and Their Implications for Processes of Desistance, *Feminist Criminology*, 15(3), 255–277.

Garland, D. (2001), *The Culture of Control: Crime and Social Order in Contemporary Society*, Oxford: Oxford University Press.

Garner, S. and Selod, S. (2015), The Racialization of Muslims: Empirical Studies of Islamophobia, *Critical Sociology*, 41(1), 9–19.

Gbowee, L. and Mithers, C. (2011), *Mighty Be Our Powers: How Sisterhood, Prayer and Sex Changed a Nation at War*, New York: Beast Books.

Gelsthorpe, L. (2007), Sentencing and Gender in R. Sheehan, G. McIvor and C. Trotter (2007), *What Works With Women Offenders* (1st ed.), Cullumpton: Willan.

(2009), What Works With Women Offenders: The Past 30 Years, *Probation Journal*, 56(4), 329–345.

(2010), *Working with Women Offenders in the Community: A View from England and Wales*, Cullompton: Willan, 153–176.

(2013), Working With Women in Probation: 'Will you, won't you, will you, won't you, won't you join the dance?' in P. Ugwidike and P. Raynor (eds.), *What Works in Offender Compliance: International Perspectives and Evidence-based Practice*, Basingstoke: Palgrave Macmillan.

Gelsthorpe, L. and Canton, R. (2020), Paradoxes of Care: Women in the CJS in England and Wales, *Spaces of Care*, 55.

Gelsthorpe, L. and Morgan, R. (2007), *Handbook of Probation*, London: Willan Publishing.

Gelsthorpe, L., Mody, P. and Sloan, B. (eds.) (2020), *Spaces of Care*, Bloomsbury Publishing.

Gilligan, C. (1982), *In a Different Voice*, Cambridge, MA: Harvard University Press.

Gilmore, R. W. and Murakawa, N. (2020), *Change Everything: Racial Capitalism and the Case foe Abolition*, Haymarket Books, 234.

Goffman, E. (1963/1990), *Stigma: Notes on the Management of Spoiled Identity*, London: Penguin.

Goldhill, R. (2016), Reflections on Working with Vulnerable Women: Connecting Cans of Worms, Closures and Coping, *The British Journal of Social Work*, 46(5), 1336–1353.

(2019), Challenges of Gender Responsivity in Probation Work with Women Service Users, *British Journal of Community Justice*, 15(2), 106–126.

Gunaratnum Y. (2003), *Researching 'Race' and Ethnicity: Methods, Knowledge and Power*, London: Sage.

Gurusami, S. (2019), Motherwork Under the State: The Maternal Labor of Formerly Incarcerated Black Women, *Social Problems*, 66, 128–143.

Hackett, L. (2015), Working with Women Experiencing Mental Distress; Creating a Safe Space for Conversations in L. Baldwin (ed.) (2015), *Mothering Justice: Working with Mothers in Criminal and Social Justice Settings*, Sherfield on Loddon: Waterside Press, 43–65

Hairston, C. F. (1991), Family Ties During Imprisonment: Important to Whom and For What?, *Journal of Sociology and Social Welfare*, 18, 87–104.

Haggerty, K. D. and Bucerius, S. (2020), The Proliferating Pains of Imprisonment, *Incarceration*, 1(1), 2632666320936432.

Hames, C. and Pedreira, D. (2003), Children with Parents in Prison: Disenfranchised Grievers Who Benefit from Bibliotherapy, *Illness, Crisis and Loss*, 11(4), 377–386.

Hamilton, L. (2010), '*The Boundary See-saw Model, Good Fences Make for Good Neighbours' Using Time, Not Doing Time: Practitioner Perspectives on Personality Disorder and Risk,* Chichester: John Wiley & Sons.

Hannah-Moffat, H. (2005), Criminogenic Needs and the Transformative Risk Subject: Hybridizations of Risk/Need in Penalty, *Punishment and Society*, 7(1), 29–51.

Harding, N. (2017), Picturing Subjugated Knowledge in K. Atkinson, A. Huber and K. Tucker (eds.), *Voices of Resistance: Subjugated Knowledge and the Challenge to the Criminal Justice System*, Bristol: EG Press Limited, 35–44.

(2020a), Co-constructing Feminist Research: Ensuring Meaningful Participation While Researching the Experiences of Criminalised Women, *Methodological Innovations,* 13(2), 1–14.

(2020b), Navigating Gendered Criminalisation: Women's Experiences of Punishment in the Community, Doctoral thesis, Manchester Metropolitan University: https://e-space.mmu.ac.uk/628739/

(2021), Playing the Game: Women and Community Punishment in I. Masson, L. Baldwin and N. Booth (eds.), *Critical Reflections on Women, Family, Crime and Justice*, Policy Press, 11–34.

Harding, S. (1981), *Feminism and Methodology: Social Science Issues,* Bloomington: Indiana University Press.

Hardy, K. (2013), Healing the Hidden Wounds of Racial Trauma, *Reclaiming Children and Youth,* 22(1), 25–28.

Harrell, S. (2000), A Multidimensional Conceptualization of Racism-related Stress: Implications for the Well-being of People of Colour, *American Journal of Orthopsychiatry*, 70(1), 42–57.

Harris, R. (1992), *Crime, Criminal Justice and the Probation Service*, London: Routledge.

Harris, M. and Fallot, R. D. (eds.) (2001), *Using Trauma Theory to Design Service Systems*, Jossey-Bass/Wiley.

Hart, E. L. (2017), Women Prisoners and the Drive for Desistance: Capital and Responsibilization as a Barrier to Change, *Women and Criminal Justice*, 27(3), 151–169.

Haslam, N. and McGrath, M. J. (2020), The Creeping Concept of Trauma, *Social Research: An International Quarterly*, 87(3), 509–531.

Hastings, A., Mackenzie, M. and Earley, A. (2021), Domestic Abuse and Housing: Connections and Disconnections in the Pre-Covid-19 Policy World, Interim Report, UK Collaborative Centre for Housing Evidence.

Hawton, K., Linsell, L., Adeniji, T., Sariaslan, A. and Fazel, S. (2014), Self-harm in Prisons in England and Wales: An Epidemiological Study of Prevalence, Risk Factors, Clustering, and Subsequent Suicide, *The Lancet*, 383(9923), 1147–1154.

Hays, S. (1996), *The Cultural Construction of Motherhood*, New Haven, CT: Yale University Press.

Hedderman, C. (2012), *Empty Cells or Empty Words? Government Policy on Reducing the Number of Women Going to Prison*, Criminal Justice Alliance.

Heidensohn, F. (1985), *Women and Crime*, New York: New York University Press.

Heidensohn, F. and Silvestri, M. (2012), Gender and Crime in M. Maguire, R. Morgan and R. Reiner (eds.), *Oxford Handbook of Criminology*, 336–369.

Henderson, K. (2019), The Role of Housing in a Coordinated Community Response to Domestic Abuse, doctoral thesis, University of Durham, Durham.

Henriques, Z. W. and Jones-Brown, D. D. (2000), Prisons as 'Safe Havens' for African-American Women in M. W. Markowitz and D. D. Jones-Brown (eds.) *The System is Black and White: Exploring the Connections Between Race, Crime, and Justice*, Sage.

Her Majesty's Government (1996), Housing Act 1996, London: The Stationery Office.

(2017), Homelessness Act 2017, London: The Stationery Office.

(2021), Domestic Abuse Act 2021, London: The Stationery Office.

(2022a), *Criminal Justice System Statistics Quarterly*, June, HM Government. https://www.gov.uk/government/statistics/criminal-justice-system-statistics-quarterly-june-2022/criminal-justice-statistics-quarterly-june-2022-html

(2022b), Tackling Domestic Abuse Plan, CP 639 Crown Copyright.

(2022c), Police, Crime, Sentencing and Courts and Act 2022, London: The Stationary Office.

HM Inspectorate of Prisons (2020)(October), *Minority Ethnic Prisoners' Experiences of Rehabilitation and Release Planning: A Thematic Review,* London: HM Inspectorate of Prisons.

HM Inspectorate of Probation (2010), *Women in Prison: A Short Thematic Review.* London: Home Office.

(2016), *A Thematic Inspection of the Provision and Quality of Services in the Community for Women Who Offend*, London: Home Office.

(2018), *Enforcement and Recall: A Thematic Inspection by H M Inspectorate of Probation,* London: Home Office.

(2020)(July), *Trauma-informed Practice,* HM Inspectorate of Probation.

HM Inspectorate of Probation and EPIC (2021), *Experiences of Black, Asian and Minority Ethnic Service Users on Probation: A Report Summarising Service User Perspectives,* London: HM Inspectorate of Probation.

Herman, J. (1992), *Trauma and Recovery: From Domestic Abuse to Political Terror.* London: Pandora.

Holly, J. (2017), *Mapping the Maze: Services for Women Experiencing Multiple Disadvantage in England and Wales*, London: Agenda, Against Violence and Abuse and Barrow Cadbury Trust.

Homeless Link (2018), *Implementing the Homelessness Reduction Act: Learning from Homeless Link's Regional Events*, Homeless Link, London.

Home Office (1984), *Probation Service in England and Wales: Statement of National Objectives and Priorities,* London: Home Office.

(1997), Women in Prison: A Thematic Review by HM Chief Inspector of Prisons, London: Home Office.

(2021), Statutory Homelessness. July–September 2021. Home Office/Dept for Levelling up, Housing and Communities. https://assets.publishing.service. gov.uk/government/uploads/system/uploads/attachment_data/file/1050291/ Statutory_Homelessness_Stats_Release_July-September_2021.pdf

Hooks, B. (2009), *Belonging: A Culture of Place*, New York: Routledge.

Hough, M. Bradford, B., Jackson, J. and Roberts, J. V. (2013), *Attitudes to Sentencing and Trust in Justice Exploring Trends from the Crime Survey for England and Wales,* Ministry of Justice.

INQUEST (2018/2019), Still Dying on the Inside. https://www.inquest.org. uk/still-dying-on-the-inside-report Update: https://www.inquest.org. uk/2019-update-still-dying

  (2019), INQUEST Finds Serious Failures at Sodexo Run HMP Peterborough Contributed to Death of Annabella Landsberg: https://www.inquest.org.uk/ . annabella-landsberg-conclusion (Accessed 10 August 2021).

Irving-Clarke, Y. (2016), Supporting People — How Did We Get Here and What Does it Mean for the Future?, doctoral thesis, De Montfort University, Leicester.

  (2019), *Supported Housing: Past, Present, and Future*, Abingdon: Routledge.

Irving-Clarke, Y. and Henderson, K. (2022), *Housing and Domestic Abuse: Policy into Practice,* London: Routledge.

Jayanetti, C. (2021) Record number of domestic abuse victims made homeless, *The Guardian*, October 30.

Jewkes, Y., Jordan, M., Wright, S. and Bendelow, G. (2019), Designing 'Healthy' Prisons for Women: Incorporating Trauma-Informed Care and Practice Into Prison Planning and Design, *International Journal of Environmental Research and Public Health*, 16, 3818 (doi: 10.3390).

Joe, J., Shillingford-Butler, A. and Oh, S. (2019), The Experiences of African American Mothers Raising Sons in the Context of #BlackLivesMatter, *The Professional Counsellor*, 9(1), 67–79.

Jones, S. (2008), Partners in Crime: A Study of the Relationship between Female Offenders and Their Co-Defendants, *Criminology and Criminal Justice*, 8, 147–164.

  (2011), Under Pressure: Women Who Plead Guilty to Crimes They Have Not Committed, *Criminology and Criminal Justice*, 11, 77–90.

Jones, A. and Pleace, N. (2010), *A Review of Single Homelessness in the UK*, London: Crisis and Joseph Rowntree Foundation.

Jordan, S. (2013), *Missing Voices: Why Women Engage With, or Withdraw from, Community Sentences,* The Griffins Society.

Karslen, S., Nazroo, J., McKenzie, K., Bhui, K. and Weich, S. (2005), Racism, Psychosis and Common Mental Disorder Among Ethnic Minority Groups in England, *Psychological Medicine*, 35(1), 1795–1803.

Katz, L. (2020), Injustice Trauma: Individual and Collective Distress: https://www.psychologytoday.com/gb/blog/healing-sexual-trauma/202006/injustice-trauma-individual-and-collective-distress (Accessed 23 October 2021).

Kelly, L. (2003), The Wrong Debate: Reflections on Why Force is Not the Key Issue with Respect to Trafficking in Women for Sexual Exploitation, *Feminist Review,* 73, 139–144.

Kinouani, G. (2021), *Living While Black*, London: Ebury Press.

Klaver, J. R., Zina L. and Gordon Rose, V. (2008), Effects of Personality, Interrogation Techniques and Plausibility in an Experimental False Confession Paradigm, *Legal and Criminological Psychology*, 13(1), 71–88.

Knight, C. (2012), Soft Skills for Hard Work: An Exploration of the Efficacy of Emotional Literacy of Practitioners Working in the National Offender Management Service with High Risk Offenders, Thesis, De Montfort University.

(2014), *Emotional Literacy in Criminal justice: Professional Practice With Offenders*, Springer.

Koons-Witt, B. and Schram, P. (2003), The Prevalence and Nature of Violent Offending by Females, *Journal of Criminal Justice*, 31, 361–371.

Kubiak, S., Covington, S. and Hillier, C. (2017), Trauma-informed Corrections, *Social Work in Juvenile and CJS*, 4(7), 92–104.

Lamble, S. (2020), Practising Everyday Abolition in Duff, K. (ed.), *Abolishing the Police: An Illustrated Introduction*, Dog Section Press, 147–160. https://abolitionistfutures.com/latest-news/practising-everyday-abolition

Lammy, D. (2017) (September), *The Lammy Review. An Independent Review into the Treatment of, and Outcomes for, Black, Asian and Minority Ethnic Individuals in the CJS*, HM Government. https://assets.publishing.service.gov.uk/government/uploads/system/uploads/attachment_data/file/643001/lammy-review-final-report.pdf

Lanskey, C., Lösel, F., Markson, L. and Souza, K. (2018), Prisoners Families, Penal Power, and the Referred Pains of Imprisonment in R. Condry and P. Scharff Smith (eds.), *Prisons, Punishment, and The Family: Towards a New Sociology of Punishment?*, Oxford: Oxford University Press.

Laub, J. H. and Sampson, R. J. (2001), Understanding Desistance from Crime. *Crime and Justice*, 28, 1–69.

LeBel, T. P., Burnett, R., Maruna, S. and Bushway, S. (2008), The 'Chicken and Egg' of Subjective and Social Factors in Desistance from Crime, *European Journal of Criminology*, 5(2), 131–159.

Lee, E., Daugherty, J. Eskierka, K. and Hamelin, K. (2019), Compassion Fatigue and Burnout, One Institution's Interventions, *Journal of PeriAnesthesia Nursing*, 34(4), 767–773.

Lee, R. (2017), The Impact of Engaging with Client's Trauma Stories: Personal and Organizational Strategies to Manage Probation Practitioners' Risk of Developing Vicarious Traumatisation, *Probation Journal*, 64(4), 372–387.

Leverentz, A. (2014), *The Ex-Prisoner's Dilemma: How Women Negotiate Competing Narratives of Re-entry and Desistance,* Rutgers University Press.

Light, M., Grant, E. and Hopkins, K. (2013), *Gender Differences in Substance Misuse and Mental Health Issues Amongst Prisoners: Results from the Surveying Prisoner Crime Reduction Longitudinal Cohort Study of Prisoners*, Ministry of Justice Analytical Series 2013, London: Ministry of Justice.

Loucks, N. (2005), *Keeping in Touch: The Case for Family Support Work in Prison*, London: Prison Reform Trust.

Loveless, J. (2010), Domestic Violence, Coercion and Duress, *Criminal Law Review*, 233–256.

Mackie, R. and Thomas, I. (2014), *Nations Apart? Experiences of Single Homeless People Across Great Britain,* London: Crisis.

Madhok, S. Phillips, A. and Wilson, K. (2013), *Gender, Agency and Coercion*, London: Palgrave/Macmillan.

Magnusson, L. and Davidge. S. (2020), *The Domestic Abuse Report 2020: The Hidden Housing Crisis,* Women's Aid.

Maguire, D. (2021), *Male, Failed, Jailed: Masculinities and 'Revolving Door' Imprisonment in the UK*, Springer International Publishing.

Maher, L. (1997), *Sexed Work: Gender, Race and Resistance in a Brooklyn Drug Market*, Oxford: Clarendon Press.

Malloch, M. S. and Stanley, E. (2005), The Detention of Asylum Seekers in the UK: Representing Risk, Managing the Dangerous, *Punishment and Society*, 7, 53.

Malloch, M. and McIvor, G. (eds.) (2013), *Women, Punishment and Social Justice: Human Rights and Penal Practices*, Routledge.

Martin, K. and Powell, C. (2023) Mother-infant Separations in Prison: Why Does Context Matter? in I. Masson and N. Booth (eds.), *Handbook of Women's Experiences of Criminal Justice,* Abingdon: Routledge.

Maruna, S. (2001), *Making Good: How Ex-Convicts Reform and Rebuild Their Lives,* Washington, DC: American Psychological Association.

Maruna, S. and Liem, M. (2021), Where Is This Story Going? A Critical Analysis of the Emerging Field of Narrative Criminology, *Annual Review of Criminology,* 4(1), 125–146.

Marshall, C. D. (2012), *Compassionate Justice. An Interdisciplinary Dialogue with Two Gospel Parables on Law, Crime and Restorative Justice,* Oregon, USA: Cascade Books.

Masson, I. (2019), *Incarcerating Motherhood: The Enduring Harms of First Short Periods of Imprisonment on Mothers,* Abingdon: Routledge.

(2021), Reducing the Enduring Harm of Short Terms of Imprisonment in I. Masson, L. Baldwin and N. Booth (eds.), *Critical Reflections from the Women, Families, Crime and Justice Research Network,* Bristol: Policy Press.

Masson, I., Baldwin, L. and Booth, N. (eds.) (2021), *Critical Reflections on Women, Family, Crime and Justice,* Bristol: Policy Press.

Masson, I. and Booth, N. (2018), Examining Prisoners' Families: Definitions, Developments and Difficulties, Howard League/Early Careers Academics Network. https://howardleague.org/wp-content/uploads/2018/12/ECAN-bulletin-November-2018.pdf (Accessed 11 October 2021).

(2022), Using Techniques of Neutralisation to Maintain Contact: The Experiences of Loved Ones Supporting Remand Prisoners, *Howard Journal of Crime and Justice,* 61(4).

Masson, I., Booth, N. and Baldwin, L. (2023). The Conversation Isn't Over: Gaining Justice for Women and Families in *Experiences of Punishment, Abuse and Justice by Women and Families,* Policy Press.

McCartan, K. F. (2020), Trauma-informed Practice, *HM Inspectorate of Probation Academic Insight,* London: Criminal Justice Insights.

McKeown, A. (2010), Female Offenders: Assessment of Risk in Forensic Settings, *Aggression and Violent Behaviour* 15, 422–429.

McIvor, G., Murray, C. and Jamieson, J. (2004), Desistance from Crime: Is it Different from Women and Girls? in S. Maruna and R. Immarigeon (eds.), *After Crime and Punishment: Pathways to Offender Reintegration*, London: Willan Publishing, 181–201.

McNeill, F. (2016), The Fuel in the Tank or the Hole in the Boat? Can Sanctions Support Desistance? in J. Shapland, S. Farrall and A. Bottoms (eds.), *Global Perspectives on Desistance: Reviewing What We Know and Looking to the Future*, Oxford: Routledge, 265–281.

McNeill, F., Farrall, S., Lightowler, C. and Maruna, S. (2012), How and Why People Stop Offending: Discovering Desistance, Insights Evidence Summary to Support Social Services in Scotland.

McNeill, F. and Weaver, B. (2010), *Changing Lives? Desistance Research and Offender Management*, Project Report, 03/2010. https://ub01.uni-tuebingen. de/xmlui/bitstream/handle/10900/81970/SCCJR_Report_2010_03. pdf?sequence=1&isAllowed=y

McNeish, D. and Scott, S. (2014), Women and Girls at Risk: Evidence Across the Life-Course, North Dalton: DMSS Research.

Meer, N. and Modood, T. (2009), Refutations of Racism in the 'Muslim Question', *Patterns of Prejudice*, 43(3/4), 332–351.

Michalsen, V. (2018), *Mothering and Desistance in Re-entry*, Routledge.

Miles, R. (1989), *Racism*. London: Routledge.

Miller, L. (2019), *'A Safe Home' Breaking the Link Between Homelessness and Domestic Abuse,* All Party Parliamentary Group for Ending Homelessness, London: Crisis.

Millings, M. N. and Ragonese, E. L. (2017), Transforming Rehabilitation During a Penal Crisis: A Case Study of Through the Gate Services in a Resettlement Prison in England and Wales, *European Journal of Probation,* 9(2), 115–131. (ISSN 2066-2203).

Milner, A. and Jumbe, S. (2020), Using the Right Words to Address Racial Disparities in COVID-19, *Lancet Public Health,* 5(8), e419-e420.

Mind (n.d.), Trauma: https://www.mind.org.uk/information-support/types-of-mental-health-problems/trauma/about-trauma/ (Accessed 11 October 2021).

Ministry of Housing, Communities and Local Government (MHCLG) (2021), Homelessness Code of Guidance for Local Authorities.

MHCLG (2021), *Delivery of Support to Victims of Domestic Abuse, including Children, in Domestic Abuse Safe Accommodation Services. Statutory Guidance for Local Authorities Across England Draft for Consultation.*

Ministry of Justice (MOJ) (2007), *Human Resources Workforce Profile Report, National Probation Service*, Issue 4, London: Ministry of Justice.

(2015), *Annual Tables — Offender Management Caseload Statistics*, London: Ministry of Justice.

(2015), *Offender Management Statistics* (October-December 2014), London: Ministry of Justice.

(2016), *Prison Population Bulletin: Weekly 31 March 2017*, London: Ministry of Justice).

(2018), *Female Offender Strategy*, London: Ministry of Justice.

(2018), *A Whole Systems Approach for Female Offenders: Emerging Evidence*, London: Ministry of Justice.

(2020), *National Concordat for Women in, Or at Risk of Entering the CJS*, London: Ministry of Justice.

(2020), *Statistics on Women and the CJS 2019: A Ministry of Justice Publication under Section 95 of the Criminal Justice Act 1991*, London: Ministry of Justice.

(2021), *Concordat on Women In or At Risk of Contact With the Criminal Justice System*, London: Ministry of Justice.

(2022), *Criminal Justice Statistics Quarterly, England and Wales, Year Ending December 2021*, London: Ministry of Justice.

Minson, S. (2019), Direct Harms and Social Consequences: An Analysis of the Impact of Maternal Imprisonment on Dependent Children in England and Wales, *Criminology and Criminal Justice*, 19(5), 519–536.

Moore, L., Scraton, P. and Wahidin, A. (eds.) (2017), *Women's Imprisonment and the Case for Abolition: Critical Reflections on Corston Ten Years On*, London: Routledge.

Morash, M. (2010), *Women on Probation and Parole: A Feminist Critique of Community Programs & Services*, New England: University Press.

Morriss, L. (2018), Haunted Futures: The Stigma of Being A Mother Living Apart From Her Child(ren) as a Result of State-ordered Court Removal, *Sociological Review*, 66(4), 816–831.

Moss, K. and Singh, P. (2015), *Women Rough Sleepers in Europe: Homelessness and Victims of Domestic Abuse*, Bristol: Policy Press.

Motz, A. (2009), *Managing Self-harm: Psychological Perspectives*, Hove: Routledge.

(forthcoming 2024), *If Love Could Kill: The Myths and Truths of Female Violence*, Alfred A. Knopf.

Motz, A., Dennis, M. and Aiyegbusi, A. (2020), *Invisible Trauma: Women, Difference and the Criminal Justice System*, London: Routledge.

Mullins, C. and Wright, R. (2003), Gender Social Networks and Residential Burglary, *Criminology*, 41, 813–840.

Munro, M. (2018), Deaths in Prison Custody of Female Prisoners, January 2006 to December 2017, England and Wales: https://www.whatdotheyknow.com/request/528196/response/1270733/attach/4/FoI%20181029016%20Matilda%20Munro%20Data.pdf?cookie_passthrough=1 (Accessed 12 August 2021).

Neale, J. (1997), Homelessness and Theory Reconsidered, *Housing Studies*, 12(1), 47–71.

Newburn, T. (2007), 'Tough on Crime': Penal Policy in England and Wales, *Crime and Justice*, 36(1), 425–470.

New Statesman (1993), From the archive: Tony Blair is tough on crime, tough on the causes of crime. https://www.newstatesman.com/uncategorized/2015/12/archive-tony-blair-tough-crime-tough-causes-crime

Nietzsche, F. (1968), *The Will to Power* (Trans. Walter Kaufmann), New York: Vintage.

Nugent, B. and Schinkel, M. (2016), The Pains of Desistance, *Criminology and Criminal Justice,* 16(5), 568–584.

Oakley, A. (1976), *Woman's Work: The Housewife, Past and Present*, New York: Vintage Books.

Office for National Statistics (ONS) (2012), *2011 Census*, London: ONS, Table 1.4.

O'Malley, S. (2018), *The Experience of Imprisonment for Incarcerated Mothers and Their Children in Ireland*, doctoral thesis, Galway: National University of Ireland.

Österman, L. A. M. (2021), Longitudinal Cross-national Perspectives on Female Desistance: The Role of Social and Emotional Capitals in Female Narrations of Maintaining Change, *European Journal of Probation* (doi: 10.1177/20662203211056463).

Österman, L. and Masson, I. (2018), Restorative Justice With Female Offenders: The Neglected Role of Gender in Restorative Conferencing, *Feminist Criminology*, 13(1), 3–27.

Pannell, J. and Thomas, C. (1999), *Almshouses Into the Next Millennium: Paternalism, Partnership, Progress?*, Bristol: Policy Press.

Park, J. (2017), *One Hundred Years of Space Standards: What Now?*, London: Levitt Bernstein.

Parry, E. (2013), 'She's Alpha Male' Transgressive Gender Performances in the Probation 'Classroom', *Gender and Education*, 25(4), 396–412.

Pemberton, A., Aarten, P. G. M. and Mulder, E. (2019), Stories as Property: Narrative Ownership as a Key Concept in Victims' Experiences with Criminal Justice, *Criminology and Criminal Justice*, 19(4), 404–420.

Petrillo, M. (2017), Double Disadvantage: The Experiences of Black, Asian and Minority Ethnic Women in the CJS, *Probation Journal*, 64, 293.

(2019), The Rising Number of Women Recalled to Prison, *Probation Journal*, 66(2), 250–251

Phillips, C. (2012), *The Multicultural Prison: Ethnicity, Masculinity, and Social Relations Among Prisoners*, Oxford: Oxford University Press.

Phipps, A. (2014), *The Politics of the Body: Gender in a Neoliberal and Neoconservative Age*, Cambridge, MA: Polity Press.

Piper, A. and Berle, D. (2019), The Association Between Trauma Experienced During Incarceration and PTSD Outcomes: A Systematic Review and Meta-Analysis, *Journal of Forensic Psychiatry and Psychology*, 30(5), 854–875.

Pirtle, W. and Brown, T. (2016), Inconsistency Within Expressed and Observed Racial Identifications: Implications for Mental Health Status, *Sociological Perspectives*, 59(3), 582–603.

Pitman, J. and Hull, J. (2021), Counting the Cost of Maternal Imprisonment, Crest Advisory Report.

Pizzi, W., Blair, I. and Judd, C. (2005), Discrimination in Sentencing on the Basis of Afrocentric Features, *Michigan Journal of Race and Law*, 10, 327–355.

Presser, L. and Sandberg, S. (2015), Introduction: 'What is the Story?' in L. Presser and S. Sandburg (eds.), *Narrative Criminology*, New York: New York University Press, 1–20.

Prison Reform Trust (PRT) (2015), *Why Focus on Reducing Women's Imprisonment?*

(2017), Counted Out: Black Asian and Minority Ethnic Women in the CJS. https://prisonreformtrust.org.uk/wp-content/uploads/old_files/Documents/Counted%20Out.pdf

(2018), *Growing Numbers of Women Returning to Prison Due to Lack of Support on Release*, London: Prison Reform Trust.

(2018), *Leading Change: The Role of Local Authorities in Supporting Women with Multiple Needs*, London: Prison Reform Trust.

(2021), Bromley Briefings Prison Fact File: Winter 2021: https://prisonreformtrust. org.uk/publication/bromley-briefings-prison-factfile-winter-2021/

Prisons and Probation Ombudsman (2018), *Independent Investigation into the Death of Ms Annabella Landsberg a Prisoner at HMP Peterborough on 6 September 2017*, Prisons and Probation Ombudsman: Independent Investigations.

(2021), Independent Investigation Into the Death of Baby A at HMP Bronzefield on 27 September 2019. https://www.ppo.gov.uk/news/ ppo-ombudsman-sue-mcallister-publishes-independent-investigation-into-the-tragic-death-of-a-baby-at-hmp-bronzefield/

(2022), Independent Investigation into the Death of Baby B at HMP&YOI Styal on 18 June 2020. https://www.ppo.gov.uk/news/ prisons-and-probation-ombudsman-publishes-independent-investigation-into-birth-of-stillborn-baby-at-hmp-styal/

Probyn, E. (2005), *Blush: Faces of Shame*, Minneapolis: University of Minnesota Press.

Quilgars, D. and Pleace, N. (2010), *Meeting the Needs of Households at Risk of Domestic Violence in England. The Role of Accommodation and Housing-related Support Services,* London: Queen's Printer and Controller of Her Majesty's Stationery Office.

Quinlan, C., Baldwin, L. and Booth, N. (2022), Feminist Ethics and Research with Women in Prison, *Prison Journal*, 102(2), 172–195 (doi: 10.1177/00328855221079265).

Randall, M. and Haskell, L. (2013), Trauma-informed Approaches to Law: Why Restorative Justice Must Understand Trauma and Psychological Coping, *Dalhousie Law Journal*, 36, 501.

Rasmusen, E. (1996), Stigma and Self-fulfilling Expectations of Criminality, *Journal of Law and Economics*, 39(2), 519–544 (doi: 10.3868/s050-004-015-0003-8).

Raynor, P. and Vanstone, M. (2016), Moving Away from Social Work and Half Way Back Again: New Research on Skills in Probation, *British Journal of Social Work*, 46(4), 1131–1147.

Rees, A., Bezeczky, Z and Waits, C. (2022), 'Together a Chance': Evaluation of the Social Worker for Mothers in Prison Pilot Project, 2021–2023,

Interim Evaluation: Year One. https://cascadewales.org/research/evaluation-of-together-a-chance/

Reeve, K. with Batty, E. (2011), *The Hidden Truth About Homelessness: Experiences of Single Homelessness in England,* London: Crisis.

Richie, B. E. (1996), *Compelled to Crime: The Gender Entrapment of Battered Black Women*, New York: Routledge.

Rodermond, E., Kruttschnitt, C. and Slotboom, A. M. (2016), Female Desistance: A Review of the Literature, *European Journal of Criminology*, 13(1), 3–28.

Russett, C. E. (1989), *Sexual Science: The Victorian Construction of Womanhood*, Cambridge, MA: Harvard University Press.

Russo, A. (2018), *Feminist Accountability: Disrupting Violence and Transforming Power,* New York: New York University Press.

Rutter, N. (2019), The Golden Thread: Service User Narratives on Desistance, The Role of Relationships and Opportunities for Co-produced Rehabilitation, doctoral thesis, Manchester Metropolitan University.

(2021), Social Media: A Challenge to Identity and Relational Desistance, *Probation Journal*, 68(2), 243–260.

Rutter, N. and Barr, Ú. (2021), Being a 'Good Woman': Stigma, Relationships and Desistance, *Probation Journal*, 68(2), 166–185.

Schaffner, A. (2007), Violence Against Girls Provokes Girls' Violence: From Private Injury to Public Harm, *Violence Against Women,* 13(12), 1229–1248.

Schur, E. M. (1984), *Labeling Women Deviant*, Philadelphia: Temple University Press.

Scott, D. (2020), *For Abolition: Essays on Prisons and Socialist Ethics*, Sherfield on Loddon: Waterside Press.

Seagrave, M. and Carlton, B. (2010), Women, Trauma, Criminalisation and Imprisonment, *Current Issues in Criminal Justice*, 22.

Selvarajah, S., Deivanayagam, T., Lasco, G., Scafe, S., White, A., Zembe-Mkabile, W. and Devakumar, D. (2020), Categorization and Minortization, *British Medical Journal Global Health*, 5, 1–3.

Sharpe, G. (2016), Re-Imagining Justice for Girls: A New Agenda for Research, *Youth Justice*, 16(1), 3–17.

Sheehan, R. McIvor, G and Trotter, C. (2011) (eds.), *Working with Women Offenders in the Community*, Cullompton: Willan.

Sim, J. (2018), We Are All (Neo-)Liberals Now: Reform and the Prison Crisis in England and Wales, *Justice, Power and Resistance*, 1, 165–188.

Singh, S., Cale, J. and Armstrong, K. (2019), Breaking the Cycle: Understanding the Needs of Women Involved in the CJS and the Role of Mentoring in Promoting Desistance, *International Journal of Offender Therapy and Comparative Criminology*, 63(8), 1330–1353.

Smith Lee, J. and Robinson, M. (2019), 'That's My Number One Fear in Life. It's the Police': Examining Young Black Men's Exposures to Trauma and Loss Resulting from Police Violence and Police Killings, *Journal of Black Psychology*, 45(3), 143–184.

Smith, J. A. (2004), Reflecting on the Development of Interpretative Phenomenological Analysis and Its Contribution to Qualitative Research in Psychology, *Qualitative Research in Psychology*, 1(3), 39–54.

Squire, C. and Newhouse, J. (2003), Racial Effects in Sentencing: The Influence of Facial Features and Skin Tone, *Journal of Undergraduate Research*, 6, 1–5.

Stalans, L. J. and Lurigio, A. J. (2015), Parenting and Intimate Relationship Effects on Women Offenders' Recidivism and Noncompliance With Probation, *Women in Criminal Justice*, 25(3), 152–168.

Stark, E. (2007), *Coercive Control: How Men Entrap Women in Personal Life*, London: Oxford University Press.

Sturges, J. and Hanrahan, K. (2011), The Effects of Children's Criminality on Mothers of Offenders, *Journal of Family Issues*, 32(8), 985–1006.

Substance Abuse and Mental Health Services Administration (2014), SAMHSA's Concept of Trauma and Guidance for a Trauma-Informed Approach, SAMHSA. https://store.samhsa.gov/sites/default/files/d7/priv/sma14-4884.pdf

Sydie, R. A. (1987), *Natural Women, Cultured Men: A Feminist Perspective on Sociological Theory*, Milton Keynes: Open University Press.

Sykes, G. (1958), *The Society of Captives: A Study of a Maximum Security Prison*, Princeton: Princeton University Press.

Thomas, M. (2021), *Developing Appropriate Strategies for Supporting Racially and Ethnically Minoritized Women within the CJS in Wales*, Cardiff: Female Offending Blueprint.

Turanovic, J. J., Rodriguez, N. and Pratt, T. C. (2012), The Collateral Consequences of Incarceration Revisited: A Qualitative Analysis of the Effects on Caregivers of Children of Incarcerated Parents, *American Society of Criminology*, 50(4), 913–959.

Tyler, I. (2020), *Stigma: The Machinery of Inequality*, London: Zed Books.

Uhrig, N. (2016), Black, Asian and Minority Ethnic Disproportionality in the CJS in England and Wales, London: Ministry of Justice.

Viglione, J., Hannon, L. and DeFina, R. (2011), The Impact of Light Skin on Prison Time for Black Female Offenders, *Social Science Journal*, 48, 250–258.

Walker, A. (1983), *In Search of Our Mothers' Gardens: Womanist Prose*, California: Harcourt Brace Jovanovich.

Walker, S. and Worrall, A. (2000), Life as A Woman: The Gendered Pains of Indeterminate Imprisonment, *Prison Service Journal*, 132.

Walker, T. and Towl, G. (2016), *Preventing Self-injury and Suicide in Women's Prisons*, Sherfield on Loddon: Waterside Press.

Walklate, S. (2001), *Gender Crime and Criminal Justice*, Devon: Willan Publishing.

Warburton, H. (2017), *An Exploration Into the Lives of Homeless Women*, unpublished thesis, University of Sheffield.

Warrington, M. (2003), Fleeing from Fear: The Changing Role of Refuges in Meeting the Needs of Women Leaving Violent Partners, *Capital and Class*, 27(2), 123–50.

Weaver, B. and Nolan, D. (2015), *Families of Prisoners: A Review of the Evidence*, Centre for Youth and Criminal Justice. https://www.cycj.org.uk/wp-content/uploads/2015/11/Families-of-Prisoners-A-Review-of-The-Evidence-FINAL.pdf (Accessed 11 October 2021).

Welldon, E. V. (1988), *Mother, Madonna, Whore: The Idealisation and Denigration of Motherhood*, London: Free Association Books.

Welle, D. and Falkin, G. (2000), The Everyday Policing of Women with Romantic Co-Defendants: An Ethnographic Perspective, *Women and Criminal Justice*, 11, 45–65.

Westmarland, N. (2015), *Violence Against Women: Criminological Perspectives on Men's Violences*, London: Routledge.

Wetherell, M., Taylor, S and Yates S. (2001), *Discourse, Theory and Practice: A Reader*, London: Sage.

Wilson, D. (2003), Playing 'The Game' Inside: Young Black Men in Custody, *Criminal Justice Matters*, 54(1), 30–31.

Wolfe, T. (1999), Counting the Cost: The Social and Financial Consequences of Women's Imprisonment. Report prepared for the Wedderburn Committee on Women's Imprisonment, Prison Reform Trust.

Women's Aid (2020), *The Hidden Housing Crisis*, Bristol: Women's Aid.

Women in Prison (WIP) (2017), *Corston + 10: The Corston Report Ten Years on. How Far Have We Come on the Road to Reform for Women Affected by the CJS?*, Women in Prison and Barrow Cadbury Trust.

Worrall, A. (1990), *Offending Women: Female Lawbreakers and the Criminal Justice System*, London: Routledge and Keegan Paul.

Worrall, A. and Gelsthorpe, L. (2009), 'What Works' with Women Offenders: The Past 30 Years, *Probation Journal*, 56(4), 329–345.

Worrall, A. and Hoy, C. (2005)(2 edn.), *Punishment in the Community: Managing Offenders, Making Choices*, Collumpton: Willan Publishing.

Worthington, M. (2014), The Road from Wigan Pier in R. Statham (ed.), *The Golden Age of Probation: Mission v Market*, Hook: Waterside Press.

Yeo, S. (1993), Resolving Gender Bias in Criminal Defences, *Monash University Law Review*, 19, 104–116.

Index

The Prison Psychiatrist's Wife
by Sue Johnson, Foreword by Charles Bronson

A gripping true story of a Herculean project as Sue Johnson's husband Bob, recruited to work with notorious offenders at Parkhurst Prison, sets out to discover whether he can change dangerous and violent men.

A rare 'outsider' view of prison which casts new light on hidden events. Of wide professional, penal and general interest — a woman's voice in a strongly male setting.

'A tremendous book. A perspective that needs to be heard'
Oliver James, author, broadcaster and clinical psychologist.

Paperback & ebook | ISBN 978-1-914603-30-3 | 2023

www.WatersidePress.co.uk

A Woman in Law

Reflections on Gender, Class and Politics

by Celia Wells, Foreword by Nicola Lacey

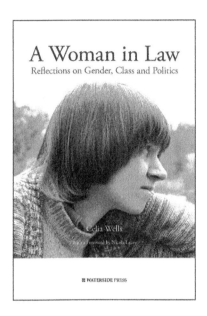

Celia Wells always felt like an outsider. Her unconventional early life was shaped by her Communist Party parents, she grew up as 'town' not 'gown' in Oxford, surrounded by books but living in a council house. She has uncovered an intriguing backstory with a bigamous grandmother, a convicted forger cousin transported to Australia in the 1840s, and the rise and fall of landed gentry.

'Well written and beautifully composed in terms of the strands [the author] interweaves so successfully'
Andrew Ashworth CBE

'Beautifully written and searingly honest… a rare resource… emotionally articulate and deeply considered'
Nicola Lacey (From the Foreword)

Paperback & ebook | ISBN 978-1-909976-66-5 | 2019

Mothering Justice

Working with Mothers in Criminal and Social Justice Settings

Edited by Lucy Baldwin, Foreword by Vicky Pryce

Written by experts with first-hand experience, *Mothering Justice* was the first whole book to take motherhood as a focus for criminal and social justice interventions. As such it is a classic work that should be on the reading list of anyone concerned with vulnerable women, their children and motherhood in general.

'I cannot help but jump around punching the air at this book. *Mothering Justice* has dared to expose the barriers both in Criminal and Social Justice Areas. Lucy Baldwin et al have delivered a stunning panoramic view of Motherhood.'
Criminal Law & Justice Weekly

Paperback & ebook | ISBN 978-1-909976-23-8 | 2015

www.WatersidePress.co.uk

Motherhood In and After Prison

The Impact of Maternal Incarceration

by Lucy Baldwin, Foreword by Lady Edwina Grosvenor

Motherhood In and After Prison focuses on how imprisonment impacts incarcerated mothers' maternal identity, emotions and role. It explores both the short and longer-term consequences for the women and society of sending mothers to prison, revealing the devastating and often underestimated impact.

'This timely book beautifully educates without judgement and is a must read for policymakers and practitioners alike, driving home a most critical message about the colossal and devastating impact of imprisoning mothers.'
Lady Edwina Grosvenor (From the Foreword)

Paperback & ebook | ISBN 978-1-914603-20-4 | 2022

www.WatersidePress.co.uk